the Kiplinger book on investing for the years ahead

PREVIOUS BOOKS BY
THE KIPLINGER WASHINGTON EDITORS, INC.

Inflation Ahead
Washington Is Like That
Success with Your Money
Boom and Inflation Ahead
How to Make More Money in the Boom Years Ahead
Kiplinger's Family Buying Guide
Florida: Land of Fortune
1975: And the Changes to Come

JOHN W. HAZARD
and LEW G. COIT

the Kiplinger
book on
investing for
the years
ahead

published for The Kiplinger Washington Editors, Inc., by

DOUBLEDAY & COMPANY, INC.

Garden City, New York, 1962

To our wives
Helen Kerr Hazard
and
Elizabeth Gray Coit

ACKNOWLEDGMENTS

It seems only proper to acknowledge the influence of the late Ralph Sayles of Loomis, Sayles & Company in the development of the basic investment philosophy of this book. His unusual insight into social, political and individual movements leading to economic and political changes in our economy and his discerning, common sense approach in periods of tension back in the Thirties (1930–1940) provided an invaluable background.

The authors also wish to acknowledge the major contribution of Margery Crane, Research Editor of *Changing Times*, who gave most generously of her time in checking and editing the manuscript.

We are indebted to Mary Widener for editorial help and to Betty Hinshon for help with the manuscript. In addition, full credit should be given Marie Roye, secretary to Mr. Coit, who stood ready at all times to help prepare the raw material that went into the book.

Our thanks go to three friends who assisted with some of the technical chapters: Leslie Douglas, Vice President of Folger, Nolan, Fleming & Company, Washington, D.C.; Richard L. Callanan, News Bureau Supervisor of the New York Stock Exchange; and William D. Horgan, Editor of *The Exchange Magazine*, published by the New York Stock Exchange.

JOHN W. HAZARD
LEW G. COIT

July, 1962

9 *how to pick companies*

The crux of the philosophy. Concentrate on quality growth stocks. List of growth industries. Examples of leading companies. How to iron out price peaks.

10 *how to get the facts and figures you need*

If you go it alone. Need for advice. Investment counselors. Trust departments of banks. Investment companies. Investment clubs. Advisory services. Brokers' market letters. Financial magazines.

11 *investment companies—how to duck part of the investment decision*

Characteristics of mutual funds and closed end trusts. Automatic diversification. Professional management. Discounts. Leverage. Funds with no load. Investment objectives.

12 *how to pick an investment trust*

What's available. Disadvantages of certain types. Common stock funds recommended. Advantages of newer growth funds. Points to watch for. Picking the best companies. How to get the facts you need. Examples of good funds.

13 *dollar cost averaging—a way to solve the problem of when to buy*

Periodic investing. Taking the guesswork out of timing. How dollar cost averaging works. Results of ten-year investment program in a growth stock—in an investment company. The front-end load.

Point and figure charts. Central Value theory. Confidence Index. Dow and Wave theories. How puts and calls are used. The ins and outs of margin trading. Pyramiding. Short selling and its dangers. The risks and rewards of speculating in commodity futures. Hedging.

Your own home. Duplex or small apartment. Second mortgages. Raw land. Syndicates. Tax-free returns. Real estate companies. New advantages from real estate investment trusts. Precautions.

Not just for the wealthy. Penalties of failing to plan. Estate taxes and settlement costs. How to minimize them. Who needs a will? Trusts and how to use them. Tax reduction by gifts. Taxes on life insurance. Lawyers' fees.

Unscrupulous advisers. The problems of a widow's securities, insurance, home, husband's business. The desperate need for income. Unbiased advice. Lawyers, bankers, investment counselors. How to invest capital safely. Life insurance options.

Skepticism. Perspective. Beware of predictions. Try for a little luck. Dangers of grabbing at profits. The feel of investing. Don't be ashamed of small purchases. The two ingredients that make stock market profits. The qualities needed for success.

---

why this book is worth reading

I like this book. I wish I had read it or something like it when I was younger. It would have done wonders for me; perhaps it will do a bit for you. Let me explain by confessing my own shortcomings in earlier years, with the hope that you may avoid anything resembling them.

Like most men I worked hard in my young and middle years, and made a good living and even accumulated a little extra which I regarded as "savings" for the rainy day or something—a bit vague as to purpose. I was in my late forties before I got a glimmer of "money sense." Then I began to get it into my head that money was not just something to be saved up, but something that could be made to grow—if managed right. It was the idea of *managing* money that was the mind opener to me. Also I discovered how many ways there are to manage—some foolish (which I did), some just so-so (which I also did), and some wise (which I finally learned after many bumps).

Another startling discovery which I made a little late in life, is that money isn't merely money. It isn't just something that you can spend for things you want. It's more than that: it's one of the products of years of work. It's the surplus energy of a life-time. It's a helper, a servant that will work for you while you are doing your own work, whatever that is. It's a college education for someone. It's a trip to Europe. It's a life saver in emergencies, for you, or members of your family, or friends, either close or distant. It's a way of giving them of yourself, for money is a sort of distillation of yourself—or it can be if you manage right.

Or another thing you can do with money is to give it away as you think best—to persons or to causes—and have for yourself the internal pleasure of seeing it brighten a number of situations. You can watch the growth of the benefits just as you have watched the growth of the money itself. Fun at both ends of the deal, a double bargain in human values, like a hobby, a prof-itable hobby.

I learned also that just as people grow with time and expe-rience, and become bigger, better and more useful persons, so money can grow and become a useful partner. These two good partners, working together, instead of just one lone individual, accomplish *much* more. Previously I had looked upon money (when I looked upon it at all) as something cold and earthy and perhaps a bit sordid, certainly not to be associated with the finer things of life. But gradually I came to see that money is one of the givers of whatever you want in life, fine or otherwise, selfish or otherwise. Not an end in itself, but a means to all sorts of ends.

Most people live on a salary, or on wages which are the equiv-alent. As they go through life they become worth more and the salary rises. But they also find that their family obligations rise proportionately. They want to live better, they deserve to live better, and sometimes they must live better to sustain a position in life that is an accompaniment of the higher salary.

They discover another fact that they had heard about—taxes. Often the higher taxes that are payable on a higher income hit them smack in the face, and they realize acutely for the first time that "this means me." The take-home pay, after taxes, does not seem to go up as much as the pay itself, and out of the take-home pay must come the higher expenses of the better living standard that has been adopted. Thus a rat race, a treadmill, and the term "salary slave."

There's one out, one escape. It involves first the saving of a portion of the salary, some sum, any sum, and the investing of it for growth, which is where this book comes in. It takes a bit of doing, but in the end is sure to lead to an extra income, a sort of independent income, independent of the salary, and a tremendous relief from the rat race. The sooner such a program is started the sooner the relief, but remember that it takes a certain amount of lead time just to prepare for it and let the beneficial forces work themselves out.

Maybe you know all this already. Maybe you are not as naive as I was in my earlier years. Maybe you have grown a money sense at an earlier age than I did, and I hope so. But just in case you have some streaks of frailty in you, I recommend this book. And if you are mature and sophisticated in these matters, I recommend it too, for it is a mature and sophisticated book.

Don't read it if you want merely to make a quick buck, for the book doesn't tell you how. Don't read it if you think only of "striking it rich," as if by some accident, stumbled upon, or searched out by superior shrewdness, such as the shrewdness that goes along with picking the daily double. And don't read the book if you are interested in getting a tip and buying some lucky stock today, selling it next week, and making a tidy gain. All these things are possible, and many a man has gotten wealthy out of a fortuitous accident, or a series of incidents. Those are not to be sneezed at, but they are not the stuff of this book.

This book shows a method of making your money grow for the years ahead, but it is not a trick or patented method. I'll steal from the authors and tell you what it is:

Buy good securities, carefully, thoughtfully, after a lot of investigation, a lot of advice: put them away and count on their growing. Count on this with a fair degree of assurance.

That's not the whole story, but that's the gist.

Can you do it? The answer in the book is YES. Can you do it with a little money, whatever you consider a little? YES. Can you apply the method if you have already accumulated a considerable substance? YES, emphatically so, more so. Can you do it even when the market is fluctuating widely and its future course seems uncertain? The answer you will find in these pages is that you don't buy or sell "the market," you buy or sell specific securities. There are ALWAYS good investments, if not in one hay field, then in another.

There are taxes to consider, always. As you progress in knowledge of investing you progress also in the awareness of taxes. There are ways and ways of dealing with taxes. You can pay the maximum under the law, or you can pay the minimum under the law. The tax laws are designed to give relief and benefit under certain circumstances, or to encourage this-or-that form of investment, or to facilitate special dispositions of money. But the tax laws do not tell you what to do, they merely prescribe what you *may* do. You are supposed to apply your own brains as to choice of methods. You are *not* supposed to overpay your taxes, although many naive persons persist in doing so.

The capital gains tax is one of the main preferential taxes in the field of investing, or of the managing of money. It is less than the income tax. A synonym for capital gains is *growth*. Note especially well those portions of this book that deal with tax saving in relation to growth.

Let me tell you about the authors of this book, and the part I played in putting them together and hatching the book itself. I had always found investment experts were a bit stuffy in their language. They knew their subject, but couldn't explain it unless you knew as much as they knew. On the other hand I had always found that mere writers were too glib, slinging the words and the terms, but not really knowing the innards of the meaning. I thought if it were possible to marry a real expert with a real human presenter or writer, the progeny ought to be good. That's what I did. That's how come this book.

The expert is Lew G. Coit, who has spent over thirty years studying the art and the science of investing, including some years as a director of one of the largest investment advisory firms in the country. He is a counselor, an adviser. He advises financial big shots, and large funds, and he also advises "little men," little in money sense. He regards such counseling as professional, like the practice of law or medicine, suitable for all, the big and the small. It's a matter of conscience with him. And he has proved out, for his counsel has made millions for his clients. He has a record, and it is established.

The writer is John W. Hazard, one of the top editors of the magazine, *Changing Times*. He is almost an investment expert in his own right, but claims not to be. He is, however, responsible for the simple, clear and straightforward presentation of investment matters.

These are the joint authors of the series of articles in *Changing Times Magazine* that have gained wide attention among all sorts of people—people with a little money, and people with scads of it—BOTH.

I have no hesitancy in recommending this book. I feel a pride in being an instigator. It will do a lot of good to a lot of people— perhaps you.

W. M. KIPLINGER

Washington, D.C.

the odds against the haphazard investor

The ordinary person can make money in the stock market but usually he doesn't. To show why he doesn't, and how he could, are the purposes of this book.

The basic causes of failure are the urge to speculate, the desire to believe in tips and rumors as a means of acquiring quick riches, the overpowering instinct to go with the herd, the tendency to drift along without a clear-cut, positive, basic investment philosophy.

The antidote to all this is to adopt a sound philosophy and stick to it.

The investment philosophy outlined in this book has been developed over a period of thirty years and has been explained from time to time in the pages of *Changing Times Magazine*. We know it works. We also realize that it is not as glamorous or romantic as many of the stories that are always going the rounds about successful coups and quick profits. So right at the start, let us investigate the idea that the nonprofessional investor, over the long run, can get rich by means of tips or inside information or by just barging into the market and trying to buy at the bottom and sell at the top.

For 350 years, ever since stock certificates have been in general circulation, investors have been trying this. And they have generally failed. But even though one generation may learn the lesson, the next generation forgets it. Look back, for a moment, to the beginnings of stock trading and note how time and time again, the small investor has been drawn into the flame and been singed.

Stock trading, as we know it, had its origins in the sixteenth century. Prior to that time investments consisted largely of tangible things: cattle, slaves, grain, great crocks of olive oil, coin, plate, and so on. But by the sixteenth century, merchants and traders had begun to sort themselves out in the great cities of Holland, France and England, the wool merchants congregating in a certain street, the weavers in another, the grocers in a third and so on. At an early date these groups had organized into guilds and begun to import shiploads of their raw materials on a cooperative basis, each merchant financing a share. Thus they furnished a source of capital when royal companies began to be chartered.

In 1600 when Queen Elizabeth chartered the East India Company to import pepper, spices, silk and tea in competition with the Dutch, capital was raised by selling 125 shares in the company for close to 600 pounds per share. Originally the subscribers to the East India Company financed each voyage separately and profits per voyage often amounted to 100%. After 1612, however, voyages were conducted on the joint stock system for the benefit of the company as a whole. As the number of the company's shares grew, the stock began to be traded.

For a while stock ownership was a privilege only of the wealthy merchants and nobility. But as England prospered under Elizabeth and wealth began to spread downward through the social pyramid, a need arose on the part of the middle classes for some medium of investment besides land. Macaulay, describing this evolution, says, "Thousands of busy men found every Christmas that after the expenses of the year's housekeeping had been defrayed out of the year's income a surplus remained; and how that surplus was to be employed was a question of some difficulty. In our time, to invest such a surplus at something more than 3 per cent on the best security that has ever been known in the world is the work of a few minutes. But, in the seventeenth century a lawyer, a physician, or a retired merchant, who had saved some thousands and who wished to place them safely and profitably, was often greatly embarrassed.

"Three generations earlier," Macaulay continues, "a man who had accumulated wealth in a trade or a profession generally purchased real property or lent his savings on mortgage. But the number of acres in the Kingdom had remained the same and the value of those acres, though it had greatly increased, had by no means increased as fast as the quantity of capital which was seeking for employment. Many, too, wished to put their money where they could find it at an hour's notice, and looked about for some species of property which could be more readily transferred than a house or a field."

To cater to this need in the early part of the seventeenth century, a breed of stock jobbers or, as we would say, dealers in shares, sprang up. They first hung around the office of the Royal Exchanger in London. This important officer operated a monopoly granted by the King and had the exclusive privilege of changing gold coins for silver, and foreign for English money, cutting himself (and the King) in on each transaction. Stock jobbers in those days were held in low esteem, being classed by the writers of the period with chimney sweeps. They soon were driven away from the Royal Exchange and set themselves up nearby in what came to be known as Exchange Alley. There they made in the middle of the street a noisy market in such shares as were available—those of the East India Company and others now long forgotten.

Stock jobbers then as now made their biggest profits when share prices fluctuated most widely and rapidly. They were on hand in the Dutch cities in 1634 to give a boost to one of the strangest booms in history, the tulipomania. Tulip bulbs, originally imported from Constantinople around 1560, had become increasingly popular until by 1634, as Charles Mackay says in his book "Extraordinary Popular Delusions," it was deemed a proof of bad taste for any man of fortune to be without a collection of them.

The rage for possessing the rarer kinds of bulb spread from the wealthy to all classes of Dutch society. By 1636, regular marts or tulip exchanges were flourishing in the major Dutch cities. Stock jobbers turned from share trading and stood ready to quote prices on the many varieties of bulbs just as brokers quote stock prices today. As speculation grew more feverish, bulb prices rose and fell rapidly and fortunes were made and lost almost overnight. Mackay says that nobles, farmers, mechanics, seamen, footmen, maid-servants and even chimney sweeps dabbled in tulips. To raise cash for speculation, people sold or mortgaged their property for far less than its real value. Foreigners heard of the boom and their money, too, poured into Holland.

As prices rose and rose there inevitably dawned on the more prudent people the realization that the boom could not go on forever. A few began to withdraw from the market, nailing down their profits while they could and investing in gold and silver plate and other more realistic values. As the word got around, selling spread and prices began to fall faster and faster. Those who had bought futures contracts refused to honor them when payment date arrived. Defaults became common and the boom collapsed with fearful rapidity. A rare tulip bulb that a few months before had changed hands for five or six thousand florins was not worth a tenth of that amount. The resulting depression lasted several years.

As stock ownership became more popular, the ruling classes were not slow to see the money-raising possibilities of setting up companies and selling shares to the public. In 1716 France was close to bankruptcy, its currency was debased and its officials, particularly the tax collectors, were utterly corrupt. Louis XIV had just died and since the heir was but seven years old, the Duke of Orléans had taken the reins as regent. At this point a Scotsman named John Law, a student of finance and at the same time an inveterate gambler, arrived on the scene and sold the Duke on a scheme to rescue the country's finances by the issuance of paper money. Law was authorized to set up a bank and to issue notes which the government would accept in payment of taxes. Law guaranteed his notes to be convertible into coin current at the time of issue. In other words, even if the government depreciated the metallic currency of the realm (which it had done on several occasions by clipping off a chunk of each coin) the notes would retain their value. Law's notes were immediately accepted by the populace and even went to a premium over gold and silver. Business began to recover.

With the success of his bank, Law persuaded the regent to allow him to set up a company to have a monopoly of trade with the area along the Mississippi River, then popularly supposed to abound in gold and silver. When stock in this Mississippi company was offered to the public, it was eagerly sought after. Naturally the directors offered additional shares. These in turn were snapped up and the regent gave the company a monopoly to trade with the East Indies, China and the South Seas. Fifty thousand more shares were issued and at least three hundred thousand applications were made to purchase them.

A frenzy of speculation thus began. Thousands of Frenchmen crowded into the square in front of the company's offices, seeking to buy stock. Three hundred thousand shares were issued and still the demand rose. Mackay reports that people of every age, both sexes and every condition of life speculated in the rise and fall of the Mississippi shares. Stock jobbers set up booths in streets adjacent to the company's offices and wherever Law went he was mobbed by aristocrats eager to have their names entered on his stock subscription lists. The price of shares sometimes rose ten or twenty percent in a few hours and people who were poor in the morning found themselves wealthy by evening. Law's own coachman soon made enough money to hire a coach of his own.

For about a year, Paris underwent an unprecedented boom. Prices and wages rose, new houses were built and all kinds of goods and works of art were ordered by those who believed themselves rich because of their enormous paper profits. In the meantime, however, very little real trading was ever done with the Mississippi territory or the South Seas or anywhere else. The whole great edifice was built on sand. Eventually a few of the shrewder speculators began to change their shares into coin. The movement grew and soon so many people were trying to cash in their shares for hard currency that in one day fifteen people were squeezed to death in the crush surrounding the royal bank. Shares of the Mississippi company plunged, Law barely escaped from France with his life, and the whole scheme came crashing down.

At the height of the Mississippi scheme the speculative fever jumped the English Channel and a similar orgy developed in London in shares of the South Sea Company. Like many a modern oil or mining venture, the South Sea Company was set up primarily to sell shares to the public and raise money for use of the promoters. In 1711 the government debt was burdensome and the Earl of Oxford persuaded a group of merchants to take it over. In return, they were to receive six percent and the monopoly on trade to the west coast of South America which was known to abound in gold and silver. The big catch, of course, was that Spain had a stranglehold on this area and had no intention of giving it up. This was glossed over, however, and rumors were spread adroitly that Spain was prepared to concede four ports on the coasts of Chile and Peru.

By 1717, the advantages of selling stock to the public had become clear to all concerned and the House of Commons permitted the South Sea Company to increase its capitalization in return for taking over more of the public debt. In the meantime, even though the Spanish had agreed to permit only one British ship a year to visit the west coast of South America, extravagant rumors were circulated to the effect that Spain was prepared to swap South American ports for Gibraltar. Exchange Alley was crowded with shouting traders and stock of the South Sea Company began to jump. The Company offered the public a million pounds of stock. It was oversubscribed by a hundred percent. In a few days the price had doubled. Another hundred million pounds worth of stock was offered and in a few hours it was oversubscribed by fifty percent.

This kind of atmosphere was utopia for the stock jobbers and very quickly they were offering shares in all kinds of joint-stock companies, some of them fairly plausible but most of them mere devices for separating the suckers from their money. One company was formed "to make deal boards out of sawdust." Another was to finance a wheel for perpetual motion. Another was "for encouraging the breed of horses in England and improving of glebe and church lands, and repairing and rebuilding parsonage and vicarage houses." One rascal offered stock in a company "for carrying on an undertaking of great advantage, but nobody to know what it is." In hopes of making a quick turn-over, crowds gathered to bid for this stock and by evening of the day it was offered the promoter was able to retire to parts unknown with two thousand pounds.

So confused was the situation in Exchange Alley during this time that shares in the same "bubble" were known to have been sold at the same instant ten percent higher at one end of the alley than at the other. The stock of the South Sea Company itself, which originally had been sold to the public at 100 pounds per share, rose to 500, at which point many people sold their government bonds to buy it. In four days it jumped from 550 to 890. It then fell back to 640 and the company agents got busy and bought in enough to restore confidence. As a result the stock ran up to 1,000. "The bubble was then full-blown," says Mackay, "and began to quiver and shake preparatory to its bursting."

Within a few weeks the stock was down to 700. Day after day it continued to fall until it eventually settled at 135. Those who had bought it or loaned money on it at higher prices were heavy losers. An investigation by the House of Commons showed that many members had accepted stock at the original subscription price in return for votes favorable to the company. Those that had done so had their estates confiscated to make partial restitution.

Not every man with a money-making idea or scheme could obtain a charter from the Crown. Some companies sold stock without a charter. Many of these "common law" companies were formed primarily to make money for the promoters but even the sound ones had a tremendous disadvantage to investors. Each shareholder was personally liable for the company's debts down to his last penny. This unlimited liability eventually was removed by Parliament. Thereafter a stockholder's liability was limited to the original subscription price of his shares. English companies having this limit on shareholders' liability thereafter were, and still are, required to use the word "limited" after their corporate name. Other reforms took place. The stock jobbers moved into a coffee house off Exchange Alley and gradually organized and adopted regulations to prevent the worst abuses.

On this side of the Atlantic the Americans went through the whole cycle again. At the start, land and mortgages were the main outlets for investment and liquidity was almost unattainable. Money itself was extremely scarce and much of the business in early Virginia was done in tobacco. Hogsheads of tobacco were taken to one of the royal warehouses where they were inspected, graded and receipts issued against them. These receipts were negotiable and could be used for payment of taxes or bills.

Most of the early American manufactures and trading ventures were family owned. Only the banks, insurance companies, canal companies, as well as the government itself, were large enough to require public financing. Stocks or bonds in these enterprises were not at first traded in the modern sense. Banks kept an inventory and sold the securities "over the counter." Many are still sold that way, not by banks but by over-the-counter dealers. Philadelphia was the first financial capital. Shares in the United States Bank and the Bank of North America were traded there before 1800. New York gradually forged ahead and brokers established an open air market under a buttonwood tree at what is now 68 Wall Street. This "curb exchange" operated in the street until 1921, long after other brokers had moved indoors.

When the railroads were organized, vigorous trading took place in their shares. Fortunes were made and lost as the various roads prospered, went bankrupt, merged and were jockeyed around by the powerful magnates of the nineteenth century.

During those days, however, the percentage of the population that actually ever owned a share of stock or a bond was extremely small. Most families had their capital tied up in land or a small business. Not only was cash scarce but there were few places available where small sums could be invested, or even deposited. Banks did business only with the wealthy. Around 1815 civic leaders began establishing mutual savings banks to provide laboring and seafaring men with a safe place for their hoard of coins and bills hidden in mattresses, stoves and secret cavities of floor or wall. Government bonds in small denominations were not available until the baby bonds of World War I.

By the Nineteen Twenties, however, money had become plentiful enough and the business outlook rosy enough for the small investor, as well as the large, to feel justified in exchanging his savings for something with growth possibilities. The most respected leaders of business and government stated confidently that a new era had arrived. Depressions, or panics as they were called in those days, were no longer to be feared. More production meant more jobs which in turn meant more money for purchasing more goods and so on in an economy that supposedly would rise forever.

The Florida land boom swelled up in the fall of 1925. Visions of the state, as the vacation and retirement land of the future inspired people to swarm to Florida and to buy up acreage and blocks of lots, subdivided only on paper, and even to begin construction of apartment houses, office buildings and hotels. Enthusiasm fed on itself and the trading in lots became as wild and hectic as any bubble in history.

Trading was possible by the use of "binders" which were merely agreements to buy at a specified price. A guest arriving in a Miami hotel at the height of the boom found the lobby so jammed with shouting and gesticulating dealers and traders in binders that he had to tip a bellboy to crawl through the legs of the crowd to the registration desk to check the room reservation. A piece of property might change hands several times a day and on the lawn in front of the Dade County courthouse more than a hundred stenographers sat at temporary desks typing away for dear life in an effort to keep up with the title transfers. Banks were so far behind in their bookkeeping that a depositor might overdraw his account with confidence that it would not become known for at least four weeks.

As in every bubble in recorded history, this one broke with a rapid collapse of paper values. In the past few years bulldozers clearing land for subdivisions outside of several Florida cities have uncovered amid the jungle of palmetto the pitiful remains of streets, curbs and gutters that some hopeful speculator had begun and abandoned during the boom of 1925 and 1926.

After the Florida land boom the stock market, leavened by an ever-increasing flow of investment money, began its inexorable rise. As it went up it attracted more investors and soon people were borrowing heavily to get in on the ride. Speculators were willing to pay 6, 8, 10 and at one point 12% for money with which to buy stocks on margin. After all, it was worth it to borrow at 10 or 12% if you could double the money in a few months—and such was the universal hope. Money to lend flowed in vast amounts not only from banks all over the country but from corporations, some of which could make more money this way than from their regular business. Commercial banks borrowed money from the Federal Reserve Banks at 5% and reloaned it in the call money market at 10% or 12%. To raise money for lending, banks even paid 4% interest on checking accounts.

By March 1929 the speculative fever had risen to such heights that speculators were willing to pay 17% and even 20% for money with which to buy on margin. The most popular stocks, strangely enough, included many of what are considered to be solid blue chips today: American Tel and Tel, Du Pont, Standard Oil of New Jersey, U. S. Rubber, Woolworth, General Electric, U. S. Steel, RCA and so on.

The Dow-Jones Industrial Average, which had been 152 in January 1927 and 200 in January 1928, stood at 300 at the beginning of 1929. At the end of June it passed 330 and three days later, 340. In August the Average rapidly crossed the 350, 360 and 370 marks and even those who previously had warned that the market was too high apparently became brainwashed. The actual historic high was reached on September 3 when the Average exceeded 381, but no one knew at the time that this was the fateful day.

A minor break took place the first week in October. Then on October 23 came the deluge. Six million shares changed hands and prices suffered the sharpest break in two years. At the close the ticker was nearly two hours late. Lights burned all night in Wall Street as margin calls went out by wire all over the country. But worse was to come. The next day was October 24, and it became known as Black Thursday. The market opened fairly steady but tremendous blocks of stock appeared on the tape, 20,000 shares at a crack. Prices began to sink, the ticker fell behind, prices sank faster, and a spiral began that seemed uncheckable. General Electric opened at 315 and soon was down to 283. RCA dropped precipitately from 69 to 44—and this in the space of a few hours. By one o'clock the high-speed ticker tape was already an hour and a half late. And the biggest bankers in New York City were meeting in emergency conference, pondering a way to stem the tide.

Shortly thereafter Richard Whitney, a Morgan partner and representative of the banks, strode about the floor of the Exchange putting in buy orders in 10,000 share blocks. This stemmed the tide but only temporarily. On Monday, October

28, the real, history-making panic began. All weekend margin calls had been going out and as the market opened, stock was dumped anew. General Electric fell 47 points that day. And the next day was Black Tuesday, the worst that Wall Street has ever known. When the market opened huge blocks of stock were thrown out for whatever they would bring. Everyone wanted to sell, no one wanted to buy. Prices plunged like an airplane hitting a giant air pocket. Over 16,000,000 shares changed hands. And at the end of the day it was clear that the great bull market was over.

More disillusioned, perhaps, than the ordinary investor was the person who had bought investment trust shares. During the Twenties these were put forth as a safe vehicle through which the small investor could turn his funds over to professional managers. But in the end, the professionals fared no better than anyone else. And worse, some turned out to be downright crooks who milked the trusts of their capital.

After the crash and the beginning of the depression, owning stocks and investment trust shares became unpopular. This was not merely because it had proved so unprofitable for so many. The so-called liberals who swarmed into power with the New Deal looked askance at money-making even when it was done by frugality and hard work. Production for use, rather than for profit, was the ideal of the young professors and reformers. Those who owned stock were thought of as living off the sweat of others.

This attitude persisted through the Thirties. Savings bonds, sold with patriotic hoop-la during the war, continued popular afterwards largely because people were more interested in safety than growth.

In 1949 when we wrote the first investment article for *Changing Times Magazine*, stocks were still unpopular as shown by a survey of consumers conducted in behalf of the Federal Reserve Board. Each person polled was asked, "Suppose a man decides not to spend all his money. He can either put it in a bank or he can invest it. What do you think would be the wisest thing for him to do with the money nowadays—put it in the bank, buy savings bonds with it, invest it in real estate, or buy common stock with it? Why do you make that choice?"

For:

Savings bonds	60%	"Safe, not a gamble"
Bank deposits	32%	"Safe, not a gamble"
Real estate	9%	
Common stock	5%	

Against:

Common stock	62%	"Not familiar with, not safe, a gamble"
Real estate	58%	"Price too high"
Bank deposits	23%	"Interest rate too low"
Savings bonds	9%	

Even among men and women with incomes of $7,500 or better, two thirds said they wanted their investments to have a fixed value.

Gradually since then, stocks have come back into favor. During the years following 1949 the number of investors tripled. Stocks that had been selling for nine or ten times earnings in 1949, were bid up until they were selling for 15, 20, 25 and sometimes 50 times earnings. In 1961 a bubble in hot new issues swelled up and caused a good deal of alarm on the part of financial writers and stock exchange officials before it subsided.

In the spring of 1962 a bear market readjusted values. The unexpected sharp drop in prices came as a surprise to a new generation of investors who had forgotten (or never learned) the lessons of the past. In recent years it has been popular to point to new ways in which today's investor is protected. It is said that markets are more carefully policed. More information is available than ever before, about the economy as a whole, about each industry, about individual companies.

All this is true. Nevertheless, no laws and no statistics can prevent a person from paying more for a stock than it is worth—or, to put it another way, more than it will bring in the market a few months or years hence.

If strict laws and regulations policing the securities markets and the general availability of financial information are guarantees that ordinary people can make money in the stock market, then you would think that officials of the stock exchanges themselves, who do much of the policing and insist on the accuracy and adequacy of published reports, would easily become wealthy. Yet at a dinner in New York in 1961 we sat next to an official of the New York Stock Exchange who confided this personal experience. The senior partner of a brokerage firm, to whom the official had been of some service, tried to repay the favor by furnishing the name of a stock to buy for a quick appreciation. The stock was bought at 32 and in a few months was down to 18. The broker was embarrassed and apologized. He then furnished the name of another stock in which he had the greatest confidence. This, in turn, went down. The official of the Stock Exchange, whose duties gave him little time to delve into individual stocks, was disillusioned.

The senior partner of a well-known brokerage firm admits that his wealth has come from his brokerage business, the income from commissions for buying, selling and underwriting securities. His own trading account over the years has produced only a five percent annual profit on capital.

These and other examples indicate that these times differ little from those past. The nonprofessional investor gropes his way into the market, getting his advice from customers' men and the writers of market letters, who themselves are dependent on their salaries or commissions for a living.

What we are saying, in short, is that the ordinary investor often does not make money in the market. What we are going to propose, in the next chapter, is that he can make money if he will follow certain principles.

an investment philosophy that has worked, and will work

No great thing was ever done without a purpose. The order of the day, issued by the general on the eve of battle; the battle cry itself, shouted by men going into action; the motto on the knight's shield; the slogan of the political party; the declaration of purpose inscribed down through the ages on parchment or on waving banner, all tell us that in order to succeed, men need to know the goal for which they strive. And even in as humble a pursuit as investing, a man must have a philosophy— a picture of what he is trying to do.

Yet very few investors have any such goal. Ask a man why he buys stocks and chances are he will say, "to make money." By this he means he hopes to buy a stock that will go up so that he can sell it at a profit and buy another that he hopes also will go up, and so on.

Despite all the evidence to the contrary, a great number of people persist in thinking that this will work. They think they can make money by devoting fifteen minutes of their lunch hour to watching the tape, consulting their broker, and buying and selling stock. It really is a kind of game, sometimes referred to as "taking a flyer in the stock market." One psychiatrist has concluded that many people have a compulsion to lose, and "play" the market to satisfy this subconscious urge. Be that as it may, the pity of it is that many of them actually could increase their capital if they would settle on a sound investment philosophy and stick to it.

Consider, first of all, the favorable currents that the intelligent investor can make use of. The investment field is one where the theoretical chance of gain is very great. The tax on capital gains amounts to only half the regular income tax. And there is a maximum of 25% of the gain itself, which means that for those in the higher income brackets, the tax is much less than half their normal tax rate.

These capital gains are more easily obtainable in the United States than anywhere else in the world. In the first place, our rate of growth has been almost unequalled in history. And there is good evidence that this dynamic growth of ours will continue. The capitalist system offers the individual great rewards for that extra effort he makes with brain, imagination and muscle.

Then, within the over-all growth of our economy, there are industries that are growing even faster than the economy as a whole. There is keen competition in steel versus aluminum and plastic; in railroads versus airlines and trucks. And within these industries, there are companies that are spurred on by the same relentless competition and are doing better than their competitors.

In the United States, too, there is more opportunity than anywhere else in the world to know the facts about growing industries and companies. The individual who reads any substantial part of what appears in the daily newspapers and weekly and monthly magazines can hardly help but know a good deal about what the economy is doing and which industries are prospering. Federal laws and New York Stock Exchange regulations make it mandatory for large corporations to give to the public the most detailed facts and figures concerning operations, sales, income and profits.

Some people do use these opportunities. And they do make consistent profits in the stock market. One way they do it, and the way that will be recommended in this book, is to select those industries and those companies within them, that are moving ahead most rapidly and consistently. Once a promising stock has been acquired, then it is held until there are signs of a change of fortune.

Most of the fortunes in securities have been accumulated in this way—not by trying to buy low and sell high time after time— but by acquiring stocks of strong growing companies, by staying with them and accumulating more. The following are true examples taken from records of an investment counselor. For example, the early records of one very substantial fortune show that the key purchase was ten shares of Standard Oil of New Jersey for $300 and ten shares of General Electric for $350. The purchasing continued and grew larger. The final result, now in the hands of a granddaughter, is millions.

Back in 1938 a widow with very slim resources invested $2,000 in the stock of Minnesota Mining & Manufacturing. Her faith in the future of the company never wavered. She may have been tempted to take a profit along the way, but she resisted. Her theory was, as long as the company was growing, why switch? In 1961 these shares had a market value of $240,000.

In Rochester, N.Y., many years ago, two young men roomed in a boarding house. One was in the buggy whip business; the other was working on a new chemical process. The young chemist needed money to finance his experiments and his friend advanced $5,000, taking it out of his buggy whip business. This was the beginning of Eastman Kodak Company and the $5,000 grew into many millions.

In the Thirties a family known to the authors scrimped and saved and put about $3,000 into the stock of International Business Machines. In 1961 this investment was worth $400,000.

The temptation to sell out along the way is, of course, tremendous. At luncheon one day, a group was talking about a man whose father, years and years ago, was counsel for a newly organized small company. He accepted stock in lieu of fees. In 1961 the stock was worth around thirty million dollars. One of the group said, "But that wasn't a result of his good judgment. He simply inherited the stock from his father. He had nothing to do with it."

To which we replied, "He did have something to do with it. Every day for years and years when the stock market was open, this man could have sold his stock at any time and nailed down his profit. Again and again he had to decide to hold his stock. The decision may have been made because of sentiment, but that is doubtful. More likely it was based on the feeling that the company would continue to grow; that its future remained bright.

"Holding onto stock, by itself, is not the whole answer—of course. The owner of stock in a street car company had to make the opposite decision. In his case he had to recognize that his stock had no future; that it should be sold and replaced."

Here is a simile to illustrate the point. A man is sitting on the bank of a meandering stream. He is dropping chips into the water. He wants these chips to move as fast as possible toward the ocean. Therefore he tries to place them in the fastest moving water. There are eddies here and there, and backwaters, so that there is danger that one chip or another will be becalmed or thrown up on the shore. When this happens, the chip will have to be relaunched. But as long as a chip is moving rapidly in the direction you want it to go, why pick it up?

So in investments. If a company becomes "mature"; if the management shows signs of standing pat, all this will soon show up in the annual reports. At this point the investor must be prepared to take his profit, pay his tax and start anew. Or, it may be he will have to step out and take a loss, and put his diminished resources into another company that still is moving. But as to those investments that are growing and moving into new fields, the investor should keep his ears stopped against the blandishments of those advisers who would have him sell merely to re-buy, only to sell again and so on.

Can the ordinary person do this? Can he afford to buy and hold over the years? Can he tie up his money so permanently? The answer is that if he cannot afford to hold, he cannot afford to invest. The stock market is no place to put money that is to be used at some specified date to meet an obligation. If a man has a debt to be repaid on a certain date, the money is better not entrusted to the ups and downs of the stock market. For stock prices do not rise or fall in a straight line. They waver up, or waver down, and the timing of the fluctuations is unpredictable.

Therefore the ability, as well as the intention, to hold should be part of the individual's investment philosophy. Too often a person invests money that really should be part of his reserves.

If a family invests money that may be needed to tide it over sickness or loss of a job, or if it invests money that will be needed to buy a new car, or pay a debt, then fate too often will decree that the need for the money will come at a time when the stock market happens to be depressed.

That leads to a set of simple precautions. Before investing, a family should have its financial affairs in good order. It should have adequate life insurance on the breadwinner; it should have its home paid for or safely financed; it should have reserve funds that will carry it through any reasonably expectable emergency. By weighing its life insurance program heavily toward real insurance, that is, ordinary life, or a combination of ordinary life and term insurance, it can obtain big protection for a relatively small annual outlay. By being conservative in its standard of living, it can pay down the home mortgage to 50%, or less, of the market value. By keeping its eyes firmly fixed on the more distant goals and withstanding the siren call of those who would sell it every gewgaw and luxury for so much down and so much a month, it can tuck away enough in savings to tide it over a six months' emergency. If a family can put itself in this posture, then it can confidently embark on a long range program of investment.

That it should make every effort toward this goal, is clear from the following facts. The United States, and indeed the world, appears to be embarked on a perpetual course of inflation. If a family feels it will need $10,000 to send a child to college at some future date, then it probably should aim for $12,000 to $14,000 because the costs of education are rising every year. If a couple believes it will need a retirement income of $500 a month, then it probably should aim at $750 or even $1,000 a month, depending on the number of years to retirement, because the cost of living goes inexorably up.

Dollars put into savings accounts, or bonds, or insurance, will not grow along with rising prices. Carefully chosen equities alone, and that means real estate or common stocks, can hold their purchasing power. And it is not inflation alone that should turn the family's eyes toward equities. Our standard of living is rising. Today we are not satisfied with the kind of life our parents led. What they considered to be luxuries, we consider to be necessities. We must have better homes, more transportation, much more elaborate recreation, better health care, higher education for our children. And this trend will continue.

Our income from salaries and wages tends to rise more or less automatically with these heavier financial demands. But our savings do not. If put into fixed-dollar investments, they lose their value as surely as if they were stolen a little bit at a time. To keep up with the rising standard of living, and the rising cost of every article and service, some savings must also be placed where they will grow in purchasing power.

To us, then, investment in stocks by the intelligently-managed family appears to be almost a necessity. And to succeed in its investments, a family must have a sound philosophy and stick to it. This means, first, making the family secure against emergencies; second, funneling money into the stocks of those companies that are growing the fastest and seem destined to continue growing; and third, resisting the temptation to sell out and trade, leaving good investments alone not for months, but if conditions continue favorable, for years.

one good reason for buying common stocks—inflation

We have explained briefly, and in a preliminary way, how the ordinary investor can successfully buy and hold common stocks. But admittedly, there are risks. Why, therefore, should he not avoid these risks and put all his money into something safe—bonds and savings accounts? Why should he even try to make money in the stock market?

One answer is that inflation, the inexorable rise in prices and decline in the purchasing power of the dollar, will eat away his savings. The economic facts of life in today's world are such that putting at least a part of one's capital into equities is a matter of self-preservation.

Let us examine this inflation for a moment and see whence it comes and what is the likelihood of its continuing. Inflation in the classical sense means simply an abnormal increase in the quantity of purchasing power without a corresponding increase in the amount of goods and services available for purchase. In theory, if the amount of goods and services produced in a country rises 5% each year, and the amount of money and credit also rises 5%, prices are stable. But if the amount of goods and services rises 5% and the amount of money and credit rises 10%, there are extra dollars floating around, chasing goods and services and bidding up prices.

Really disastrous inflations have occurred in the past in countries like France and Germany. Once the disease gets past a certain point, it begins to feed on itself and the government simply begins printing money without any backing in hopes of giving citizens enough to pay the soaring prices of goods. But each addition to the money supply sends prices up faster. After World War I Germany experienced one of these galloping inflations and the mark dropped so far in value that it took millions and later hundreds of millions to equal a dollar. In two days in the fall of 1923 the mark fell from 20,000,000 to the dollar to 60,000,000 to the dollar and Berlin insane asylums were admitting victims suffering from the obsession of multiplying zeros.

These disastrous inflations of the past, of course, have wiped out bonds, savings, life insurance, pensions, currency and anything else with a fixed monetary value. A 50,000,000 mark life insurance policy which once would have represented a fortune, would, of course, have become worthless after the mark had fallen to the level of 60,000,000 to the dollar.

The classical type of galloping inflation does not seem likely to occur in the United States. Nevertheless, bonds, savings, life insurance, pensions and currency, while they are eroded more slowly, have been eroded just as surely by the creeping inflation that has occurred in recent years.

When credit and currency are increased faster than the supply of goods and services, the result is known as "demand-pull" inflation. Since World War II economists have been talking about another type described as "cost-push" inflation. The idea is that costs can rise and push up prices regardless of the relation between supply and demand. Take as an example the steel industry, which is highly organized by labor unions. A centralized policy-making body guides the union wage demands made on the large steel producing companies. These unions thus have it in their power to force up wages throughout the steel industry. Some of these increases in the cost of making steel can be offset by labor-saving and cost-saving machinery. But to the extent that increasing labor costs cannot be so offset, steel prices must rise.

Since the beginning of World War II, the United States has been in an inflationary period. On the average, prices have been rising at around 3% a year. This is just about enough to cancel out the income from a conservative investment such as a savings bond. *Chart 1* indicates the course of prices.

CHART 1

See how prices tend to go up
Consumer Price Index

How much of this price rise is due to the classical, demand-pull inflation and how much to the newer cost-push inflation, is a matter of argument among economists. Both influences undoubtedly are at work. The quantity of money, particularly credit, has been inflated. At the same time, organized labor has been able to push up its wage scales faster than the increased costs can be offset by labor-saving and cost-saving machinery.

It would appear that inflationary forces will continue to erode the dollar and the value of fixed-dollar savings. Consider the following points:

Prices have become so sticky that they no longer go down even in circumstances in which they have always gone down in the past. Historically, prices go up during wartime and down soon thereafter. The explanation is that during wartime, much of a nation's productive capacity is diverted to armaments and munitions. The supply of consumable goods and services decreases. At the same time, a great deal of money is paid out to defense workers, soldiers and sailors, who use the money to bid up prices of the consumer goods and services that already are scarce. After the war is over, the inflation usually continues for a while until pent-up demand for civilian goods is satisfied. Then a reaction sets in and prices, inflated by wartime scarcity, collapse.

Prices hit peaks during the War of 1812, the Civil War, World War I and World War II. In each case they fell back drastically— except after World War II and the Korean War. The traditional peacetime stability of prices also has disappeared. Between wars, in the past, prices have not risen. During peacetime recessions prices actually have declined. Yet in the years following the Korean War, when the country was at least technically at peace, prices continued to rise. They did not decline during the recessions of 1953–54 and 1958–59.

There are several explanations of all this. Some economists prefer one; some another. All are pertinent to some degree. First, although the country is nominally at peace, the cold war keeps expenditures for national defense at a very high level, some fifty billion dollars a year. Even though our capacity to produce civilian goods has expanded so that autos, houses, clothes, appliances and so on are in plentiful supply, this tremendous national defense expenditure pumps money into the economy with no offsetting increase in the supply of consumer goods. As far as can be seen ahead, this inflationary cause will continue.

Not only are defense expenditures large, but the political trend is toward ever-increasing government expenditure for civilian projects. Politicians love to spend and hate to tax. Thus instead of financing these ever-growing expenditures on a pay-as-you-go basis, the government tends to spend more than it takes in and make up the difference by borrowing. In the years following World War II the federal budget generally showed a deficit. Such borrowing often is inflationary as will be shown by the following example.

Non-inflationary Treasury Financing. Suppose the Secretary of the Treasury wants to borrow $100,000,000. If he sells $100,000,-000 worth of long-term bonds to the public, this will soak up that amount which might otherwise be spent by consumers, and give it to the government to spend. This is not considered inflationary. But neither is it the only way the Treasury raises money.

Inflationary Treasury Financing. When government bonds are not popular and investors prefer stocks, the Treasury tends to borrow a good deal of its money from banks, and this is inflationary.

A former Secretary of the Treasury, Robert Anderson, has explained why this is so. "Suppose (as Secretary of the Treasury) I wanted to write checks of $100,000,000 starting tomorrow morning, but the Treasury was out of money. If I called up a bank and said, 'Will you loan me $100,000,000 at 3½% for six months if I send you over a note to that effect?' the banker would probably say, 'Yes, I will.'

"Where would he get the $100,000,000 with which to credit the account of the United States Treasury? Would he take it from the account of someone else? No, certainly not. He would merely create that much money, subject to reserve requirements, by crediting our account in that sum and accepting the government's note as an asset. When I had finished writing checks for $100,-000,000, the operation would have added that sum to the money supply. Now certainly that approaches the same degree of monetization as if I had called down to the Bureau of Engraving and Printing and said, 'Please print me up $100,000,000 worth of greenbacks which I can pay out tomorrow.'"

The Treasury and the Federal Reserve Board do not like this method of financing. But as long as the politicians keep shoveling out the money faster than it comes in from taxes, a certain amount of such inflationary borrowing seems likely. Thus unless there is to be a sharp change of administration policy, which seems remote, this cause of inflation will continue.

The assumption by the government of the responsibility for maintaining full employment, as outlined by the Employment Act of 1946, should not necessarily be inflationary, but it is. The weapons it uses are spending and control of credit. In theory, these weapons are to be used to iron out the ups and downs of the business cycle. But inevitably, by the very nature of politics, they are more often used as a stimulant than as a restraint. When the Federal Reserve Board increases available credit and lowers interest rates to counteract a recession, politicians applaud. But when a boom develops that might eventually lead to a bust, and the Board tries to lean against the wind by contracting credit and allowing interest rates to harden, politicians threaten and complain. This gives an inflationary bias to most of the economic and monetary moves made by the government. And this bias appears likely to continue.

It is generally conceded that if workers produce more goods

per hour, they should receive more pay. An increase in wages that exactly matched an increase in production per man-hour would not be inflationary because the additional money would be absorbed by the additional goods produced. In recent years, however, wages have been increasing more than twice as fast as productivity. Businessmen so far have been able only partly to compensate for this additional cost by cutting costs with labor-saving equipment. The balance of increased labor costs have been met by raising prices. These price rises have occurred at a time when goods were fairly plentiful, in violation of the classical law of supply and demand.

From time to time the government calls on unions and business-men voluntarily to hold down wages and prices. But since the union leader's prestige depends partly on his record of obtaining continual wage increases for his members, such appeals so far have been ineffective. And the so-called wage-price spiral may be expected to keep on spiraling.

What are the forces opposing inflation? Are they strong enough to stop the seemingly endless rise in prices? One contra-inflationary force is industry's never-ending fight to keep costs down. To offset the constant union pressure for higher wages, industry is shifting to automation, designing and producing machines to do the work of people. Even this trend, however, has some temporary inflationary side effects. A new automatic machine may cut labor costs for the company that buys it, but it takes labor to produce it. And this labor is akin to labor in a munitions plant. The product created is not consumable, so that the money spent to construct it goes into competition for other consumer goods and services.

Another contra-inflationary force is the reward the capitalist system offers to the man or the business that can discover a new product, or a better or less expensive way to produce an old one. This desperate race to produce what people will buy has led to cheaper compact automobiles, less expensive materials for cloth-ing, bargain airline fares and so on.

Although the classical contra-inflationary force, the law of sup-ply and demand, seems to have been suspended, it still is work-ing beneath the surface. As the rest of the world improves its manufacturing techniques, foreign goods compete more and more with goods made by high paid American labor. Foreign autos, textiles, transistor radios, sporting goods and a host of other products already have had a lowering effect on domestic prices.

Then, too, the lessons of history are not lost on everyone. The Federal Reserve Board was conceived by President Woodrow Wilson and Senator Carter Glass of Virginia, to be a central bank in the classical tradition, free of political control. As long as it remains thus independent, it could be a force against inflation.

Other leaders in politics, business, finance and education can always be counted on to point out the fate of almost every nation that started down the primrose path of deficit financing. But on the other hand, in recent years a good many well-known economists have embraced the idea that a little inflation is a good thing, that it oils the wheels of progress.

These forces that oppose inflation are not new. They have been in existence all along since World War II. At no point have they been completely effective.

If we are, then, in a continuing era of creeping inflation, what are the consequences? Consider one or two examples from the past that give a glimpse of what the future may be like.

Back in 1948 a couple might have started a savings program designed to send their son, then aged five, to college when he reached the age of eighteen. At that time a boy could go to a state university for four years for about $4,000. The couple might prudently have figured that a savings program of $22 a month at 3% compound interest would produce the required amount.

In the meantime, however, tuition, room and board, all went up rapidly. The necessary amount became closer to $7,000. The savings program as it turned out, would have been far from sufficient. Actually, the couple should have been saving $40 a month instead of $22 or else should have put the money where the principal would grow.

Similarly, the couple that started a savings account some years ago to provide money for retirement might have had as their goal a fund that would furnish them $200 a month. Upon retirement they found that they could not live as they had planned on $200 a month. Their needs were closer to $400. The "prudent" method of salting away dollars turned out to be not prudent, after all.

In the light of history, then, the family that is looking fifteen or twenty years ahead cannot assume that cost of a college education, or an adequate retirement income, or any other expense, will be the same as it is today. Rather, the really prudent family must assume that college costs, retirement costs and general living costs will continue to rise in the future as they have in the past.

There are two ways to cope with this problem. One is to set aside half again as much, or twice as much, as would now seem to be required. This is the life insurance company's answer to inflation. If living costs are going to rise, says the life insurance salesman, then you should buy just that much more insurance. If the dollar is going to be worth half as much fifteen years from now, then just save twice as much. This pat answer, however, is seldom practical. Taxes and other financial demands make savings difficult. Most families have to scrimp to keep up any sort of a savings program.

The other alternative, and the one that this book will recommend, is to put at least a part of savings where they may be ex-

CHART 2

Why Stocks Can Protect You Against Inflation
Note how stocks have gone up,
while value of a dollar has dropped

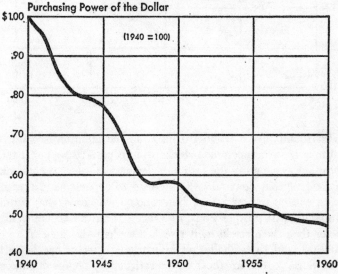

pected to grow, not at a fixed rate of 3% or 4%, but faster, say
6–10%. Suppose that in 1947 a family had put $5,000 in a 3% sav-
ings account and $5,000 into good quality common stocks—those
that make up the Dow-Jones Industrial Average. Fifteen years
later, the $5,000 in the savings account would still have been
worth $5,000 but would have bought only ½ as much as it would
fifteen years previously. But the $5,000 in common stocks would
have grown to over $14,000 not counting dividends and would
thus have bought 40% more than it would have 15 years before.

CHART 3

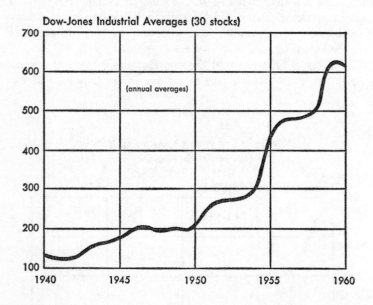

This sounds like a wonderful program—IF inflation is going to
continue, IF certain common stocks will keep on rising faster than
average prices, and IF the ordinary person can select such stocks.
We believe that demand will catch up to capacity and that inflation will be resumed, that the economy will grow, that certain
companies will prosper and grow faster than the economy as a
whole, that their stocks will rise faster than the general price
structure, and that, finally, an industrious investor can learn to
select those particular stocks with a satisfactory degree of success.

a better reason
for buying stocks
—the dynamic
future of America

Protecting yourself against inflation is a valid, but somewhat negative reason for buying stocks. Here's a more positive, more exciting reason: to participate in the dynamic growth of America that lies ahead. Glance for a moment at the prospects for future prosperity, in which you can share via common stocks.

Disregarding the short-term swings in business, which will always be with us, take a long look ahead. Note these prospects. There will be more people. They will have more money to spend. They will have more intriguing things to buy. They will have more time for travel and leisure. Business itself will be under heavier pressure to spend more on research and development, which will result in more new materials, new products and new ways of getting things done. The federal government has undertaken heavy commitments to keep employment high and the cold war seems destined to continue for years and keep military expenditures up.

If you are skeptical, remember that Americans, even though they are notorious for their optimism, have consistently underrated their own future. Benjamin Franklin thought it would take hundreds of years to settle the American continent. Thomas Jefferson figured on 25 generations for the occupation of the Louisiana Purchase.

Even the forecasts made but a few years ago have already fallen short. So it is dangerous to shrug off predictions of growth and prosperity. The truth is that this great dynamic America has for nearly two hundred years exceeded all expectations. Therefore, today's forecasts should be taken seriously. Here are some, based on U. S. Census Bureau figures and other sources.

This decade will show a 20% increase in the number of people, an ever-increasing market. There will be a 30% to 40% increase in spending money. There will be a rise in the number of families in middle-to-high brackets and these are the best buyers. There will be more marriages than ever before which means more homes and home furnishings and equipment sold. There will be more babies, even with a stable birth rate. There will be a sharp upsurge in teen-agers, 15 to 20 years old, about 41% up. And there will be about a 40% increase in young adults, 20 to 30 year olds. No great increase is forecast in the middle-aged group, 30 to 55, but they'll have higher incomes, and they are great buyers. And there'll be a substantial increase in older people, ages 55 and up, and they will be better heeled than at any time in the past.

Looking further ahead to 1975, here are some of the things we see. Population will top 230,000,000. Gross national product, recently $550 billion, will be in the neighborhood of $1,000 billion; in other words, a trillion. Inflation will have shrunk the dollar another 25% but individual incomes will be up 50%. The working force, now over 75,000,000, will be around 100,000,000—over 30,000,000 of them women. And they won't be the industrial workers of yore. A higher and higher percentage of them will be white collar workers operating and administering an automated economy.

Let us try to break these staggering figures down into pictures that will give a better perspective on a changing, growing, prospering America. In the years ahead there will be more *people*. And these people will have more *time* to live fully, enjoy life and leisure. They also will have more *money* to spend on the necessities of life, and increasingly on the luxuries, the better things. And there will be more *things* available to spend on. By things is meant goods and services. Finally, there will be great changes in our *ways;* our ways of living, working, and doing business.

There are other arbitrary ways of labeling the great changes ahead, but these five, perhaps, will do. People, time, money, things and ways.

PEOPLE

From 1960 to 1975, population will grow, according to estimates of the U. S. Census Bureau, 30%. But all age groups will not grow by the same amount, and this makes an interesting story. There will be more young folk and more old folk, and fewer middle-aged folk to carry the burden. The following list shows how the age "mix" of the population will change. Biggest percentage increase will be in the age groups over 65 and under 21. Smallest percentage increase will be in the age group 22 to 64.

Age Group	Increase in Numbers 1960 to 1975	Percentage Increase 1960 to 1975
Under 5	8.1 million	40%
5–13	9.2 "	27%
14–17	5.8 "	52%
18–21	6.7 "	70%
22–44	11.8 "	22%
45–64	7.4 "	20%
65 and over	6.1 "	39%

You can see that there will be lots of small fry and teen-agers clamoring for toys, clothes and roomy houses and classroom space in schools. There will be relatively huge numbers of college-age youngsters and young adults, studying, wooing, wedding, house-hunting, car-buying and baby-planning. At the other end of the scale will be hordes of elders, most of them retired. In the middle will be relatively fewer working men and women on whose shoulders will rest the burden of keeping the whole shebang going. But the burden may not be as great as might be supposed, and there will be compensations.

For one thing, with the tremendous growth of social security and private pension plans, more and more older people will be economically self-sufficient. Less and less will they live in the spare bedroom in the home of a son or daughter. More and more they will have their own quarters in cottage, apartment or retirement hotel in Florida, Arizona, California or some other state.

As for the small fry, they will be a burden, of course. But the chores of raising a family will be greatly lightened by labor-saving, time-saving devices that today are still on the drawing boards of manufacturers of home appliances and housing equipment.

The middle group will have another advantage. Because there will be relatively few of them, they will be in great demand. Management, needing their energy, brains and youth, will compete for their services. And as business increases its emphasis on labor-saving methods, more and more of the working population will become white collar workers, technicians and operators of complicated machines.

TIME

Although we may seem to be busier and more harassed than our parents or grandparents were, actually we have more time today than ever before. We live longer, retire earlier, have shorter work weeks and longer vacations. We can go places faster, get jobs done quicker and many chores and much drudgery that consumed the daylight hours of grandfather and grandmother are performed for us automatically.

Look at *Chart 4* for a glimpse of these changes in time that have taken place in the past generation or two. Note how life expectancy has risen just since 1940. In the meantime, retirement age is dropping steadily from the old-fashioned level of 72 or upwards, to 65, 62, and in many cases, 60.

Along with this longer life and earlier retirement, come many more golden years of leisure for the country's mothers. Study the chart for it packs a wealth of family significance. On the average, men and women marry earlier and have their children sooner than did their parents or grandparents. And note particularly the relatively carefree period available to the mother and her husband beginning with the date of marriage of their last child. In 1890, in the typical family, the last child was married when the mother was about 52. Thereafter she had only another year or so before her husband died and 16 years before her own death. Today, the last child, on the average, is married when the mother is only 48. Thereafter she has 13 years of companionship with her husband and beyond that another 16 years.

CHART 4

Stages of the Life Cycle
of the Family in the United States:
1890, 1940 and 1950

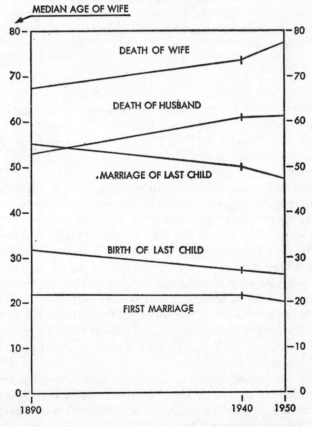

The trend toward shorter work days, shorter work weeks and longer vacations is obvious to everyone. Other changes are perhaps more imperceptible, but nonetheless significant. An example or two will suffice. Think, for example, of the time consumed in hanging out the wash in the old-fashioned way compared with drying it in an automatic dryer. Think back, also, to the early days of aviation when it took 48 hours to *fly* across the country. Such flights, of course, were far removed from today's nonstop journeys. In 1929 a transcontinental air passenger flew only by day and took the train by night. Thus he would start in the evening in New York and go by rail to St. Louis. Thence he would fly during daylight hours and get as far as Waynoka, Kansas. Then another night train ride to Clovis, Oklahoma and finally a daylight flight to Los Angeles. Ever faster planes are constantly shrinking the size of our country.

MONEY

In less developed countries such as India or Red China, where little free enterprise is permitted, there is little incentive to force upwards the standard of living. Mere growth of population does not bring increasing prosperity. Every new mouth is simply another drain on the meager production of food and services. But in the United States where ambitious men are permitted freedom to invent, produce, distribute and make a profit on what they do, every new mouth is simply a new customer, a new opportunity. It is like the old story of the two boys who were put to work by their fathers digging wild onions and dandelions out of the front lawn. One boy was paid a dollar for the job, and it took him all day. As he worked he was discouraged by the number of weeds remaining to be pulled. But the second boy was offered a penny apiece for all he dug and he finished the job in two hours. He worked fast because he was *encouraged* by the number of weeds still available. He even wished he could pull some out of the neighbor's yard.

So in the United States an increasing population is a signal that continuing prosperity lies ahead. The assumption is, and it has proven correct in the past, that the additional people have as much—and more—money to spend as people have had in the past. It is a fact that in spite of increasing population and in spite of the decreasing value of the dollar, people's real purchasing power has been rising. Look at *Chart 5* showing per capita disposable (after taxes) personal income in terms of constant dollars; that is, dollars that have been adjusted to correct for the decrease in purchasing power due to rising prices. From 1950 to 1961 population rose from 152,000,000 to 184,000,000 but disposable income in constant dollars rose from $1,675 per person to nearly $2,000 per person.

CHART 5

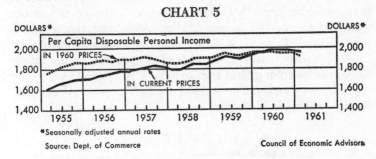

*Seasonally adjusted annual rates

Source: Dept. of Commerce   Council of Economic Advisors

CHART 6

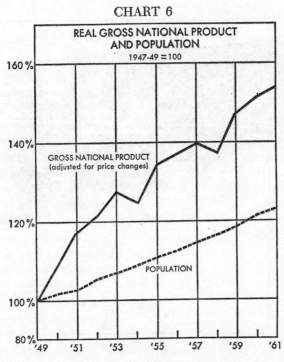

The tendency of our production to run ahead of population is shown in a different way in *Chart 6*. Note that while the population line rises steeply, the line showing gross national product in constant dollars (corrected for price rises) goes up more steeply yet.

Back in the Thirties, President Franklin Roosevelt complained that he saw "one-third of a nation ill-housed, ill-clad and ill-nourished." That could hardly be said of today's population. The lowest income group has been shrinking as people crowd upward into the middle income bracket. And there also is a considerable shift from the middle income into even high brackets. *Chart 7* shows that the percentage of people earning under $4,000 shrank from 57% in 1940 to 33% in 1960. At the same time the $4,000 to $10,000 bracket rose from 37% to 50% and the over-$10,000 bracket from 6% to 17%.

CHART 7
Income Distribution Before Taxes in 1960 Dollars

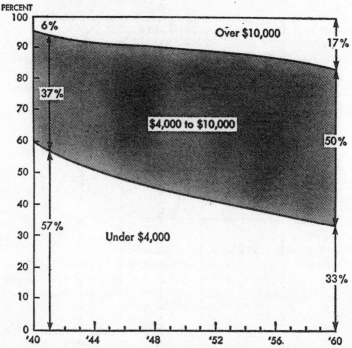

But will this prosperity, in truth, go on and on? Isn't it likely that just when we think we have it made, another great depression will strike as it did in the years after the crash of 1929? This is possible, of course, but there are good arguments that it won't happen. For one thing, there are financial cushions under the economy that were not in existence in the Thirties. Bank deposits and savings and loan accounts are largely insured. A very big percentage of debt obligations outstanding, particularly home mortgages, are insured and in addition, are being paid off in monthly instalments. Remember that in the Thirties many debts, including mortgages, came due in large lump sums and had to be renewed periodically at the option of the lender.

Keep in mind, too, that the federal government, under the terms of the Employment Act of 1946, has assumed the responsibility for keeping the economy going at forced draft. Its weapons are control of credit, taxes and spending. Inevitably, by the very nature of politics, these weapons are used more often as a stimulant than as a depressant, which gives an inflationary bias to most of the economic and monetary moves that the government makes.

The government provides other underpinning in the form of expenditures that will continue, come boom or recession. Roads, bridges and superhighways, with their steel and concrete consuming interchanges, will continue to be built, as will airfields, schools and hospitals. Other projects are sewage disposal plants, the cleaning up of rivers and the extension of parks and recreation areas.

There is unemployment insurance and a great body of people—veterans, farmers and older men and women under social security and pension plans—have guaranteed incomes.

Military expenditures continue, and they pull money out of the economy and produce nothing usable in return; thus, they are inflationary. Billions will be spent on space exploration.

Of course, the growing extension of the government into what once was the private sector of the economy could exert a deadening effect on business. Overall, this has not greatly dampened the dynamic initiative and energy that a free economy engenders. But the trend is disturbing to businessmen and could become serious. Another danger lies at the other extreme, the possibility that government fiscal policies could bring on a runaway boom and galloping inflation. It is to be hoped that prudence will prevent both of these contingencies and that business and government, each using restraint and discretion, can live safely side by side, complementing each other.

THINGS

In this modern world of ours we are surrounded by new things that were unknown to our grandparents when they were in their early and middle years. Under the category of things, we include, of course, jet planes, space satellites, superhighways, radar, synthetic fibers, nylon gears, glass fishing rods, aluminum boats, computers and electronically controlled factories. But we also should include more intangible things that not many years ago were either nonexistent or available only to the wealthy few. We mean such things as broad coverage health insurance, pension plans, ways to invest money in small amounts, unemployment insurance, insured and self-liquidating home mortgages with low down payments, easily obtained credit and inexpensive travel abroad.

It is not only the existence of these new things, but it is the ever-widening distribution of them that so significantly affects our economy and its future. Mass merchandising, vast advertising and the creation of consumer wants and desires have brought what once were luxuries into the easy grasp of everyone. Sometimes we take this wide distribution of the good things of life for granted. But when reduced to charts and tables, the increase is impressive. Look, for example, at the two following charts which were selected at random. One shows the widening distribution of a certain product, a symbol, in a way, of the age in which we live. It is the outboard motor. This is not a cheap item, nor a necessity. It is the modern equivalent of the wealthy person's yacht of 75 years ago. Yet look how it is becoming a part of the furniture of modern living.

CHART 8
Outboard Motors in U.S.A.

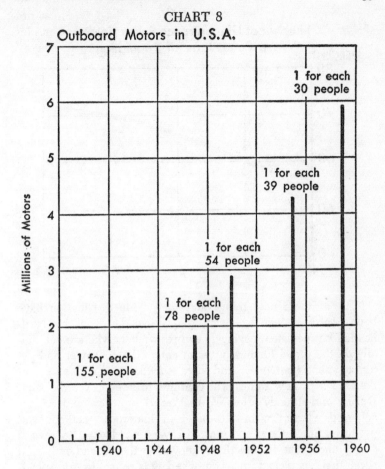

The next chart gives another glimpse of how wealth and security are spreading down through the economic pyramid.

CHART 9

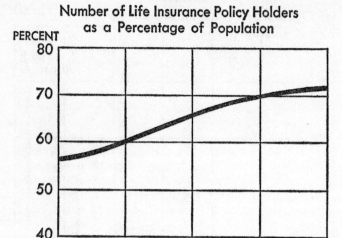

Number of Life Insurance Policy Holders
as a Percentage of Population

Most of these new things and their wide distribution have been contrived, not by starry-eyed do-gooders, but by hard-headed businessmen, engineers and researchers who are continually on the prowl for new ways to entice the consumer and get him to spend his money. And there is evidence that this tremendous flood of new things will continue to sweep over the land. During and directly after World War II, industry and science achieved a massive breakthrough in materials, methods and products. Since then, one new discovery has led on to several others and what is sometimes known as the second industrial revolution has picked up speed. The key is research. And spending on research is climbing in what appears to be a geometrical progression. From 1920 to 1940 it ran at an insignificant level. But it jumped in the early 1940's and from 1945 to 1955 it tripled. It appears that it will triple again from 1955 to 1965 and go on up from there.

CHART 10

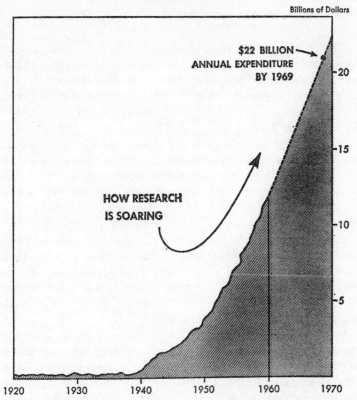

Billions of Dollars

$22 BILLION
ANNUAL EXPENDITURE
BY 1969

HOW RESEARCH
IS SOARING

Since it takes from 7 to 10 years for a dollar put into a research project to come out at the other end in the form of usable goods or methods, you can see that a tremendous flow of new things lies ahead. These new products will be designed and produced to entice the consumer to spend. And as he spends, he will create more purchasing power for himself and his fellows. This will be a continuation, and probably a stepped-up one, of the widening circle of research, production, advertising, selling and consuming that has broadened and raised our standard of living since World War II.

WAYS

The changes in the ways of doing things in the past 20 years have been as spectacular as the creation of new materials, products and services. Changes in the way we live are known to all of us but sometimes we take them for granted. As older people become more self-sufficient, they create additional households, a large net addition to what the Census Bureau calls spending units. In the same way, unmarried women tend to take jobs and set themselves up in apartments, moving out from under the parental roof. This, too, adds to the spending units.

Longer weekends and longer vacations, coupled with universal ownership of automobiles, enables millions of families to travel around the country. A wide variety of industries have sprung up to cater to this leisure time: resorts, motels, boats, motors, cameras, sports equipment. Shorter work days and time-saving home appliances enable families to spend hours of each week in diversions that our grandfathers would have deemed sinful—television watching, bowling, movie going, sports watching and entertainment of every kind.

Bank accounts, charge accounts and credit cards have converted what once was largely a cash economy into one that is vastly fluid. The modern family has little need of cash. Every kind of goods and service is charged. Checks may be cashed at the local supermarket or service station. Almost anything may be bought on time and the amount of consumer credit outstanding shows a long-term upward trend.

Looking into the modern home, we see that servants have almost disappeared, being replaced by mechanical gadgets—washing machines, dryers, floor waxers, power lawn mowers, and a host of do-it-yourself tools from versatile electric drills to small home concrete mixers.

The same trend goes forward in retailing: vending machines and cavernous discount houses, where self-service is the rule and clerks are hardly discernible, replace the store where every customer is waited on.

In industry we find human beings being replaced even faster by machines of unbelievable complexity. Basic to this whole change is the ability of one man or woman with mechanical or electronic help to do the job that once occupied many. We note it in agriculture where fewer and fewer farmers produce more and more food and fibers. We note it in industry where manual laborers are fast being replaced by the operators of machines. The result is a smaller percentage of farmers and manual laborers, a growing percentage of white collar workers. See *Chart 11*.

CHART 11

White Collar Workers as a Percentage of the Labor Force
Farm Population as a Percentage of Total Population

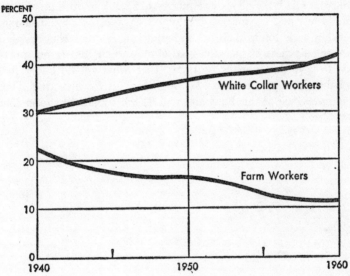

As the percentage of workers required to produce goods becomes smaller, more of the business community turns to supplying services. A great army of accountants, business machine operators, clerks and stenographers is needed to keep track of bank accounts, charge accounts, credit card buying, insurance, investing, social security, retirement plans, tax collecting, and payroll deduction, and the rest of the great web of financial transactions in which the average family is enmeshed.

The truth is that today we have achieved a way of life that our grandparents and great-grandparents slaved and scrimped to attain. We have what they dreamed of—financial security, home ownership, retirement income, physical comfort, minimum back-breaking labor, leisure time, entertainment, travel, health protection. Yet it is one of the great ironies of our time that these wonderful achievements have not brought happiness. Speaking before the 1961 annual meeting of the American Medical Association, Dr. Dana L. Farnsworth of Harvard University said, "The great sickness of our age is aimlessness, boredom, and lack of meaning and purpose."

Be that as it may, America apparently is destined to go on and on and on in the same direction. More people, with more time to live fully (if they will), more money to spend, more things available to buy and use and continuing changes in the ways of living, working and doing business. Whether these great changes will cure the sickness of boredom and aimlessness is not in our province to say. But there is no doubt that they will do one thing, and that is to provide fabulous opportunities for investing. That is the province of this book and will be the subject of succeeding chapters.

about bonds, savings accounts, life insurance

We have recommended the purchase of common stocks of strong companies in fast growing industries as a way to protect against inflation and to participate in the future growth of America. But certainly not all of a family's assets should be so invested.

The anchors and lifeboats that the prudent person carries against emergencies are life insurance, savings and probably the ownership of a home. Life insurance should be as nearly adequate as possible to enable the family to carry on if the breadwinner should die. Savings should be enough to carry the family over a period of sickness or unemployment. The house should be owned outright—or if there is a mortgage, it should be no larger than 50% of market value. These safe investments should be acquired before much money is put into stocks.

The reasons are obvious. Stocks continually fluctuate in value. You cannot ever count on being able to swap them for a specified amount of cash. Although they rise over the years on the average, they do not rise in a straight line. They undulate upwards. And it is the usual fate of the shoestring investor to encounter a financial emergency just when stocks are at the low point in the cycle. When an investor is forced to sell at a time not of his own choosing, he cannot expect to take advantage of the long-term upward trend.

Life Insurance. As written by a modern company, a life insurance contract is an ingenious device. Look at *Chart 12* to see its several possibilities.

CHART 12

HOW LIFE INSURANCE WORKS
To Provide Both Savings and Protection

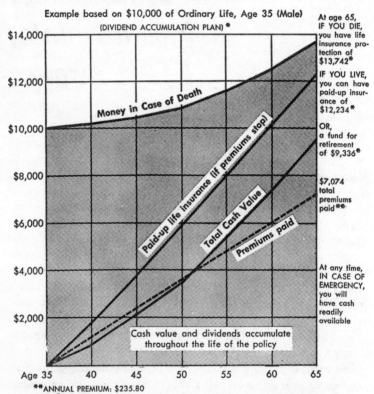

Example based on $10,000 of Ordinary Life, Age 35 (Male)
(DIVIDEND ACCUMULATION PLAN) *

At age 65,
IF YOU DIE, you have life insurance protection of $13,742*

IF YOU LIVE, you can have paid-up insurance of $12,234*

OR, a fund for retirement of $9,336*

$7,074 total premiums paid **

Money in Case of Death

Paid-up life insurance (if premiums stop)

Total Cash Value

Premiums paid

At any time, IN CASE OF EMERGENCY, you will have cash readily available

Cash value and dividends accumulate throughout the life of the policy

$14,000 — $12,000 — $10,000 — $8,000 — $6,000 — $4,000 — $2,000

Age 35   40   45   50   55   60   65

**ANNUAL PREMIUM: $235.80

*Dividends and interest are computed on the 1962 dividend scale and are neither estimates nor guarantees for the future. A terminal dividend is payable upon surrender, lapse or death after at least fifteen policy years, but only if declared by the company at such time. The illustration on this page applies only to amounts between $5,000 and $14,999.

Courtesy of New England Mutual Life Insurance Company

By the stroke of a pen, a man can create an estate overnight. In the example, the estate so created by a man aged 35 starts at $10,000 but it could be any multiple of this amount, $20,000, $50,000, $100,000, etc. If he keeps on paying the premiums and lets the dividends accumulate, this $10,000 estate will increase to $13,000 by age 65. After the first few years, the paid-up insurance will be worth a good deal more than the money actually paid in. And after 17 years, the cash value of the policy itself will be worth more than the total payments made. The protection offered by this ordinary life policy could be increased in its early years by adding to it decreasing term insurance. Thus a man with small children could pile up his insurance at the start of his marriage and let it run down slowly as the children grew up, finally ending with an ordinary life policy worth, in the example, $13,000 face value.

Savings Account. A savings account, in bank or savings and loan association, is the traditional anchor to windward. In this day when credit is so plentiful, and life, health and even jobs are insured to some extent, savings may seem unnecessary—a bit old-fashioned. But savings are far from being a waste. They can grow at 3% or even over 4% and money put periodically into savings at these rates grows quite surprisingly. A look at *Chart 13* will show you the snowballing effect of compound interest. It shows how long it would take for a man making $7,500 a year after taxes to save up an emergency fund equal to half a year's take-home pay.

CHART 13
Monthly Savings to Produce $3,750

	At 3%	At 4%	At 5%
In 2 years	$152.77	$151.63	$150.51
3 years	100.32	99.08	97.84
4 years	74.11	72.81	71.32
5 years	58.39	57.07	55.78

A Home. A well-built and well-located house, kept modernized and repaired, is an excellent investment. Roy Wenzlick, a St. Louis real estate counselor, selected such a house and traced its value back over the years, noting the price at each sale. He found that over the long pull it did not depreciate. Rather, its value rose faster than the cost of living—as *Chart 14* will show.

CHART 14

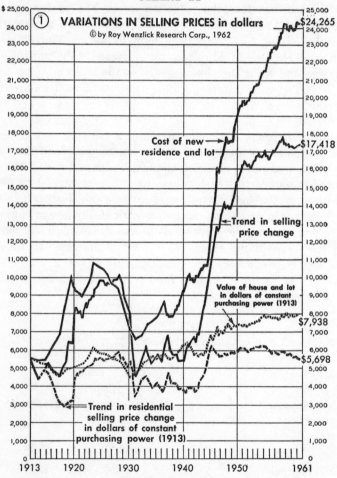

Courtesy of *Roy Wenzlick & Company, St. Louis, Missouri*

A house bought with an initial mortgage has other advantages. Payments on the mortgage are a kind of forced savings. The interest is deductible from income for tax purposes. If inflation continues and the dollar declines in value, the mortgage payments will be made in ever cheaper dollars.

Once the family does have these backstops, it naturally turns to the more glamorous possibilities of stocks and bonds. In large investment funds, bonds and preferred stocks are used to balance the risk of common stock. A family should strive for a somewhat similar balance. Remember, though, that many families start rather heavily overbalanced on the side of fixed-income investments such as savings bonds. At the start, they may need to concentrate on purchase of common stocks to even up.

As an example of what is meant by a balanced portfolio, look at an old plan started by Andrew Carnegie in 1905 to provide pensions for college teachers. The original plan is known as TIAA (Teachers Insurance and Annuity Association). Its reserves always have been conservatively invested in bonds and mortgages. For a long time the program worked well, being especially satisfactory during the depression of the Thirties when prices were down and a retired teacher's fixed monthly pension went a long way.

But after World War II when prices began to soar, the retired teachers saw the purchasing power of their fixed retirement pay going steadily down. So the officers of TIAA cast about for a supplementary plan that would counteract the forces of inflation. By 1951 they had worked up a companion program known as CREF (College Retirement Equities Fund). This is the way it works:

Up to 50% of the annual contribution toward a pension may now be invested in CREF, which reinvests the money in common stocks. For each payment into CREF, the teacher is credited with so many units, each unit being a tiny cross-section slice of all the common stocks in CREF's portfolio. Then, upon the teacher's retirement, the accumulated units (translated currently into dollars) are paid back on a monthly basis for life.

The results so far have been excellent. Managers of CREF have invested consistently in top quality growth stocks, and CREF's annuity units, which started out with a value of $10 each, rose within ten years to a value of over $22. In the meantime, of course, the bonds and mortgages in TIAA continue to guarantee a safe and fixed income at the traditional rate.

How a family may arrive at a good balance between bonds and preferreds, on the one hand, and common stocks on the other, will be explained in the next chapter. In the meantime, let us examine the characteristics of the various kinds of stocks and bonds that may be used to make up the "mix."

Bonds versus Stocks. A bond is a promise to pay a specified amount of money at a specified date in the future, along with a stated amount of annual interest. The issuer may be the federal government, a state, a city, a county, a turnpike authority, a railroad, a utility, a manufacturing company or even a monastery or convent. Note that in the case of a bond, a fixed sum of money is *owed* the holder. Regardless of how well or poorly the issuer is making out, it must continue to pay the stated interest, and the principal when due.

In contrast, the holder of common stock *owns* part of the enterprise. In buying his stock he assumes all the risks and uncertainties that face every business from the corner delicatessen to the largest steel company. His share of the profits, the dividends on his stock, are unpredictable. The value of his stock, how much he can sell it for, rises and falls as the business prospers or runs in the red.

Savings Bonds. The U. S. Savings Bond perhaps is the safest dollar investment available. It is non-negotiable; that is, the owner cannot sell it to another person. If he wants cash he must turn it in to the government for the value stated on the back. Other bonds are traded in the bond market and their values rise and fall daily. But the savings bond, with its predetermined value printed on the back, is removed from the vagaries of the market place. You always know to the penny how much you can get for it.

A savings bond is not issued at par (the value stated on the face of the bond) with a stated interest payable semi-annually as other bonds are. It is sold at a discount from par and as the years go by the interest accumulates so that the value of the bond approaches par or 100%. The interest does not accrue in equal instalments, but it starts off at a rather low rate and ends up at a

UNITED STATES SAVINGS BONDS - SERIES E

TABLE OF REDEMPTION VALUES AND INVESTMENT YIELDS FOR BONDS BEARING ISSUE DATES BEGINNING JUNE 1, 1959

Table showing: (1) How bonds of Series E bearing issue dates beginning June 1, 1959, by denominations, increase in redemption value during successive half-year periods following issue; (2) the approximate investment yield on the purchase price from issue date to the beginning of each half-year period; and (3) the approximate investment yield on the current redemption value from the beginning of each half-year period to maturity. Yields are expressed in terms of rate percent per annum, compounded semiannually.

Maturity Value——	$25.00	$50.00	$100.00	$200.00	$500.00	$1,000.00	$10,000	APPROXIMATE INVESTMENT YIELD	
Issue Price——	18.75	37.50	75.00	150.00	375.00	750.00	7,500	(2) on purchase price from issue date to beginning of each half-year period¹	(3) on current redemption value from beginning of each half-year period to maturity¹
Period after issue date	(1) Redemption values during each half-year period¹ (Values increase on first day of period shown)							Percent	Percent
First ½ year——	$18.75	$37.50	$75.00	$150.00	$375.00	$750.00	$7,500	0.00	3.75*
½ to 1 year——	18.91	37.82	75.64	151.28	378.20	756.40	7,564	1.71	3.89
1 to 1½ years——	19.19	38.38	76.76	153.52	383.80	767.60	7,676	2.33	3.96
1½ to 2 years——	19.51	39.02	78.04	156.08	390.20	780.40	7,804	2.67	4.01
2 to 2½ years——	19.90	39.80	79.60	159.20	398.00	796.00	7,960	3.00	4.01
2½ to 3 years——	20.28	40.56	81.12	162.24	405.60	811.20	8,112	3.16	4.03
3 to 3½ years——	20.66	41.32	82.64	165.28	413.20	826.40	8,264	3.26	4.05
3½ to 4 years——	21.07	42.14	84.28	168.56	421.40	842.80	8,428	3.36	4.06
4 to 4½ years——	21.50	43.00	86.00	172.00	430.00	860.00	8,600	3.45	4.06
4½ to 5 years——	21.95	43.90	87.80	175.60	439.00	878.00	8,780	3.53	4.04
5 to 5½ years——	22.40	44.80	89.60	179.20	448.00	896.00	8,960	3.59	4.03
5½ to 6 years——	22.86	45.72	91.44	182.88	457.20	914.40	9,144	3.64	4.02
6 to 6½ years——	23.32	46.64	93.28	186.56	466.40	932.80	9,328	3.67	4.01
6½ to 7 years——	23.79	47.58	95.16	190.32	475.80	951.60	9,516	3.70	4.01
7 to 7½ years——	24.27	48.54	97.08	194.16	485.40	970.80	9,708	3.72	3.99
7½ years to 7 years & 9 months——	24.75	49.50	99.00	198.00	495.00	990.00	9,900	3.74	4.06
MATURITY VALUE (7 years and 9 months from issue date——	$25.00	$50.00	$100.00	$200.00	$500.00	$1,000.00	$10,000	3.75	------------

*Approximate investment yield for entire period from issuance to maturity

¹3-month period in the case of the 7½ year to 7 year and 9 month

higher rate. This makes it disadvantageous to cash in the bond early in its life, as *Chart 15* will show.

Negotiable or Marketable Bonds. Most bonds, unlike savings bonds, are negotiable and are bought and sold in the market place. Their value goes up and down according to the law of supply and demand. Every bond is a promise to repay a certain number of dollars. But even the most sincere promise sometimes cannot be fulfilled. Hence if some doubt creeps in as to whether the issuer of a bond is going to repay in full, the worth of the bond will decline in the public's estimation. Then if the holder of such a bond wishes to sell it, he will find that it no longer is worth 100 cents on the dollar but will bring only 95 or 80 or, if the financial prospects of the issuer seem really bad, 50 or less.

Government Bonds. There is no doubt about the federal government's ability to pay its obligations. Therefore a government bond is as safe as a church. Paradoxically, however, even a bond issued by the federal government may fluctuate in value due to changes in the level of interest rates. To see how this works, suppose you bought a $1,000 3% 20-year bond. In effect, you have lent the government $1,000 for which you will receive $30 a year interest for 20 years, at the end of which time you get your $1-000 back. Now suppose that several years elapse and the general level of interest rates changes. Money is a bit scarcer or investors prefer stocks to bonds. As a result, the government no longer can borrow at 3%, it must pay 3½%. Who is going to buy your 3% bond for $1,000 when he can buy a new 3½% bond for the same amount? Obviously, if you want to sell your 3% bond, it will bring less. How much less will depend, in part, on the number of years the bond has to run. In any event, you receive $30 a year on your bond and this dollar amount will not change. So the price must adjust.

Assume that interest rates have risen and that the 3% government bonds sold several years ago for $1,000 apiece now are trading at $860 on the market. If you buy such a bond you will receive $30 a year interest on an investment of $860, or nearly 3½%. In addition, if you hold the bond until maturity, you can cash it in for $1,000, or $140 more than you paid for it. This $140 profit will be considered a capital gain by the Internal Revenue Service but bond dealers generally will spread it over the life of the bond for purposes of computation and figure it as part of the "yield to maturity."

To figure this yield to maturity is a bit complicated and bond dealers use prepared tables. For example, if you paid $860 for a $1,000 3% bond with 17 years to run, the yield to maturity would be 4.15%. On the other hand, if you paid $1,100 for a 3% bond with 17 years to run, the yield to maturity would be 2.28%.

Look at *Chart 16* to see how widely a typical issue of government bonds has fluctuated over the years.

CHART 16

Price and yield each 6 months for the past 10 years
on government 2½'s of 1967-72 (December)

	Price	Yield
July 1951	$ 97.04	2.68%
Dec.	96.05	2.74
July 1952	97.27	2.64
Dec.	95.16	2.80
July 1953	92.20	3.01
Dec.	96.14	2.75
July 1954	100.16	2.46
Dec.	98.25	2.59
July 1955	94.01	2.94
Dec.	94.30	2.87
July 1956	92.31	3.05
Dec.	87.22	3.52
July 1957	86.26	3.62
Dec.	93.10	3.06
July 1958	92.30	3.12
Dec.	85.22	3.82
July 1959	83.24	4.09
Dec.	79.26	4.58
July 1960	88.26	3.62
Dec.	88.18	3.69
July 1961	87.00	3.93
Dec.	85.26	4.12

Before 1953, the yield was figured from a mean of the bid and asked. Since 1953, it has been figured on the basis of the bid alone.

Short-term Government Bonds. If you bought a government bond on the open market that had only a few weeks to run, it naturally would sell pretty close to par. Buying such a bond would be almost like putting money in the bank, only safer. Similarly, bonds due in five years or less usually sell pretty close to par. It takes a very large change in interest rates to change their value substantially. Since there is so little risk of their value changing, they are known as practically the most riskless investment you could find. And since the buyer doesn't take much risk, he ordinarily can't expect much yield. *Chart 16* shows prices and yields on a government bond as they have been from time to time in recent years.

Municipal Bonds. Tax-exempt or "municipal" bonds are sold by states, cities, counties, various highway authorities, school districts, toll bridge authorities, and so on. These bonds have a special feature. The owner does not have to pay federal income taxes on the interest. Some states also exempt from state income taxes the interest on their own municipal bonds provided the owners are state residents. Thus a resident of Virginia who owns Virginia municipal bonds pays neither federal nor state income taxes on his interest.

"General obligation" municipal bonds are those of states, counties, cities and school districts and are backed up by the general taxing power of the issuer. "Revenue" bonds are those issued by toll road and toll bridge authorities and the like, and are backed up only by the earnings of the toll road, toll bridge, etc.

Municipal bonds are not considered quite as safe as government bonds. Although most are sound enough, a few issuers in the past, notably turnpike authorities, have had trouble meeting interest payments when due. And back in the depression days of the Thirties some municipalities defaulted. Yields, because of the attractiveness of the tax-free feature, generally run lower than yields of other bonds.

Tax-free bonds are best suited for investors in the 40% or higher income tax brackets. As an illustration, consider the married person having a net taxable income after deductions and exemptions of $10,000. His federal tax would be $1,680 plus 26% of everything over $8,000. Now if such a person had $10,000 worth of corporate bonds yielding 4¾%, he would receive interest of $475 and pay 26% of this, or $123, leaving around $350 after taxes. If, on the other hand, he had $10,000 of municipal bonds paying 3½%, he would receive $350 tax-free, approximately the same net amount. If the same married person, however, had a $25,-000 net taxable income and $10,000 face value of 4¾% corporate bonds, he would receive $475 in interest, pay a tax of 43%, or $204, leaving $270 after taxes. But if the $10,000 were invested in municipal bonds at 3½%, he would receive $350 tax-free, or nearly $80 more. Those in higher brackets would benefit proportionately.

Corporate Bonds. Although a long-term government bond may fluctuate in price as interest rates change, it is riskless in the sense that if you hold it to maturity you are bound to get par or the face amount of the bond. Other bonds issued by private corporations are not riskless because the financial picture may change, the company may suffer losses and be unable to meet its interest payments and even come up to the date of maturity without sufficient money to make good on the principal. A doubt, even a small one, about the issuer's eventual ability to pay off a bond, will affect its price and yield. Naturally, the riskier the bond is, the more the issuer must offer in order to persuade people to buy it. A company that is financially shaky, or whose future is questionable, must pay very high interest on its bonds, perhaps 8% or 10% to persuade people to buy. On the other hand, a top quality utility company whose business is very stable and dependable, is considered quite safe and is able to sell its bonds at a relatively low rate.

Corporate bonds come in a wide variety and the quality, generally speaking, is measured by the yield, the higher the yield, the lower the quality. The quality also is measured and tabulated by several stock market services. The higher quality bonds are those rated A-1+, A-1, A and B-1+ by Standard & Poor's, or Aaa, Aa, A and Baa by Moody's. The average investor looking for a municipal or corporate bond probably should confine himself to those rated A-1, A and B-1 (Standard & Poor's) or Aa, A and Baa (Moody's).

Investors buy bonds because they are safe and more stable

in price than common stock. Bonds are known as "senior" securities. A company must pay the interest on its bonds before it can even think of paying dividends. In the event of liquidation of the company, the bondholders are paid off first. If anything is left, it goes to the preferred stockholders, then last to the holders of the common.

Even though bondholders come ahead of stockholders, the safety and stability of a bond still depend on how much you can count on getting the full interest and also the principal when due. To reassure the investors, mortgage bonds are secured by real property. A railroad may pledge so many miles of track. A manufacturing company may put up real estate.

In cases where the interest or principal is not paid on time, the trustees for the issue, usually a group of banks, will take action in behalf of the bondholders. When a case of default goes to its ultimate conclusion, the pledged property is sold and the proceeds are distributed among the bondholders. This seldom happens in actual practice. The court usually permits the company to reorganize and to replace a defaulted bond issue with a new bond or with a combination of bonds and preferred stock and maybe some common stock.

A bastard kind of bond, known as an income bond, pays interest only when the issuing company earns it. A debenture bond has no security pledged behind it in the form of corporate property. It is a note. This additional risk usually gives these bonds a higher yield. Nevertheless, the debenture or income bond of a strong, profitable company earning enough to pay interest charges several times over might be safer than the first mortgage bond of a company financially weak and only able to meet interest payments by the skin of its teeth. The A T & T bonds, for example, are debenture bonds.

Preferred Stocks. These also are senior securities in the sense that they rank ahead of the common. The word "preferred" means that preferred dividends must be paid before dividends may be paid on the common. Preferred stock usually carries a fixed dividend expressed either in terms of a percentage of par, or a dollar amount. A $100 par, 6% preferred stock would pay $6 a year dividends. If this were a cumulative preferred and if one or more dividends were passed over, all back payments would have to be made before any dividends could be paid on the common. In case of liquidation of the company, the par value of the preferred, whether $50 or $100, would have to be paid before anything was distributed to holders of the common.

The same measures of risk and quality that apply to bonds, apply also to preferred stocks. That is, the higher the quality the lower the yield. Thus if a government bond yielded 3%, then a corporate bond might yield 3¾% to 4% and a high quality preferred stock probably 4½%. A preferred with this yield undoubtedly would have its dividends well covered by expected earnings so that there would be little doubt about their continuance.

Where there is a narrow margin between a company's earnings and the preferred dividend it has pledged to pay, the risk is greater, the quality of the preferred is lower and the yield higher. There are also noncumulative preferred stocks on which the company need not pay the dividend unless it is earned. Here, again, the quality is lower and the yield higher. The ordinary investor probably should use preferred stocks for their inherent advantage of safety and therefore should stick to those of higher quality, say, A grade, leaving those of questionable value to the sophisticated professionals who have the time and facilities to delve into their special characteristics.

Convertibles. Convertible bonds and convertible preferreds are, in some respects, the ideal way for a conservative investor to acquire an interest in stocks. They are defensive securities with a kick; defensive because they are senior to the common and have a fixed yield and therefore should fall less if business slumps or the stock market declines. The kick comes into play when the company prospers and the common stock rises. In this event, the convertible can be exchanged for a designated number of shares of common. It's like having your cake and eating it, too. The number of shares of common into which a convertible preferred may be changed can be expressed in two ways: the price at which the conversion can be made, or the number of shares of common into which the preferred may be changed. Thus a $100 par convertible preferred might be exchanged for two shares of common, in which case the conversion price would be $50. If the conversion price were set at 33⅓%, the conversion rate would be three shares of common for one of preferred.

The important characteristics of a convertible are the soundness of the company behind it, the interest or dividend rate, the call price, the conversion price, any limitations on the option to convert and, of course, the price at which the issue may be purchased by the investor. For example, if a company's common stock were selling at $45 a share, and it wanted to raise new capital, it might offer a convertible preferred at $100 a share, the conversion price being set at $50, or slightly above the going price of the common. Thus each share of the preferred could be converted into two shares of common. As long as the common remained at $45, the conversion privilege would have little effect on the price of the preferred. The two shares of common would be worth only $90. But if the price of the common rose above $50, it would automatically cause the price of the convertible preferred to rise, too. If the price of the common went to $55, two shares would be worth $110 and therefore the price of each share of the preferred would have to go to $110, also. If the common and the convertible both rose by large amounts, the company might call the preferred in order to save the expense of paying the 4½% dividend. The call price of preferreds and debentures is set at the time of original issue. Suppose the call price was $104 and the issue was called. In this case the holders of the preferred stock or debentures would either have to accept $104 a share, which they would certainly not do, or convert into common.

Back in the late 1940's when there was little interest in common stocks, these convertible securities were available at prices and yields in line with those of preferreds and debentures that had no conversion privilege. In other words, the investor was not asked to pay a large premium for the potential value of the conversion feature. Also, the price at which the convertible could be converted into common usually was only slightly above its value in common stock so that if the common rose by even a small amount, it would leaven the price of the convertible.

In later years the fashion changed, there was more interest in common stocks and convertibles became popular. The demand rose until companies were able to sell convertible preferreds bearing a lower dividend than that carried by straight preferreds of similar quality. In addition, companies were able to set the conversion price way above the going price of the common. As an example, early in 1961 when Minneapolis-Honeywell common stock was selling for around $160, the company offered a $100 par 3% convertible preferred which was convertible at $180. Not only was there a 20-point spread between the price of the common and the conversion price but short-term government bonds were available that paid more than 3%. Thus in theory, the actual value of this issue should have been below $100. But so great was the interest in convertibles that the price jumped to a premium of five points on the day of the offering.

Someday the fashion probably will change again and it will be possible to buy attractive convertibles at near the going price of straight preferreds, with the conversion price not much above the current price of the common.

Common Stock. Imagine, if you will, a faucet and three containers. The first container is an ordinary 8-ounce tumbler labeled "bond interest." The second is a similar 8-ounce tumbler labeled "preferred stock dividends." The third is a 10-quart pail labeled "common stock dividends." As the water flows from the faucet, the bond tumbler is filled first. Then if enough water is forthcoming, the preferred tumbler is filled. If there is no more water, the common stock bucket remains empty. But if water keeps coming, it all goes into this bucket.

This illustrates the risks and rewards that come with ownership of common stock. If earnings are barely sufficient to pay the bond interest and preferred dividends, then the common stockholder stands to get nothing. But if earnings are large, then the possibilities of profit for the common stockholder are unlimited. Some companies, of course, have neither bonds nor preferred stocks outstanding. All profits then accrue to the common stockholders, either in the form of dividends or retained earnings which increase the value of the stock indirectly.

This question of retained earnings is important. After interest and preferred dividends have been paid, the balance of earnings usually is divided, a part going into common stock dividends and the rest being retained and reinvested in the company. If these retained earnings are plowed back into the business and put to work with vigor and intelligence by the management, they will snowball and eventually push up the price of the stock.

Without this kind of growth potential, a common stock is a questionable investment. If there is no particular prospect of growth, then the only attraction is the yield. And if yield is what the investor wants, a good preferred would better suit his needs.

Bonds and preferreds are used by investors to balance the risk of common stock. A balanced portfolio might have half its capital in equities or common stock designed to provide growth and protection against inflation. The other half would be in bonds and preferreds, whose fixed income would hold up during times of deflation or business recession. Here again, the common stock portion of the portfolio would not serve its function unless the stocks themselves were of the type that consistently showed increasing earnings.

Many managers of portfolios try to shift back and forth toward common stocks when business prospects appear good, and toward bonds when they appear poor. Businesses use short-term governments as a place to put cash that will be needed on short notice. Unlike a savings account, these bonds need not be held through any particular date for the interest to become payable. They earn interest from the date of purchase. There are certain government bonds, notably the 2½'s of 1967–72 which may be used for paying estate taxes. When so used, their value is par, even though they often sell at a considerable discount. In 1960, for example, you could have bought these bonds for 82 to 86. In other words, for an investment of $820 to $860, a man whose estate would be subject to taxes could have acquired an investment that eventually would be worth $1,000 and would be worth $1,000 immediately if he died (but only to the amount of the estate tax).

The uses to which the various types of securities may be put, are unlimited. For example, in 1933 when President Roosevelt closed the nation's banks and millions of people had their money tied up indefinitely, a famous authoress accepted the events with serenity. A wise investment counselor had put part of her funds into $100,000 of short-term government bonds which were then past due. When the banks closed, this lady had a call on the U. S. government for $100,000 in cash which at that particular time, at least, was safer than money in the bank.

For most families, however, the bond-stock mix will consist largely of growth common stocks and high quality corporate bonds and preferreds. The next chapter will show examples of how, in our opinion, a family's portfolio might well develop as the family prospers and grows older.

how to achieve a balance among stocks, bonds, cash, real estate

That word "balance" is important. Stocks should not be bought and sold in a vacuum. Rather, they should be fitted into a person's over-all financial picture. If you don't have a clear picture of your financial situation, you should take the time and trouble to make one. In any such picture three features should stand out. They might be described simply as answers to three sets of questions.

• *What is your present financial situation—in what are your assets invested?* It is surprising how few people really know the true answer to this one.

• *What will be your financial situation over the years if you live into retirement?* In other words, how much should your assets grow? Will you be protected against inflation? Will you be able to send your children to college? How much income will you have at retirement?

• *What will be the financial situation of your family if you should die before attaining old age?* How would you and your family make out in the face of emergencies?

To answer these questions, no matter what your age, it is necessary to distinguish three categories of assets.

• *First* are equities, such as stocks and real estate. They should be the kind that will grow over the years.
• *Second* are fixed-dollar or "riskless" assets, such as high-grade corporate bonds and preferred stocks, government bonds such as savings bonds, and savings accounts. They should provide safety of principal and a reasonable income.
• *Third* are forms of protection such as life insurance, health insurance and provisions for fixed-retirement income such as a pension plan and social security.

Each type of asset has its own role to perform. At various ages, each type will bear a different proportion to the whole. But each will always be present to some degree. For example, in the early years, before a man has had time to save up much money, his estate will consist largely of life insurance and fixed-dollar savings for emergencies. As he grows older and his estate builds up, he will be able to put more money into equities that should grow over the years. As he reaches retirement age, his need for insurance may diminish. He will retain a good proportion of his equities but, nevertheless, will shift his emphasis toward income.

What's needed is some kind of orderly method for showing these relationships. Every investor should work up his own table. The examples shown on following pages have been filled in with hypothetical figures for ages 30, 45, 60 and 70. They do not indicate that a man of a given age should have any arbitrarily fixed amount of bonds, stocks or life insurance. The figures are chiefly for illustration and to show what we believe to be desirable proportions or ratios. The stocks used have been selected from sample lists that will appear later in this book. Glance at one set of these tables to see how they are constructed.

Chart 17 shows how a man might have his assets distributed as between safe, fixed-dollar investments and equities, or risk investments.

CHART 17
Age 30

Summary of Assets

Description	Principal Amount	Percent of Total	Income	Yield
Fixed-dollar or Riskless Assets				
Cash	$ 500	7.7%		
Government Bonds and Savings Accounts	1,500	23.1	$ 60	4.0%
Short-term Corporate Bonds (Baa or better)				
Medium-term Corporate Bonds (Baa or better)				
Long-term Corporate Bonds (Baa or better)				
Preferred Stocks (Baa or better)				
Equities				
Risk Bonds				
Risk Preferreds				
Common Stocks	3,000	46.1	44	1.5
Real Estate (value of house minus mortgage debt)*	1,500	23.1		
TOTALS	$6,500	100%	$104	2.1%

*The family's equity in a house is not considered an income-yielding asset.   (on $5,000)

Chart 18 shows how well the investor's stocks are diversified among various industries.

CHART 18
Age 30

Common Stock Diversification

	Principal	%
Agric. Equip.		
Automobile		
Aviation		
Bank		
Building		
Chemical		
Container		
Drug		
Elec. Equip.		
Food		
Glass		
Insurance - Fire		
Life		
Inv. Trust	$3,000	100.0
Machinery		
Metals		
Off. Equip.		
Oils		
Paper		
Railroad		
Retail		
Rubber		
Tobacco		
Utility		
Misc.		
TOTALS	$3,000	100.0%

Chart 19 lists the stocks and bonds, giving such information as cost, market value, yield, and so on.

CHART 19

Age 30

ACQUIRED		Rating	Amount	DESCRIPTION	Yield $/Sh	Maturity	APPROXIMATE		
Date	Price						Price	Principal	Income
				COMMON STOCKS					
				Investment Trust					
		M	100	National Investors	.25*		$17	$1 700	$25
		E	100	Chemical Fund	.19*		13	1 300	19
								$3 000	$44

* Usually plus capital gains distribution

Chart 20 shows how well the investor has protected his family against the possibility of his untimely death.

CHART 20

Age 30

Protection

Description	Principal Amount	Monthly Income if Husband Should Die
Life Insurance	$25,000	$ 78.12*
Social Security (assuming widow & two minor children)		254.00**
Income from Investments (omitting house)***	5,000	14.58
Pension Plan (if any)****		
TOTAL		$346.70

* It is assumed that if the breadwinner should die and leave a widow, she will elect to leave the proceeds of life insurance with the insurance company at interest and that the interest will amount to 3¾%, the rate paid by leading mutual companies in the early Nineteen Sixties. In actual practice, the widow might elect some other option such as monthly income for life.

** It is assumed that there are a wife and two minor children. For more than two children, $254 remains the maximum monthly payment. For widow and one minor child, payment would be $191. For widow with no children,

Now consider the first case, that of a man 30 years old. His life insurance should be adequate to take care of his family in the event of his untimely death. He should also have an investment program. This should be roughly 25% in savings bonds, savings accounts, and so on, and 75% in equities, notably stocks in well-managed companies in promising fields to be held for the long pull.

In the beginning, when the equity investment necessarily is small, it is difficult to achieve a broad diversification by buying stocks in individual companies. Therefore it is suggested that the young man start out with investment trusts. National Investors Corporation, used in the example, is one that concentrates mostly on good quality growth stocks. Chemical Fund, in spite of its name, is broadly invested in high quality companies in a variety of industries including chemicals, drugs, oils and steels.

By age 45, barring troubles or unusual circumstances, a man should have acquired an attractive list of common stocks. Such equities, including his interest in his own home, should constitute about 75% of his total assets. The non-stock part should be in bonds, savings accounts and high grade preferreds. In *Charts 21–24*, it is assumed that when this man still was in his early thirties he continued for a while to buy investment trusts and acquired an interest in Tri-Continental Corporation, one of the better performers which generally sells at a discount from liquidating value. The common stocks in the list are good quality growth stocks. If the past is a guide, an investor gets a chance to benefit from one bull market—or at most two. Therefore the man at age 45 must get his chance in the next 20 years.

---

payments would not start until she reached age 62. Then the maximum would be $105.

*** This could be increased by a shift a bit toward income-producing securities.

**** Since not all people are covered by a company pension plan, hypothetical income figures for such a plan are not included in the tables but space is provided for those who wish to insert their own figures.

CHART 21

Age 45

Part I

Summary of Assets

Description	Principal Amount	Percent of Total	Income	Yield
Fixed-dollar **or Riskless Assets**				
Cash, Savings Accounts and Government or Savings Bonds	$5,000	8.7%	$125.00	2.5%
Short-term Corporate Bonds (Baa or better)				
Medium-term Corporate Bonds (Baa or better)	5,000	8.7	200.00	4.0
Long-term Corporate Bonds (A or better)				
Preferred Stocks (Baa or better)				
Equities				
Risk Bonds				
Risk Preferreds				
Common Stocks	37,520	65.2	732.20	1.9
Real Estate Equity	10,000	17.4		
Totals	$57,520	100.0%	$1,057.20	2.2%
				(on $47,520)*

*House is not considered income-producing asset.

CHART 22

Age 45

COMMON STOCK DIVERISFICATION

	Principal	%
Agric. Equip.		
Automobile		
Aviation		
Bank		
Building	$1,980	5.3
Chemical	2,250	6.0
Container		
Drug	2,600	6.9
Elec. Equip.	1,890	5.1
Food		
Gas Trans.	2,300	6.1
Glass	1,700	4.5
Insurance - Fire Life		
Inv. Trust	11,900	31.8
Machinery	4,780	12.7
Metals		
Off. Equip.	1,880	5.0
Oils	1,800	4.8
Paper		
Railroad		
Retail		
Rubber	2.100	5.6
Tobacco		
Utility		
Misc.	2,340	6.2
TOTALS	$37,520	100.0%

CHART 23

Age 45

ACQUIRED		Rating	Amount	DESCRIPTION	Yield $/Sh	Maturity		APPROXIMATE		
Date	Price						Price	Principal	Income	
				Cash & Savings Bonds				$5 000	$125.00	
				Corporate Bonds				5 000	200.00	
				COMMON STOCKS-Bldg						
		E	15	Sherwin-Williams	3.00		$132	1 980	45.00	
				Chemical						
		E	30	Dow Chemical	1.45		75	2 250	43.50	
				Drug						
		E	50	Upjohn	.74		52	2 600	37.00	
				Elec. Equip.						
		S	15	Litton Industries	--		126	1 890	--	
				Gas Transmission						
		M	100	Tennessee Gas Transmission	1.12		23	2 300	112.00	
				Glass						
		E	10	Corning Glass Works	2.00		170	1 700	20.00	
				Investment Trusts						
		M	200	Natl. Investors	.25**		17	3 400	50.00	
		S	200	Putnam Growth Fund	.22**		19	3 800	44.00	
		E	100	Tri-Continental	1.50**		47	4 700	150.00	
				Machinery						
		M	40	Black & Decker	1.60		60	2 400	64.00	
		M	70	Signode Steel Strapping	.60		34	2 380	42.00	
				Office Equipment						
		E	4	Inter. Business Machines	2.30		470	1 880	9.20	
				Oil						
		E	30	Phillips Petroleum	1.70		60	1 800	51.00	
				Rubber						
		E	50	Goodyear Tire & Rubber	.90*		42	2 100	45.00	
				Miscellaneous						
		E	30	Minnesota Mining & Mfg.	.65		78	2 340	19.50	

* plus stock dividend   ** usually plus capital gains distribution
E - excellent   M - medium   S - speculative

CHART 24

Age 45

Protection

Description	Principal Amount	Monthly Income if Husband Should Die
Life Insurance	$50,000	$156.25*
Social Security (assuming widow & two minor children)		254.00**
Income from Investments (omitting house)***	47,520	138.60
Pension Plan (if any)****		
TOTAL		$548.85

* It is assumed that if the breadwinner should die and leave a widow, she will elect to leave the proceeds of life insurance with the insurance company at interest and that the interest will amount to 3¾%, the rate paid by leading mutual companies in the early Nineteen Sixties. In actual practice, the widow might elect some other option such as monthly income for life.

** It is assumed that there are a wife and two minor children. For more than two children, $254 remains the maximum monthly payment. For widow and one minor child, payment would be $191. For widow with no children, payments would not start until she reached age 62. Then they would be $105 a month.

*** The above example allows for a shift toward securities producing an increase in income.

**** Since not all people are covered by a company pension plan, hypothetical income figures for such a plan are not included in the tables but space is provided for those who wish to insert their own figures.

At age 60, a man is close to retirement. He may be considering whether he prefers current income or whether he still is willing to forego some current income in order to acquire further growth of capital. We believe that barring special circumstances, he should concentrate on further growth. First, his pension probably will be based on a fixed-dollar return and its buying power could decrease sharply over the remaining years of his life. Second, if he starts switching out of growth stocks into income stocks, he will pay a substantial capital gains tax. On the other hand, if he holds his stocks and leaves them in his estate, there will be no capital gains tax. Third, if he holds onto his growth stocks, their yield, as well as their value, should continue to grow. Thus his income would increase.

We believe, therefore, that at age 60 a man's equities still should be kept at a high proportion of his total assets. In the next table two investment trusts, concentrated on younger and more speculative investments, have been added. Since the man himself would find it difficult to appraise and select this kind of newer company, we believe he would best leave that task to investment trust managers. All in all, while the character of the common stocks in this man's portfolio are somewhat more conservative than those listed for younger ages, there still is a preponderance of good growth issues. The diversification table shows the shift in emphasis.

CHART 25
Age 60

Summary of Assets

Description	Principal Amount	Percent of Total	Income	Yield
Fixed-dollar or Riskless assets				
Cash, Savings Accounts and Government or Savings Bonds	$ 5,000	4.9%	$ 125	2.5%
Short-term Corporate Bonds (Baa or better)				
Medium-term Corporate Bonds (Baa or better)	10,000	9.9	400	4.0
Long-term Corporate Bonds (A or better)				
Preferred Stocks (A or better)				
Equities				
Risk Bonds				
Risk Preferreds				
Common Stocks	61,400	60.5	1,436	2.3
Real Estate (House paid for)	25,000	24.7		
TOTALS·	$101,400	100.0%	$1,961	2.6% (on $76,400)*

*The house is not considered as an income-producing asset.

CHART 26
Age 60

COMMON STOCK DIVERSIFICATION

	Principal	%
Agric. Equip.		
Automobile		
Aviation		
Bank	$6,700	10.9
Building	3,000	4.9
Chemical	3,960	6.4
Container		
Drug	2,000	3.2
Elec. Equip.	5,500	9.0
Food	6,750	11.0
Glass	3,520	5.7
Insurance - Fire		
Life		
Inv. Trust	7,400	12.1
Machinery		
Metals		
Off. Equip.	4,700	7.7
Oils	5,960	9.7
Paper		
Railroad		
Retail		
Rubber		
Telephone	4,760	7.8
Tobacco		
Utility	7,150	11.6
Misc.		
TOTALS	$61,400	100.0%

CHART 27

Age 60

ACQUIRED		Rating	Amount	DESCRIPTION	Yield $/Sh	Maturity	APPROXIMATE		
Date	Price						Price	Principal	Income
				Cash-Savings Bonds				$5 000	$125.00
				Corporate Bonds				10 000	400.00
				COMMON STOCKS -Bank					
		E	50	Chase Manhattan	2.50*		$80	4 000	125.00
		E	60	Northwest Bancorporation	1.30		45	2 700	78.00
				Building					
		E	30	U.S.Gypsum	3.00		100	3 000	90.00
				Chemical					
		E	30	Union Carbide	3.60		132	3 960	108.00
				Drug					
		E	50	Pfizer	.85		40	2 000	42.50
				Elec. Equipment					
		E	25	Minneapolis-Honeywell	2.00		140	3 500	50.00
		M	50	Square D	1.40		40	2 000	70.00
				Food					
		E	60	Corn Products	1.20		55	3 300	72.00
		E	50	National Dairy Products	2.00		69	3 450	100.00
				Glass					
		E	40	Owens-Illinois Glass	2.50		88	3 520	100.00
				Investment Trusts					
		M	200	National Investors	.25**		17	3 400	50.00
		S	200	Fidelity Capital Fund	.11**		20	4 000	22.00
				Office Equipment					
		E	10	Inter.Business Machines	2.30		470	4 700	23.00
				Oil					
		E	80	Gulf Oil	1.10*		37	2 960	88.00
		E	50	Phillips Petroleum	1.70		60	3 000	85.00
				Telephone					
		E	40	American Tel & Tel	3.45		119	4 760	138.00
				Utilities					
		E	50	American Electric Power	1.90*		67	3 350	95.00
		E	100	Gulf States Utilities	1.00		38	3 800	100.00

*plus stock dividends   **usually plus capital gains distribution
E - excellent   M - medium   S - speculative

CHART 28
Age 60

Protection

Description	Principal Amount	Monthly Income if Husband Should Die
Life Insurance	$50,000	$156.25*
Social Security (assuming no minor children and widow under age 62)		--- --**
Income from Investments (omitting house)***	76,400	222.83
Pension Plan (if any)****		
TOTALS		$379.08

* It is assumed that if the breadwinner should die and leave a widow, she will elect to leave the proceeds of life insurance with the insurance company at interest and the interest will amount to 3¾%, the rate paid by leading mutual companies in the early Nineteen Sixties. In actual practice, the widow might elect some other option such as monthly income for life.

** Widow would receive $105 a month when she reached age 62.

*** This could be increased by a shift a bit toward income-producing securities.

**** Since not all people are covered by a company pension plan, hypothetical income figures for such a plan are not included in the tables but space is provided for those who wish to insert their own figures.

The assumption is, of course, that the 70-year-old man is retired or about to retire. Therefore, for him we have suggested a reduction in total common stock holdings and a shift to preferred stocks that will produce a larger income. We also have shifted his common stock holdings to more conservative issues. Note that the income from securities is 2.5% versus 2.1% for the man aged 45. Nevertheless, we have kept a representation in growth stocks and growth stock investment trusts. Even at age 70, this man still could live another 20 years and during that time the purchasing power of the dollar could depreciate another 40% or 50%. Some of his investments, certainly, should be designed to offset such a rise in the cost of living.

From time to time, the question arises of suggesting growth stocks for a man of 70 if he had his assets almost entirely in cash, bonds and a pension. In particular, should such a man enter the market when the price-to-earnings ratio of good growth stocks is relatively high? In answer, we would say: Yes, go ahead and invest up to one third of your assets in these stocks. Spread out your purchases, so as to make some during the recessions that appear every several years, and try to pick the more conservative issues such as foods, utilities and banks.

We have assumed, also, that the 70-year-old man has cashed in his life insurance and has left it at interest with the insurance company. As an alternative, he could convert it to an annuity payable monthly. The result of this alternative is shown in a footnote.

CHART 29
Age 70

Summary of Assets

Description	Principal Amount	Percent of Total	Income	Yield
Fixed-dollar or Riskless Assets				
Cash, Savings Accounts and Government or Savings Bonds	$ 3,000	2.9	$ 75	2.5%
Short-term Corporate Bonds (Baa or better)				
Medium-term Corporate Bonds (A or better)	5,000	4.8	200	4.0
Long-term Corporate Bonds (A or better)				
Preferred Stocks (Baa or better)	15,697	15.2	747	4.7
Equities				
Risk Bonds				
Risk Preferreds				
Common Stocks	54,680	53.0	1,357	2.5
Real Estate (House paid for)	25,000	24.1		
TOTALS	$103,377	100.0	$2,379	3.0% (on $78,377)*

* The house is not considered an income-producing asset.

CHART 30
Age 70

COMMON STOCK DIVERSIFICATION

	Principal	%
Agric. Equip.		
Automobile		
Aviation		
Bank	$ 5,600	10.3
Building		
Chemical	2,700	4.9
Container		
Drug		
Elec. Equip.	4,800	8.8
Food	8,350	15.3
Glass		
Insurance		
Inv. Trust	6,800	12.4
Machinery	4,100	7.5
Metals		
Off. Equip.		
Oils	5,960	10.9
Paper		
Railroad		
Retail		
Rubber		
Telephone	4,800	8.8
Utility	6,200	11.3
Misc.	5,370	9.8
TOTALS	$54,680	100.0%

CHART 31

Age 70

ACQUIRED		Rating	Amount	DESCRIPTION	Yield $/Sh	Maturity	APPROXIMATE		
Date	Price						Price	Principal	Income
				Cash & Savings Bonds				$3 000	$75.00
				Corporate Bonds				5 000	200.00
				PREFERRED STOCKS					
		E	30	Cleveland Elec. Illum	4.50		$98	2 940	135.00
		E	30	Consumers Power	4.50		94	2 820	135.00
		M	30	Florida Power	4.00		80	2 400	120.00
		E	30	General Mills	5.00		107½	3 225	150.00
		M	25	Radio Corp.Amer.	3.50		72	1 800	87.50
		E	300	Union Pacific	.40		8 3/8	2 512	120.00
				COMMON STOCKS-Bank					
		E	50	Bankers Trust	1.97		64	3 200	98.50
		E	50	First Wisconsin Bank Shares	1.65		48	2 400	82.50
				Chemical					
		E	20	Union Carbide	3.60		135	2 700	72.00
				Elec. Equipment					
		E	20	Minneapolis-Honeywell	2.00		140	2 800	40.00
		M	50	Square D	1.40		40	2 000	70.00
				Food					
		E	50	Corn Products	1.20		55	2 750	60.00
		E	40	National Dairy Products	2.00		69	2 760	80.00
		E	40	Quaker Oats	2.05		71	2 840	82.00
				Investment Trust					
		M	200	Mass. Investors Growth Stock Fund	.23**		15	3 000	46.00
		S	200	Putnam Growth Fund	.22**		19	3 800	44.00
				Machinery					
		M	40	Black & Decker	1.60		60	2 400	64.00
		M	50	Signode Steel Strapping	.60*		34	1 700	30.00
				Oils					
		E	80	Gulf Oil	1.10*		37	2 960	88.00
		E	50	Phillips Petroleum	1.70		60	3 000	85.00
		E	40	Telephone					
				Amer. Tel & Tel	3.45		120	4 800	138.00
		E	50	Utilities					
				Amer. Electric Power	1.90*		67	3 350	95.00
		E	50	Cleveland Elec. Illuminating	1.90		57	2 850	95.00
		E	30	Miscellaneous					
		E	30	Eastman Kodak	2.25		101	3 030	67.50
				Minnesota Mining	.65		78	2 340	19.50

* plus stock dividends   ** usually plus capital gains distribution

E - excellent   M - medium   S - speculative

CHART 32
Age 70

Protection

Description	Amount	Monthly Income	
		To Wife if Husband Dies	To Husband & Wife if Husband Lives
Life Insurance, cash value	$35,000	$109.37*	$109.37*
Social Security		105.00**	175.00 or 190.00***
Income from Investments (omitting house)****	78,377	228.60	228.60
Pension Plan (if any)*****			
TOTALS		$442.97	$512.97, or $527.91

* If left at interest assuming 3¾%. Payment would be $290 per month if taken in the form of an annuity, ten years certain.

** For widow with no minor children, payments would not start until she reached age 62. Then they would be $105 a month.

*** Depending on whether wife's benefit begins at age 62 or 65.

**** This could be increased by a shift toward income-producing securities.

***** Since only a small percentage of families are covered by a company pension plan, hypothetical income figures for such a plan are not included in the tables but space is provided for those who wish to insert their own figures.

Keep in mind when considering the four tables above that they were made up for a hypothetical family. If you were to use such a table for your own situation, the figures necessarily would be somewhat different—perhaps radically different. The form of the tables is important, however; so is the concept of balance. It is important to know the relationships between fixed-dollar assets, equities and protection. It is also important to be able to tell at a glance what industries are represented and what industries are omitted in a list of common stocks. The stocks used in the examples were not picked at random. You will find them listed among desirable stocks in a later chapter.

the basic criterion in the selection of stock—earnings, not dividends

Mention a common stock to most people and they will ask, "What does it pay?" This tendency to appraise a company by its dividend is understandable but, in our opinion, outdated. Nowadays, because of taxes and inflation, earnings and their trend are truer measures of a company's worth.

Take as an example two companies, each showing earnings of $8 a share. Company A pays a dividend of $6 a share. Company B pays a dividend of only $3 a share. Assuming that the stocks are selling at the same price and the company managements are equally competent, which would be a better buy? For most people, Company B, the one that pays the smaller dividend, would be better. Here is why.

Company B retains $5 a share of its earnings (compared with only $2 in the case of Company A) and puts it to work in the business. This $5 belongs to the stockholders and is invested for them by the company's management. In many cases the managers can reinvest these plowed-back earnings better than the stockholders could invest their dividends. In the case of leading growth companies, retained earnings are reinvested by the best minds in American industry. Many well-managed growth companies operate at higher than average profit margins. Thus their reinvested earnings not only increase sales, but may produce an operating income before taxes of 15% to 35% of such sales. These profits produce more earnings. Over the years the snowballing effect should raise the market value of the stocks and, gradually, the dividend rate.

The advantages of concentrating on growth of earnings, rather than on dividends, has been explained by Herbert P. Buetow, president of Minnesota Mining & Manufacturing Company. "What appears at first glance to be a conservative dividend policy may prove in the long run to be most rewarding for the stock owner," he said. "Any company dedicated to growth, but disinclined toward borrowing money or diluting its stock must retain a substantial part of its earnings to provide funds for expansion of facilities and activities. This policy of 'postponed dividends' ultimately leads to appreciation of the stock as well as to greater dividends by stimulating sales and profits. Dividend policies of growth companies should not be measured in terms of a percentage of the current market value of the stock. Instead, current dividends should be expressed in terms of a percentage of the market value of the stock five or ten years earlier. A current Minnesota Mining & Manufacturing dividend may look conservative based on the current price of 3M stock but it represents a return of 17% to the investor who bought 3M stock ten years ago."

After the stock market decline of early 1962, this growth stock theory was questioned by some investors. In many cases these were people who had been caught up in the speculative fever of the previous year and who had put a disproportionately large amount of money in the market near its top. With the market down, these fair-weather investors had swung from overoptimism to deepest depression. They tended to conclude that high dividend stocks had suffered less in the 1962 break and therefore that investment for income would have been wiser than investment for growth.

No human being yet has been able consistently to predict stock movements and be right even 55% or 60% of the time. Despite many reforms and improvements, the stock market still is driven up and down unpredictably. In the old days, when margins were low and investors few, many violent ups and downs were caused by manipulation. Today, with strict regulations against manipulation, with several times as many individual stockholders and with a large increase in the number of stockholding institutions, one might think that fluctuations would have died down. But manipulation has been replaced by emotion. Investors are no different from anyone else. They have their weaknesses, including avarice, enthusiasm, and the tendency to go to extremes.

The investment philosophy of this book takes into account these drastic swings due to emotional shifts. We have evolved a method of practical operation that we think offers the best promise of gain, providing the country will continue to grow, that capital will continue to be owned by individuals, that industry will continue to be able to retain earnings and that managers with initiative, aggressiveness and inventiveness can continue to increase the earnings of their companies.

This philosophy stresses: (1) study of facts, figures and trends; (2) selection of companies best able to meet competition and to come out with above average gains in earnings; (3) long-term objectives, which means purchasing consistently over a period of time and holding.

To indicate how this method proves out, we have compiled figures showing the performance of sample growth stocks over a ten year period up to 1962, but substituting for 1961 prices the price level after the panic of the early 1962 break had subsided. We deliberately omit 1961 prices as an antidote to those pessimists who, even using hindsight, were so myopic that after the 1962 break they could see no further back than the abnormal, emotion-produced peaks of the previous year.

The price figures we use here are the average between the annual high and low except for 1962 when we have used the midyear level. You will note that in three out of the four cases the 1962 price level was above any pre-1961 year. In the case of one stock the 1962 level was below 1960 but above any prior year.

Year-to-year prices of FMC, for example, beginning in 1952 and ending in 1962 (omitting 1961) were $-12-9-11-13-16-13-17-24-27-34$. For IBM these ten-year prices were $-26-31-47-66-90-132-185-272-336-374$. For Chas. Pfizer prices from 1952 to 1962 (omitting 1961) were $-12-10-12-14-15-18-27-38-32-40$. In the case of Corning Glass Works, the 1962 price was still below 1960 but the growth trend is unmistakable.

Prices, beginning in 1952 and ending in 1962 (with 1961 omitted) were $-31-32-49-64-74-82-88-122-155-135$.

These growth companies were selected at random. Many more could be shown that would illustrate the point. And the point is, of course, that over the long pull, growth stocks are attractive. The upward trend in earnings and prices cuts through temporary sags and bulges resulting from investors' emotional depression or overenthusiasm. Remember, also, that if the investor had been averaging over the years, as we recommend, he would have made only one or two purchases in the abnormally inflated year of 1961.

The investor who values dividends above all, may argue that a bird in the hand is worth two in the bush. But in our judgment most investors would be better off leaving their birds in the bushes to lay eggs, raise families and multiply. If this is done, many more birds may be trapped in the end.

Here are other reasons why we value increasing earnings over large dividends. Taxes take a portion, and in some cases a very large portion, of the stockholder's dividend income. In the long run it is better to leave the money with the company in the expectation that reinvested earnings will keep sales, earnings and the price of the stock rising over the years. By foregoing dividends, the investor shifts away from the regular income tax and toward the capital gains tax which, of course, is half the regular tax and, for those in the upper income brackets, less than half.

Glance at *Chart* 33 to see the tax advantages of growth stock investing. Even at the lower end, taxable income above $4,000 but less than $6,000 is subject to an income tax of 26%. This in itself is a higher rate than would be paid by the person with an income of $100,000 or even $500,000 if that income came from capital gains. This, of course, is because the maximum rate on long-term gains is only 25%.

Even the person in the 26% bracket saves half his tax on that part of his income that comes from long-term capital gains. The same situation prevails up through the 50% bracket and thereafter the saving is even more pronounced as the 25% maximum comes into play. The person with $70,000 taxable income, for example, would pay 81% on ordinary income but only 25% on capital gains.

Another point is that dividend checks usually come in small sizes. They are easily cashed and spent. If they are reinvested,

CHART 33

For Single Taxpayers

Taxable Income	Income Tax	Long-term Capital Gains Tax
$ 4,000	$ 840 plus 26% above $ 4,000	13%
$ 6,000	1,360 plus 30% above $ 6,000	15%
$ 8,000	1,960 plus 34% above $ 8,000	17%
$10,000	2,640 plus 38% above $10,000	19%
$12,000	3,400 plus 43% above $12,000	21.5%
$14,000	4,260 plus 47% above $14,000	23.5%
$16,000-$18,000	5,200 plus 50% above $16,000	25%
$50,000-$60,000	26,820 plus 75% above $50,000	25% (would be 37.5% except for 25% limit)
$70,000-$80,000	42,120 plus 81% above $70,000	25% (would be 40.5% except for 25% limit)

the income tax must be paid first, then brokerage commissions. But if earnings are retained by the company and reinvested, the stockholder never sees the money. He can't fritter it away. If he wishes to build up an investment fund, this method forces him to do it.

Why does the emphasis on dividends persist? Partly it is a holdover from the Twenties and Thirties. In those days a steady cash income was fine. Taxes were low and the cost of living was stable. Since World War II the situation has changed.

To be more specific, let us consider four men aged 25, 45, 60 and 70. The first three are making investment plans with the object of building up an estate for their old age and to pass on to their heirs. The 70-year-old man already is retired and needs income to live on but also wants to leave as large an estate as is reasonably possible.

Take the youngest man first. He has before him perhaps 40 years until retirement. If he is prudent, his present financial program may be something like this. He very properly is paying premiums on life insurance. He has approximately $1,000 in a bank or savings and loan account as a reserve against emergencies. In addition, he is contributing to some kind of retirement plan. So far, the young man's savings are of the fixed-dollar type; that is, he is putting away dollars. In 40 years he will still have these dollars and be getting them back as retirement income.

The question then arises, how much will these dollars be worth in relation to the cost of living? From 1942 to 1962 the consumer price index, the generally accepted measure of the cost of living, rose about 87%. To be sure, this period included one full-scale war and the so-called Korean police action. But who knows what may cause consumer prices to jump again in the future?

From 1950 to 1962, a shorter period, the cost of living rose, about 26% or over 2% a year. If the young man is trying to look ahead to his needs at age 65, it would seem prudent for him to assume at least an annual rise of 1.5%. This figure not only is accepted by many economists, it is welcomed by some as being a mild stimulant or lubricant to the economy and therefore healthy.

Now the man working for a corporation with a pension fund will be able to counteract inflation to some extent by gradual cost-of-living increases in wages or salary. The amount set aside for him in the pension fund, being based in part on his pay, will increase during his working years. Nevertheless, there is a built-in lag as the pension is based on *past* income levels. And once the man has retired he is off the inflation train; his pension is paid at a fixed rate, and he has no more protection against rising prices. Yet he could live for another 20 years of rising prices so that his pension would buy only half of what was originally contemplated.

Boil it all down and you will see that if the young man maps out a retirement plan on the assumption that he could get along on $4,000 a year, prudence suggests that he revise this goal upward to $7,000 or $8,000. But how can he double the number of dollars he is putting into insurance and a retirement plan? He can't, but what he can do is to begin at some point along the line to put dollars into an investment that might increase in value at least as fast as the cost of living. That means putting money into stock of companies that seem destined to grow over the years. And this doesn't mean one or two years. It means possibly ten or twenty.

But how about the man of 45? Isn't he almost at the point where he could use the extra income that would come from high dividends? His children may be getting ready for college or already in college. His expenses are heavy.

The answer even here is of course that he would be better off foregoing the high income. A 45-year-old man has 20 years to go until retirement. Suppose that during this 20 years prices go up as much as they did from 1942 to 1962. That means that what costs $1 today may cost nearly $2 when he retires. The Federal Reserve Board estimates that the cost of operating a household increased nearly 30% from 1954 to 1962.

What this amounts to is that even the man of 45 must expect that by the time he retires, the cost of living could be nearly double what it is today. He probably cannot afford to put twice as much into his retirement fund. His expenses are already heavy. But here is what he can do. If he has not by now invested at least 65% of his assets in the stocks of strong, growing companies or similar equities, such as well situated real estate likely to increase in value, then he should certainly begin paying especial attention to the growth side of his investment picture. He should not jump into the stock market overnight. But he could begin working his way into a position in growth stocks, making purchases at regular intervals, perhaps through the medium of an investment trust.

When counting up his assets so as to see the balance between those that will pay off in a fixed number of dollars, such as bonds, life insurance, savings accounts, etc., and those that will pay off in a variable number of dollars, such as stocks and real estate, the 45-year-old man may be in doubt as to how to evaluate his social security or pension plan. Suppose that by means of the pension plan and social security he expects to receive $4,000 a year when he retires. That expectation is the equivalent of a large fixed-dollar investment. It would take a fund of $100,000 invested at 4% to produce such an income. Therefore, in theory at least, he should put a phantom asset of $100,000 on the fixed-dollar side of his list. This means, of course, that even those who own a considerable amount of common stocks may still be overbalanced with fixed-dollar investments.

Take, now, the case of the man who is 60. He has a life expectancy of 20 years and so still needs some protection against inflation. But he is quite close to retirement. So he also has a need for investments that will soon begin to produce an income. If he is fortunate enough to have bought good growth stocks early in life and held on to them, he is probably well off both as to income and capital. The dividends, which were once relatively small, should have grown over the years so that today they provide a good income—maybe as much as 10% to 50% of their original cost.

If this income still is not enough, this man could increase it by the following program. On January first each year he would valuate his stocks and plan to spend during the ensuing year 4% or 5% of that value. Or, he could make his valuation twice a year and draw out 2% or 2½% of the valuation each time. The money would come from cash in the investment account plus sale of stocks from among those thought to be least desirable. In the meantime, all dividend checks would be deposited in the investment account and reinvested as opportunity arose.

This man's problem may thus be one of sitting tight if his stocks still have potential growth. Where a company is in the later years of its growth cycle, he might switch to something more stable. Nevertheless, not too large a part of his holdings should be changed to more stable stocks. After all, the cost of living could double during his remaining lifetime. There is another factor. Whenever he sells a stock in which he has a sizeable profit, he must pay a capital gains tax. But if he holds on to such stocks and leaves them intact to his heirs, no capital gains tax is paid. Or he might have in mind delaying the changes until he retires and his tax bracket is lower.

Now consider the far more common case—that of the man who has reached 60 without having foreseen or provided for the rise in the cost of living. His assets are in life insurance, savings bonds, and bank accounts; his retirement plan, which once looked adequate, now looks skimpy. Suddenly he becomes aware of the advantages that would have come from owning good common stocks. Yet if he purchases high-priced growth stocks, there will hardly be time for them to increase their earnings enough to provide the income he will need within five years.

The 60-year-old man starting an investment program must now do what he should have done 20 years earlier—put down on paper his fixed-dollar assets, such as bonds, and his equities, which may consist entirely of real estate. If his pension and social security income is to be, say, $4,000 a year, he should count that as a theoretical fixed-dollar asset of $100,000. To balance the fixed-dollar assets and protect himself against a cheaper dollar, he probably should buy common stocks. Also in need of income, he might compromise and, instead of buying all simon-pure growth stocks, concentrate on stocks having a higher yield and more stability but still some growth potential. Examples of such stocks will be listed in a later chapter.

At 60, the man approaching retirement without having made adequate provision for the rising cost of living may become panicky and try for higher yields than he can safely afford. He may be tempted to put a small down payment on a small apartment building, hoping to pay off the mortgage and at the same time get an income. Or he may toy with buying second mortgages advertised as offering yields of 8% to 10%. But unless such a man is experienced in the real estate business, he would probably do better to make safer investments. Stocks are not the safest investment in the world. But much information and help are available to the investor, and if the stocks are chosen carefully and held for the long pull, they can be safer than many investments purporting to give high yields and quick gains.

Remember, there are millions of people looking for 10% yields and quick profits combined with safety. If there were such an investment, the demand for it would soon run up the price until the percentage yield was down to 1% or less.

Now, how about the 70-year-old? His life expectancy is shorter, ten years. He probably does need income, and if years ago he bought stocks of well-managed companies in growing industries, he probably has it. If his assets are, say, 85% in such stocks and his income is barely enough to cover his living expenses, then he might wish to withdraw a certain percentage of capital each year, taking a capital gain on his least desirable stocks. Or he might shift some of his assets from these growth stocks into good-grade preferreds or bonds, leaving 50% to 60% in common stocks.

Otherwise, he is better off holding his growth stocks for the following reasons. He can avoid paying a capital gains tax by leaving his stocks directly to his heirs. On the other hand, if he sells, much of his profit will go to pay a capital gains tax and he will have less to reinvest, less to leave to his heirs, and less for payment of estate taxes. If he has a family to leave his money to, they will be better off if the estate is left in growth stocks where it will continue to increase in value. And finally, this 70-year-old man *could* live longer than his life expectancy and there *could* be a real inflation, even during that relatively short period, that would radically cut the purchasing power of his investments.

If at the age of 70 a man has never bought stocks, he should proceed with caution. He might convert up to a quarter of his assets into common stocks chosen from more stable and higher yielding stocks having some growth potential. These more stable stocks mentioned in connection with investors who are 60 or 70 years old are not as high-priced in relation to earnings as the much-sought-after leaders. And because their prices have not been bid up as high, they offer a somewhat larger income. A list will be given later.

Looking back over the needs and resources of investors of various ages, it is easy to see that in order for the nonwealthy investor to get income when he will most need it—in other words, in the later years of his life—he must pretty well forego investment income during earlier periods. The intriguing thing about this theory is that if the young man, or even the middle-aged man, does forego income and invests in well-selected growth stocks, the income problem should eventually take care of itself. Those two birds left in the bush will have multiplied and their descendants will be ready for the oven.

general
observations on
stock selection

The problem of selecting stocks that will grow in value over the years looks easy—at least to those who haven't tried it and experienced the results. An investment counselor chatting at dinner with two spinsters was trying to explain his business. He expounded on the desirability of saving money and problems involved in investing it wisely. After an hour of serious conversation on this subject, one of the ladies spoke up and said that it all sounded very interesting. While she never had saved nor bought anything, she thought it would be fun, and beginning the next day she would look at the stock quotations in the newspaper and pick out something to buy.

That kind of casual approach may be all right for someone who wants to dabble. But a person who seriously wants to save and invest must recognize that the problem is much more formidable. For one thing, it has become extremely difficult to save money. A generation ago, and for generations before that, a goodly percentage of income was saved automatically in many families. A man of 76 once told us that the preceding year had been the first year of his adult life in which he had not been able to save half his income.

The cost of living is high for the necessities. And the power of modern advertising has made yesterday's luxuries into necessities today. To top it off, income taxes, sales taxes, real estate taxes, excise taxes, transportation taxes, and so on, pinch back a family's income to the point where saving becomes difficult.

This difficulty makes it doubly important that the individual invest his hard won savings wisely. Yet investing wisely may be the more difficult job of the two. Even professional money managers, when faced with the task of selecting stocks, sometimes throw up their hands in despair. A conservative New England banker recently advanced the opinion that it was dangerous to own common stocks because of the possibility that investment trusts might some day be forced to dispose of a substantial part of their holdings and thus break the market. That banker has held this theory for many years and it explains why he owns few stocks. The comment has been common in all sections of the country.

Members of the investment committee of another bank ride along with the same old stocks they have had for years, fearing that if they buy new ones they will expose themselves to criticism. As one of them has put it, "If I sell one stock and replace it with another, I take two chances of being wrong, one on the sale and one on the purchase."

The truth is that investing is neither as easy as the spinster lady assumed, nor as impossible as the bankers feared. While the difficulties are formidable, the nonprofessional can derive comfort from the fact that there is no magic formula, even for the professionals. It is estimated that they spend hundreds of millions of dollars a year on research and analysis. But even this vast perusal of facts and figures yields a variety of conflicting answers. One investment trust will buy a stock and another will sell the same stock in the same month. And these opposite decisions are based on the same general facts and figures about the economy as a whole, the industry concerned and the company itself. The point is that while the amateur has plenty of competition, at least he is not competing with anyone who has the secret touchstone of investing.

The investment counselor often is criticized for being unable, or unwilling, to try to answer the question, "What is a good buy?" An effort will here be made to provide a basis for the answer.

There are many possibilities, but let us narrow them down and discuss five groups.

1. Income stocks, or those that pay relatively high dividends. We do not favor these for reasons that appeared in the last chapter.

2. Cyclical stocks; that is, companies whose earnings generally swell during periods of good business and shrink during recessions. We do not favor this group, either. The up-and-down pattern pretty much repeats itself over the years, and earnings reach roughly the same ceiling and drop back to about the same floor with each change in the business weather. Prices of these stocks are likely to follow earnings up and down. Examples are heavy industry stocks such as the steels, steel foundries, coppers, etc. When an investment manager feels that growth stocks are too high in relation to earnings, he may turn to these cyclical stocks for short term purchases, attempting to buy them at the low point in the cycle. This is extremely difficult, even for professionals.

3. Growth stocks. These are the stocks that this book primarily recommends. They have the following characteristics. Earnings, on the average, rise gradually year after year. Prices fluctuate with the business cycle, but have an upward bias. In other words, over the years growth stock prices continue to make new highs, while each low point is somewhat above the previous low. This is the group that must be counted on to maintain the investor's purchasing power and to build up his capital.

4. Stocks of sound companies, including growth stocks, that seem temporarily depressed. Assume, for a moment, that Stock X was highly thought of for its satisfactory long-term trend of earnings. The management was excellent, finances strong and long-term outlook good. The stock dropped, say, 25%. This appears to be due to a temporary set-back in the industry which will be corrected within a reasonable period. At some time in the future this industry once again will be attractive.

In 1961 the oils, chemicals, papers and cements might have been tagged as industries in this situation. Their productive capacity appeared temporarily to have outstripped demand but the expectation was that demand once again would catch up and profits climb.

At a time when prices of top quality growth stocks are high in relation to earnings, sound companies in temporarily depressed industries may be appealing. To the successful investor the depressed price of the oils, cements and papers for example, was not a warning but perhaps an indication of opportunity.

5. Stocks with more stability, yet some growth in earnings. This is a group with some appeal consisting of stocks providing income that is relatively stable, yet rising slowly from year to year. Such stocks should appeal to two types of investors. First would be the older person who wants income, some growth, but minimum risk of fluctuation. Second would be the investor who already has a large proportion of growth stocks, and has additional money to invest but is reluctant to buy more top quality growth stocks because of their high price in relation to earnings.

Examples in this group of slowly growing income stocks are the foods, such as General Foods, National Dairy, some of the chain stores such as Woolworth, utilities such as Baltimore Gas & Electric or Cleveland Electric Illuminating and bank stocks.

Of these five groups we recommend primarily Group 3. Under certain circumstances Groups 4 and 5 have their place.

The following twelve points enter into stock selection.

1. Price-to-earnings ratio. This ratio has been so high in many top quality growth stocks that it has become an obstacle to their purchase in the minds of many investors. Around 1949 the Dow-Jones Industrial Average was selling at less than ten times earnings. Since then earnings have risen with the almost uninterrupted boom in business. But prices of stocks, particularly certain growth stocks, have risen even faster than earnings. Thus while IBM was selling for 15 times earnings in 1950, it went to 23 times in 1955, and 50–60 times in 1961.

Even so, if a growth stock is selling at 30 to 40 times current earnings and continues to show an annual earnings increase of between 12% and 20%, then eventually earnings will reach a level that will justify the price the investor pays in the beginning. As a matter of fact, there are organizations and individuals that try to measure mathematically what a stock will be selling for five years from now. They assume that earnings will continue to grow at the same rate as during the past ten years, and that the price-to-earnings ratio will remain steady. To many such investors, these calculations justify the purchase of growth stocks even at high price-to-earnings ratios.

A few examples of this kind of company, although by no means a complete list, would include Virginia Electric and Power, Florida Power, Minnesota Mining & Manufacturing, International Business Machines, Addressograph, most of the drugs and most of the glass stocks.

2. Labor costs. An investor should note carefully how heavily labor costs figure in a company's operations. Successful growth companies are likely to have been able to hold down the ratio of labor cost to price. This can be done in various ways. For example a chain store installs help-yourself tables thus cutting down on the number of clerks. Companies having equal success are the drugs, chemicals, and particularly producers of office equipment. These latter companies not only have mechanized their own operations but produce machines enabling other companies to do the same.

In contrast, steel and other heavy industrial companies have been by their very nature the least successful in reducing the ratio of labor costs to the price of the product. Competition tends to hold steel prices down, for example, but strongly organized labor unions inexorably keep pushing wage costs up. Despite efforts at automation, wage costs still bulk large in steel operations. The result is a profit squeeze.

3. Research. The proportion of gross income that a company plows back into research may be an indication of its potential growth. Companies that plow back a large percentage are known as research companies. An example is Corning Glass. Not all expenditures on research are converted into profitable products but certainly the effort in that direction is significant and very important for growth!

4. Freedom from government control. Over the years there has been a consistent tendency for government to enlarge its control over private industry. This tendency, known by some as the approach of the welfare state, by others as creeping socialism, can be argued pro and con. However, to the extent that it may impose control of prices on an industry without corresponding control of wage costs, it is detrimental to health and growth. Therefore, it behooves the investor seeking growth companies, to beware of those most susceptible to governmental control. In this connection, some of the steels, which produce the same basic product year after year, fall into an unfavorable category. On

the other hand, companies that constantly are developing and putting on the market new products, largely escape this deadening influence.

The utilities are a special case. Regulatory agencies have good reasons both for keeping rates low and also for keeping them high enough to permit reasonable profits. Low rates help consumers and also attract new industry and new residents to the area served. Reasonably high rates are recognized as necessary, however, to give the utilities earnings with which to finance new facilities to meet increasing demands.

5. Equity-to-debt ratio. Some companies have outstanding equity capital (stock) and debt capital (bonds and debentures). In the case of industrial companies, the bonds should be a small portion of the total. A sound ratio from the point of view of the stockholder might be $500,000,000 of stock versus $100,000,000 of bonds, or five to one. In even more favorable instances, the company will have no bonds outstanding at all. In such a case, none of the earnings would go toward paying interest on bonds or reducing outstanding debt. All earnings could go toward research, expansion or payment of dividends to stockholders. Utilities, having more stable operations, can safely carry a larger percentage of debt in relation to capital.

6. Current assets versus current liabilities. These are figures that the investor should scrutinize although the companies strong in growth generally are strong financially, as well. The ideal ratio varies from one industry to another, but in good quality industrial companies it traditionally is two or three to one. Utilities, with their more predictable income, can operate safely with ratios somewhat smaller.

7. Operating profit. This is the result realized from the actual conduct of the business, expressed as a percentage. Accountants obtain it by taking the company's gross income, subtracting operating expenses (cost of goods sold, selling and administrative expenses) and dividing by net sales.

A good company to buy into is one that is increasing its sales year after year and at the same time is converting 15% to 30% of these sales into operating profits.

Figures on operating profit for most listed companies are shown in Standard & Poor's Listed Stock Reports. It will be found that growth companies generally show the highest operating profit ratios. In recent years IBM has shown an operating profit of around 34–38% while a more stable company, Safeway Stores, has shown a ratio of only 4.3% to 4.5%. Growth companies, having these high ratios, usually spend heavily on research and expansion. The resulting pyramiding process raises sales and earnings and justifies the high price the investor must pay in relation to earnings.

8. Quality. Since the nonprofessional investor can devote only a modest amount of time to study and since the investment field is so complicated, it would seem best for him to stick to stocks of good quality. A company deserving the label of good quality will probably have these characteristics: an upward trend in earnings over the past ten years reflecting alert and imaginative management, good cost control and ability to compete in a rapidly changing world; a sound ratio of current assets to current liabilities; manageable debt; aggressive officers and directors. The advisory services also give ratings which are helpful in judging quality. Standard & Poor's Stock Guide, for example, rates companies as A plus, A, A minus, B plus, B, B minus and C.

Good quality stocks may well be relatively high priced in terms of dollars per share. This should not scare off the investor. Nor should he succumb to the idea that more money can be made on 100 shares of a $2 or $10 stock than on one or two shares of a $500 or $600 stock. If this frequently held belief actually were true, then everyone would buy $10 stocks and IBM would be on the bargain counter instead of selling for 30 or 50 times earnings.

As a matter of fact, those who have purchased a few shares of IBM years ago have done very well. Twenty-three years ago present shares were worth about $6 and were too high even then to interest most investors or advisers. However, we know of a man and wife who daringly managed to buy ten shares each and their joint holdings in 1961 were worth $400,000. In another case a wealthy man was advised by his investment manager to put about $20,000 into IBM. In 1961 this had grown to over $3,000,000.

9. Diversification. Owning any common stock is a risk since there is no guarantee that it will pay any certain dividend or that the owner can get back any specific sum of money if he should sell. Diversification, or spreading a sum of money over

more than one stock, is the common way of decreasing the risk. Big funds spread their capital over 50 to 75 stocks. While they thus decrease the risk, they also dilute the performance of their best stocks and bring their records closer to the averages. Of course, if they could hold only the best performers they would be better off. But even these professionals cannot always spot in advance which will be the best performers.

Some managers have insisted on diversification for its own sake and have been afraid to permit more than 8% or 10% of their funds to be concentrated in any one industry even when stocks in this industry clearly are outperforming many others. This has led some funds to cut back on holdings of their best stocks such as IBM, Minnesota Mining, Corning Glass, etc. The philosophy set forth in this book, on the contrary, is that a growing company, once purchased, should be held until there are signs that growth is faltering. The great fortunes were not made through diversification to the nth degree. However, it is a protection.

10. Statistics on growth. Much information is available to the interested investor. One of the newest investment services is "America's Fastest Growing Companies" by John S. Herold, Inc. It covers not only such leading stocks as IBM, Minnesota Mining, Proctor & Gamble and Reynolds, but also less well-known and younger companies. The mortality rate among these younger companies is high, however, and therefore they are risky. One issue of this service stated that 25% of the stocks were dropped from the list in one year.

Moody's Investors Service provides a listing of nearly 700 active stocks, showing their dividend stability, price growth and recent price behavior. It is available in most brokerage offices and well worth studying. The Value Line Service rates companies as to quality and growth. It also provides factual material in a manner so easy to understand that it is worth using for this reason alone. Two other services that try to rate the growth are published by Supervised Growth Leaders in Detroit, Michigan and Clark, Dodge & Company.

11. Timing purchases. During everyone's lifetime there are several opportunities to make attractive purchases. The rise and fall of business traces a rough pattern. About every ten years there seems to be a rather serious recession or setback. Less severe recessions seem to come every three or four years. These intermediate recessions usually are caused by a too fast accumu-

lation of inventories which in turn causes businessmen to hold off buying until stocks are cut back to more realistic levels. In the past these periods of recession have provided opportunities for buying stock.

In addition to buying opportunities that come during recessions, individual stocks continually move up and down in price in response to special but temporary situations within the company or industry. An investor having patience and nerve, and perhaps a little luck, may be able to profit by these annual fluctuations and pick up shares of selected stocks at favorable prices. Often these erratic movements of individual stocks are larger than might be supposed. Here are some random examples of stocks along with their highs and lows for the years 1958 and 1961.

	1958*	1961*
Addressograph	45–21	109–80
Pitney-Bowes	33–17	68–39
American Electric Power	55–38	77–57
Tampa Electric	22–17	49–37
Gulf States Utilities	27–19	47–35
Corning Glass	102–74	194–145
Owens-Illinois Glass	89–50	104–82
J. C. Penney	37–27	59–37
General Foods	39–24	107–68
National Dairy	49–37	79–59
Corn Products	27–16	63–37
Black & Decker	30–18	71–41
FMC	46–23	93–59
Signode Steel Strapping	18–10	38–28
Phillips Petroleum	49–36	64–51
Gulf Oil	38–29	43–32
Continental Oil	64–38	60–46
Minneapolis-Honeywell	126–76	170–123
General Electric	79–57	80–60
Square D	24–15	51–29
Dow Chemical	77–52	85–70
Rohm & Haas	116–72	164–122
Eastman Kodak	74–48	119–97
Minnesota Mining & Mfg.	38–24	87–66
Aetna Life Insurance	89–63	157–95

* Adjusted for stock splits and dividends.

While in theory it is a sensible plan to make purchases only during recessions or price dips, in practice it is not so easy. Unless the investor has his list of desirable stocks made up in advance and unless he has the courage to stick to his convictions, he is likely to lose his opportunity to buy at recession levels.

In the first place, the money might disappear. There will be many tempting ways to spend it during the interval before a buying opportunity appears. Secondly, the market may start up, instead of down, and the investor may get panicky and buy at even higher levels than he would have had he gone into the market at once. Thirdly, if he does manage to wait until there is some kind of recession or dip in prices he may still miss out. The reason might be that during recessions the great mass of people become uncertain and fearful of the future. This mood of pessimism is catching and even the investor who believes fundamentally in the long range growth of the economy begins to wonder whether there ever will be a recovery. If he doesn't watch out, not only will he fail to buy additional stocks but will find himself selling those that he has in an effort to grab what profits are left.

Therefore, unless the investor is cool-headed and strong-willed he probably should not try to time his purchases but should save up his money and buy once or twice a year as outlined later in Chapter 12.

12. Timing sales. The philosophy of this book is to put a certain part of capital into top quality, growth common stocks and pretty much leave it there. If the original selection is good, why sell? Of course if conditions change and the company that once looked so promising begins to look a little sour, then selling would be justified. But the object is to keep those situations to a minimum.

Possible causes of such a change might be increasing competition from other companies or other products, or a weakening of the aggressiveness of management. Incidentally, the age of the executives of a growth company are not necessarily a measure of the company's long range future. It is commonly thought that youth must be in the saddle. But in recent years the key officers of Minnesota Mining & Manufacturing Company have been in their sixties and seventies and the company has still enjoyed a splendid period of growth.

But what about selling to nail down an exceptionally good

profit? An economist of international standing, discussing the investment philosophy outlined in this book, once said, "Isn't it possible for a perfectly good stock to do even better than you expected and to rise to a point where it is overpriced, even though its growth and prospects are just as good as you thought they were originally? I bought quite a bit (for me) of Thermo King in 1958 at $7, thinking that it might double in price in two or three years. It went up much faster than I expected and rose to more than $20, and I sold half of what I had at $19, not because I thought it had turned sour but because it seemed to have over-discounted its prospects. Is this wrong?"

To these questions, the following reply was made. "Five out of six times the tendency to sell is due to the desire to grab a profit before it disappears. It looks too good to last. You estimated that your stock would double in two or three years, but as it turned out this happened in less than one year. Well, just how good was your estimate? How much did you know about the company and how it would fit into the growth of the country? Also, you bought it at roughly seven times earnings and sold it at, say, 15 times earnings. The growth in earnings had been quite spectacular, and what made you think that that growth was to be checked? Is there any reason to believe now that it will be checked in the near future? It was undervalued when you bought it and perhaps only more reasonably valued when you sold it. If the earnings double in a few years, as they have in the past, there should still be substantial price growth.

"If you take your profit, you also have the problem of reinvesting the funds. Are you sure that you will put the money into a stock that is going to do better than the one you sold? The one you select may have doubled or tripled in approximately the same period, but since you did not own it during that period, its history is not as firmly impressed on your mind. Or the new stock may have gone to 90 and been split three for one, so that at 30 it actually seems cheap and a bargain, whereas if you had bought it originally at 30, had retained it up to 90, and then seen it split three for one, you would feel that at 30 it was very high.

"There is always the danger that your judgment is unbalanced because you remember too well some particular period in the past, such as the 1929 boom or the record boom in business and prices during the past ten years. Such memories make it difficult to fight the impulse to grab a profit before it disappears.

"Back in 1942 a financial adviser bought some Pfizer when it was first offered to the public. In a few years he had tripled his purchase price and took his net gain of 200%, thinking that he had been very smart and that the stock was undoubtedly as high as it was likely to go. A few years ago he repurchased some at 30, and today it is worth five times what he had paid for it the second time (allowing for a 3-for-1 split). Thus he doubled his money once and increased it fourfold the second time. This sounds pretty good. However, if he had held it from the beginning, it would be worth today 40–50 times what he paid for it originally. Yet today you still see it listed as an attractive purchase for the long term."

All of the foregoing may make the matter of investing seem very complicated. And as a matter of fact, it is. If it were not, we would all know the answers and all get rich overnight. Of course this could not happen because if most investors knew exactly when and what to buy, all would jump in at once and bid up prices of the favored stocks until they would be hopelessly overpriced and completely unattractive.

One philosophy of investing calls for going counter to the mob. This is sometimes known as "the theory of contrary opinion." When Wall Street is bearish, it calls for buying and when Wall Street is bullish, it calls for reducing common stock holdings. Actually such a program would have worked out fairly well over the past. However, fighting mass psychology is most difficult. The individual seldom can doctor himself. Almost always his actions are based on emotion and he ends up tailoring the facts to fit his preconceived desires rather than vice versa.

The fact is that most fortunes in securities have been accumulated not by trying to buy low and sell high, but by slow steady acquisition of stocks of strong growing companies, by staying with them and accumulating more.

how
to pick
companies

The selection of securities that the investor will buy and hold is the crux of any investment philosophy. A theory will stand up, perhaps, for ever. But when a person puts down in black and white a list of stocks for all to read, not just this week or this month, but a list that perhaps will repose in a book on a library shelf and be perused years hence, the challenge is an awesome one. Yet stock selection is the investment counselor's business. So he will undertake it, even though he may have (as always) some misgivings.

The investor to whom this book is addressed (and that is what might be called the average, if there is such a thing) should confine himself to good quality stocks. Primarily this means companies having a rather long history of good management, strong financial position and a good performance evidenced by an increasing trend in earnings for ten years back.

In suggesting stocks of good quality, the investment counselor opens himself to a certain amount of panning. If he recommends IBM, the inquirer is likely to laugh. "Anybody could suggest that." On the other hand, if he mysteriously brought forth the name of a company that no one had ever heard of, it undoubtedly would make a great impression. The inquirer would say, "He must have done some digging to come up with that one."

In the same way, the investment counselor probably would make a bigger hit if he came up with something selling for $10 a share. This kind of stock sounds as though it had a much better chance of going up than the stock selling at, say 150.

Financial circles are, of course, always buzzing with "tomorrow's IBM" and "tomorrow's Minnesota Mining." A few of these so-called baby growth stocks will pan out. But the investor who happens to select one will do so largely by luck. He will resemble the economist who told a group of investment managers that he had accurately predicted the sudden depression of 1921—based on the wrong reasons.

It may be well to look back a few years. In 1939 IBM was selling for six—still not a cheap stock. Twenty-two years later, after adjusting for splits and stock dividends, it was worth almost 100 times as much. In 1961 Gillette was worth 60 times its 1939 price. The manager of an investment trust or adviser who recognized the possibilities of IBM and Gillette in 1939 would have much to be proud of today. But he would have had to do more than spot the potential of these stocks. He would have had to recommend their purchase and then for 22 years recommend against selling them, even though in the interim they sold for five to ten times what he paid for them.

There are a good many other stocks, besides these two, that have had this kind of astonishing performance. Below is a random list to illustrate the fact that it is not necessary to buy unheard of or low-priced stocks to make a profit. Of course, you hear it said that anyone could have bought these top growers. But usually the person who makes this remark is the very one who did not buy such stocks himself.

Growth stocks of good quality, then, in our opinion are what the readers of this book should concentrate on. What do we mean by growth stocks of good quality? Unfortunately, the selection can't be done scientifically or mathematically. The whole field of investing is based on human judgment, subject to human error. Nevertheless, we shall present a list. It is not intended to be all-inclusive. Neither can it be entirely uniform in quality. Some stocks inevitably will do better than others. The investor should diversify and try to balance the fastest growing companies with those that are semi-conservative or recession resistant.

	1939 Prices*	1961 Prices*
Black & Decker	4 –2	71–41
Continental Oil	7⅞–5	60–46
Corning Glass Works	11¾–9¼	194–145
FMC	7⅜–4⅛	93–59
General Foods	12 –9⅛	107–68
Gillette	¾– ⅝	57–29
IBM	6½–5⅞	607–386
International Paper	1½– ⅝	38–29
Minnesota Mining & Mfg.	1¼– ⅞	87–66
Signode Steel Strapping (1952)	3⅞–2⅞	38–28
Square D	3 –1½	40–23

* Adjusted for splits and stock dividends.

UTILITY INDUSTRY

Until recently this was known as a defensive industry, since earnings tended to be relatively stable regardless of the trend of business. This was particularly true of utilities with large residential loads. But in recent years there has come a realization that there probably is no field where growth is as certain as in the utility industry. While the rates are regulated, which is generally an unfavorable characteristic, the State Commissions allow the companies to earn enough money to finance expansion. Also, utilities borrow a great deal of money, often at low rates. Thus they have been able to earn 6% or 7% on money borrowed at say 4%.

Some bank trust departments bought utilities years ago because they were the most reliable, stable and conservative purchases they could make. Later, these banks found that they owned a growth industry.

Some managers recommend that you have 20% to 25% of your funds in utilities. It would have been better to have made the purchases around 1959 or 1960 when utility stocks were rather low-priced in relation to earnings. However, higher price-to-earnings ratios may be justified by very favorable growth rates, 17% a year, for example, for Florida Power & Light and also for Florida

Power. Those listed below also have had favorable rates of growth which seem likely to continue.

Faster growth—Higher P.E.R.   *Good growth—more conserva-tive in price*

American Electric Power	Central Illinois Public Service
Florida Power & Light	Cleveland Electric Illuminating
Florida Power	Dayton Power & Light
Gulf States Utilities	Duke Power
Houston Lighting & Power	General Public Utilities
Texas Utilities	Montana-Dakota Utilities
Virginia Electric & Power	Oklahoma Gas & Electric

* Price earnings ratio.

GLASS INDUSTRY

Another promising field is the glass industry. Products include glass textiles, fiber glass with uses ranging from insulation to powerboats and the intricate tubes and containers produced by Corning Glass for television sets and laboratories. The companies benefit greatly from money spent on research. Corning Glass and Owens-Corning Fibreglas are two of the most promising. Corning Glass owns 50% of Pittsburgh Corning, 50% of Dow Corning and 31.2% of Owens-Corning Fibreglas.

Owens-Illinois has had a steady, if not as spectacular, growth. Management feels that foreign consumption of its glass will grow twice as fast as U.S. consumption. The company has fourteen foreign plants to produce for foreign markets. In addition, this company has interests in the paper industry, through National Container, and also makes metal and plastic enclosures, as well as scientific glassware and bulbs. Owens-Illinois owns about 30% of Owens-Corning Fibreglas and has large holdings in Monsanto Chemical, Continental Can, Container Corporation and Pennsylvania Glass Sand Corporation.

Gustin-Bacon and Thompson Fiber Glass are two smaller and more speculative issues.

Corning Glass	Owens-Corning Fibreglas
Owens-Illinois	Gustin-Bacon
	Thompson Fiber Glass

OIL INDUSTRY

Some oil companies are primarily crude producers, some are distributors, (Standard Oil of Kentucky) while others are integrated, (Continental Oil). The prosperity of the different segments of the industry varies from year to year. Years ago the crude producers were considered the more desirable because they could pretty well determine their own prices. The distributors operated at that time on a very narrow margin and often were squeezed. In those days it seemed best to buy the stocks of companies which produced their own crude oil, refined and distributed it. In 1960 and 1961 they were all in the dumps and their stocks were selling at 10 to 12 times earnings versus 30, 40 or 50 times earnings in the case of other growth stocks.

Remember, too, that ownership of natural resources is thought of as a protection against inflation. Probably over the years that judgment will prove sound.

The foreign consumption of oil continues to grow at nearly twice the rate of the United States. The big international oil companies have this advantage. Their activities are so broad that what might upset a company in one place is not likely to hurt the company as a whole.

Another point: most of the oil companies have large interests in natural gas and chemicals made from natural gas—a fast growing field. Here are some of the more interesting oils for long pull:

Domestic Companies
> Continental Oil—integrated
> Standard Oil Indiana—more of a distributor
> Phillips Petroleum—heavy in natural gas reserves and petrochemicals.
> Union Oil California—California oil producer and distributor. Phillips has large stock interest.
> Shell Oil—controlled by Royal Dutch and Shell Transport & Trading.

Some of the most attractive international companies: with activities broadly distributed throughout the world, including the new fields in Africa.

Texaco—has been one of the more successful companies
Socony Mobil—world-wide—doing a good job
Royal Dutch Petroleum—large, strong, aggressive, world-
wide interests
Gulf Oil—increasing earnings from domestic business
Standard Oil New Jersey—largest world factor in oil

METAL INDUSTRY

Aluminum is another industry which was depressed in the early
1960's because production was greater than consumption. Despite
the setback, the companies listed below should show very substantial growth. Falconbridge Nickel is more speculative but the
growth record has been spectacular.

Aluminum Company of America
International Nickel
Falconbridge Nickel

CEMENT INDUSTRY

Here is another industry that was over-producing in 1960–61
but which, over the years, inevitably will grow along with demand for its products. The stocks shown are of good grade.

Giant Portland Cement
Ideal Cement
Penn-Dixie Cement

TOBACCO INDUSTRY

This is an industry generally considered stable but Reynolds
Tobacco, General Cigar and American Tobacco have shown outstanding, good and fairly good growth, in that order.

American Tobacco
Reynolds Tobacco
General Cigar

CHEMICAL INDUSTRY

This bluest of blue chip industries historically has shown an outstanding growth rate. Large sums are spent on research. New products are continually coming off the production line. New fields such as petrochemicals and plastics have contributed greatly to growth. Most of the companies are widely diversified and thus are not so much affected by a contraction in any one business. Development of new products helps the industry over short recessions. This industry, although suffering from very severe competition, still deserves an important place in any investment account.

Rohm & Haas, heavy in plastics, resins and organic chemicals, showed a sales increase of 267% from 1947–49 to 1962, compared with a rise of only 104% in the nation's Gross National Product. Its 1960 return on net worth was 14.9%. Dow Chemical with its broad range of products including magnesium and plastics, increased its sales in the 1947–49 to 1962 period almost four times faster than the Gross National Product. American Cyanamid, deep in plastics, but still very diversified, showed a slower but steady annual increase in sales. Union Carbide, in chemicals, gases, metal alloys and plastics, showed a sales increase of 167% from 1947–49 to 1962, versus 104% for the Gross National Product. Monsanto, maker of plastics, synthetic fibers and industrial chemicals, has grown more slowly, but future prospects are favorable.

Rohm & Haas	Monsanto Chemical
Union Carbide	American Cyanamid
Dow Chemical	

DRUG INDUSTRY

This is a fast growing industry with a promising future. The consumption of drugs in the United States increases as new kinds are developed and as people live longer. American companies also supply the rest of the world. Below are a few companies which seem to have the most interesting futures. The investor should buy several if possible.

Pfizer   Smith Kline & French
Merck   Schering
Upjohn

A buyer of these stocks should be aware that market prices are often very high in relation to earnings. It takes sharply increasing earnings to justify such prices.

RECREATION INDUSTRY

Because of the shortening work week, longer vacations and earlier retirement, this industry has achieved growing importance. There are not as many proven companies but those available probably will continue to grow and prosper.

Outboard Marine—primarily maker of outboard motors, but also builder of inboard motorboats, scooters, yard and garden equipment.

Eastman Kodak—fibers and plastics make up one-fifth of production; professional and amateur photographic products about 60%.

MACHINERY INDUSTRY

The shortening work week and rise in hourly wages have raised costs and put a price squeeze on a large part of American industry. To offset such costs and maintain competitive advantage, companies turn to labor-saving equipment and automation. There seems to be no end to the struggle. Black & Decker has built a big business out of producing small tools for "do it yourself" homeowners. It also has a complete set of auto repair tools for garages. FMC (formerly Food Machinery & Chemical) Corporation makes garden equipment, spraying material, insecticides and machines to sort and package fruits.

Signode Steel Strapping Company has been busy developing new ways of tying together bulk material for easier handling. This strapping can be used with sawed boards or steel pipe, waste paper or magazines. Although not too well known, Signode is one of the leading companies in its field with a good record running back over many years.

With unlimited road building ahead, expansion for Caterpillar Tractor seems limitless. Ex-Cell-O is one of the successful machine tool companies. Standard Packaging has expanded largely through acquisitions, and while it is speculative, there seems to be a reasonable chance that the speculation could prove very profitable. One of the company's developments is a vending machine for selling greeting cards for all occasions. The company estimates 15,000 to 20,000 machines will eventually be in use.

Black & Decker	Caterpillar Tractor
Signode Steel Strapping	Ex-Cell-O
FMC	Standard Packaging

OFFICE EQUIPMENT INDUSTRY

The pressure on banks, insurance companies, etc., to find some means of reducing costs of handling paper work has brought a number of companies into the field of labor-saving office machinery. There are machines that do bookkeeping, control inventories, do billing, run industrial machinery and make intricate mathematical calculations for government and industry. Unfortunately the best office equipment companies traditionally sell high in relation to earnings. However, it is an industry in which the investor should own stocks.

International Business Machines	Xerox
Addressograph	Moore Corp., Ltd.
Pitney-Bowes	

ELECTRONIC INDUSTRY

This has been a glamor industry. Any company, no matter how new or insecure, that carried in its name anything to indicate electronics or nuclear development has found a ready market for its shares. A number, of course, will survive, but a great many will not. Also, many of the smaller companies that do succeed will be taken over by the larger companies. Or the larger companies, through their own research departments, will develop products which will be competitive with the smaller ones.

One of the great battles is in the field of computers. IBM, of course, was the first to achieve a profitable computer business. Sperry Rand, RCA and Minneapolis-Honeywell each spent many millions of dollars, but were slow in achieving a volume that would offset the cost of developmental work.

Microwaves, transistors, and long distance communication between computers and bookkeeping machines is part of this business.

International Business Machines	Thompson Ramo
Litton Industries	Wooldridge
Minneapolis-Honeywell	General Electric
RCA	McGraw-Edison
American Tel & Tel	Square D

BANKING INDUSTRY

This is a field which has appealed largely to the institutional or the professional investor. However, it has shown considerable growth. Bank deposits increase along with the volume of business, the supply of money and credit. As business expands, so does the demand for loans and it appears that future levels of interest rates should be satisfactory for the production of steadily rising earnings. Bank stocks add a touch of strength, stability and quality to any investment account.

Chase Manhattan	First National Bank of
Morgan Guaranty Trust	Chicago
First Wisconsin Bank Shares	Bankers Trust
Northwest Bancorporation	Irving Trust
Marine Midland	Empire Trust

CHAIN STORES

The whole chain store industry, including food stores and variety stores, recently began to undergo a major revolution. The future is difficult to foretell, especially as to whether it will be profitable. However, certain companies should thrive. It has been true for years that Woolworth's interest in its British subsidiary alone was worth about as much as the price at which Woolworth sold on the New York Stock Exchange. Now, Woolworth's foreign holdings have grown and prospered and as it has been able to bring back to this country some of its foreign earnings, the stock has become even more interesting. In addition it has entered the discount field.

Woolworth
J. C. Penney
Sears, Roebuck

BUILDING INDUSTRY

This is a highly competitive industry, but during periods of growth has been very profitable for some companies. With the increase in population we probably will see 2,000,000 housing starts a year instead of 1,200,000. This should bring continued profits to companies shown below.

United States Gypsum   National Lead
National Gypsum   Sherwin-Williams

PAPER INDUSTRY

This industry has grown with the development of the country. Like some of the others, such as the oils and cements, it had problems of over-capacity in the early 1960's. Certainly one of the outstanding companies in the industry, and one that has been very profitable over the years and no doubt will be in the future, is Scott Paper.

International Paper
Scott Paper

RUBBER INDUSTRY

The rubber industry has gone into other lines in an effort to get rid of the continual ups and downs. In particular, it has gone aggressively into chemicals.

Goodyear Tire & Rubber (large foreign interests)

INSURANCE INDUSTRY

The fire insurance companies have suffered from periods of heavy losses and rate regulation. The growth in earnings often has been disappointing. Earnings of life insurance companies, on the other hand, have grown and should continue to grow as more life insurance dollars are needed by the survivors to offset the decrease in the dollar's purchasing power. Also, new drugs prolong life and thereby increase profits of life insurance companies. For one thing, much insurance in force today was written on the basis of shorter life expectancies of years ago. For another, longer life brings a demand for retirement plans and endowment policies. This industry should continue to be a good place to invest. The individual companies are a bit difficult for the average person to appraise. However, money put into the better ones should provide a good return over the years.

Aetna Life Insurance
Connecticut General Life Insurance
Jefferson Standard

GAS AND TRANSMISSION INDUSTRY

Here is an industry that produces gas, transmits it from coast to coast and distributes it to consumers. The industry's biggest trouble has been in getting rates favorable enough to offset rising costs.

Tennessee Gas Transmission
Oklahoma Natural Gas
Panhandle Eastern Pipe Line

FOOD INDUSTRY

This is one of the more conservative industries, generally thought of as stable and depression resistant. Nevertheless, it includes companies that have shown very satisfactory growth. Some companies, such as Pillsbury, produce packaged foods for the working housewife. All five of those listed below have had a satisfactory, consistent record of growth.

Corn Products   National Dairy Products
Pillsbury   Quaker Oats
General Foods

MISCELLANEOUS

Under this heading we are listing only one company which has been a top grower over the years: Minnesota Mining & Manufacturing. It is hard to classify a company that makes sandpaper, tape to cover surgical wounds, reflectors to put along roadways and also owns a broadcasting system. Anyway, it is reasonable to suppose that 3M's extensive research will continue to develop many new and profitable products. The growth in earnings has been constant, with the dividend payments doubling in less than four years. Many a prospective purchaser who held off buying because the price was high now regrets it.

Perhaps the reader will be worried about the frequent references to high prices and high price-to-earnings ratios. It is true that in recent years growth stocks became exceedingly popular. But since the future is so unpredictable, we would warn against any effort to try to find the botom of the market and buy only then. It is very doubtful whether anyone, amateur or professional, can do this consistently. A better and safer approach is to buy these stocks in small bites over a period of time and thus average out the highs and lows. More detailed ways of doing this will be discussed in a forthcoming chapter.

how to get the facts and figures you need

The list of stocks in the previous chapter gives concrete examples of what we mean by leading growth stocks. No list, however, will provide the prospective investor with everything he wants to know, and should know—facts, figures, current prices and earnings, comparisons, the history of this company or that. How much of this can he ferret out himself? How much of it should he get from professional sources? To what extent should he depend on his own judgment? To what extent should he lean on the advice of others?

There are no general answers to these questions but let us discuss the problems involved and the ways of getting good help and advice. Perhaps one of the most important reasons an investor needs some outside judgment is to get perspective. Doctors who unhesitatingly prescribe for and diagnose the ills of others often do not care to prescribe for themselves or their families. They fear that doubts and hopes may cloud their judgment. Many an investor, too, can prescribe a sound policy for a friend, but when it comes to his own investments, his decisions may be based not on the facts as he should see them, but on artificial reasoning manufactured to justify an emotional reaction.

The minute an individual buys a security, various forces begin to bear on him: avarice, hopefulness, pessimism, restlessness for gain, conceit if he does well, depression if he doesn't. He wants to see a profit in his stocks. And if he sees it, he is prone to grab it for fear it will be lost. If his stocks go down instead of up, he may refuse to sell when he should because of a dislike of admitting he is wrong.

Moreover, lack of patience may push him in the direction of trading in and out of the market. Brokers naturally live on commissions and are not likely to discourage this kind of trading. Yet the chances of the average investor's making money by frequent purchases and sales are not good. The so-called experts can rarely do it.

Rare is the investor, then, who can rely solely on his own judgment. Almost everyone, to some extent, finds it necessary to seek the advice of others. The kind and amount of advice he should seek is not easy to determine. For one thing, good advice is hard to identify and harder to come by. That which is the most blatantly advertised, usually is of the least value. The best costs money and unfortunately is not available to everyone.

Nevertheless, if the investor will strive for perspective on himself and learn his strengths and weaknesses, he usually can combine his own judgment with outside help in the proper proportion to make a success of his investment program. Here are the possibilities.

Investment Counselors. These are professionals in the business of providing individual investment advice for a fee. Nevertheless, it should be remembered that investing, even when done by professionals, is not an exact science. Whether an investment counseling firm is large or small, it is subject to human errors. Some firms, of course, have good records. The largest ones have the most money to spend on research and intelligent, informed counselors. But even some of the largest have mediocre records. The variance is wide. And generally speaking, the records themselves are not made public.

Another drawback—you must have capital of at least $100,-000 or you cannot afford the fees that most of the better-known investment counseling firms charge for giving you individual attention. The reason is the cost. Treating each client individually is expensive. First, the counseling firm must determine the client's needs, circumstances and desires so that a special bundle of securities may be put into his account. Then this portfolio must be reviewed constantly so that it may be kept up to date. The investor usually is consulted on all changes. These may come about as the result of a bond falling due, a preferred stock being called, a right to purchase additional stock received and so on.

Such constant supervision, plus research and overhead, costs money. Investment counselors commonly charge ½ of 1% annually of the capital involved, with minimum annual fees of from $500 to as high as $2,000. Obviously a person with only a few thousand dollars to invest cannot afford fees of $500 a year.

A few investment counseling firms have tried to supply the needs of the small or medium-sized investor. Some counseling firms manage investment companies in which anyone may purchase shares, sometimes without payment of any sales commission, or load.

The account records of most counseling firms are not available for comparison, either with each other or with the stock market averages. If a firm does reveal the record of an individual account, the account selected probably is the best available and not typical. But there are ways to make a judgment. The firms that manage investment trusts provide the public with a kind of showcase, revealing the results of their operations. The performance of these trusts, of course, is a matter of public record.

An additional way to check on a firm is to ask for the names of several of its clients, then interview them and ask for their experience.

Or write to the Investment Counsel Association of America, 100 Park Avenue, New York 17, N.Y., and ask for the names of members in your area. This is a professional society with high ethical standards.

Trust Departments of Banks. About 20% of the banks in the United States have trust departments. Some of these offer possibilities. It should be remembered, however, that banks invest their funds very conservatively. Depending on the policy of the bank, an investor with, say, $50,000 can either open an investment advisory account or set up an individual living trust. Banks that offer an investment advisory service will do the selecting of stocks subject to the investor's approval, furnish statements, collect dividends, and so on.

In the case of the living trust, the investor turns the money over to the bank for investment and specifies how the principal and income are to be handled. The trust agreement, supplemented by a will, would also determine what would happen to the principal upon the investor's death.

Bookkeeping and handling charges are proportionately too great for a bank to accept small trust accounts. Many banks, however, have an arrangement for pooling small trusts and investing them as a whole in what is called a "common trust fund." By this device, amounts ranging from $15,000 upward can be put in trust and the principal and income paid out in the same way as they would be under a separate trust. It is sometimes possible to get a record of the performance of the bank's common trust fund.

Investment Companies. One of the most satisfactory methods of obtaining professional management of small and medium-sized sums is through the purchase of shares in a well-managed investment company. This amounts to buying investment advice, not on an individual, but on a mass basis. The idea is that instead of owning stocks direct, you might prefer to own an interest in a bundle of securities selected by someone else—in this case the managers of the investment company or, as it is sometimes called, the investment trust. One advantage is that you spread a relatively small number of dollars over a number of different stocks or bonds and thus diversify your risk. Another is that if the trust is well managed, these stocks or bonds are selected on the basis of careful research by professional analysts. Quite possibly the professionals can do a better job of selecting than you could yourself.

That is the investment trust theory, but the practice of it is not so simple. There are over 350 trusts available today, so that the task of selecting the right one for any given investor, or even the one with the best record, is comparable to the job of combing through the stock market to find a good stock. Investment trusts provide such a valuable tool to the investor that the next two chapters will be devoted entirely to this subject.

Investment Clubs. According to the old adage, there is safety in numbers. Some people feel more confident investing in a group. One way to do it is to start, or join, an investment club. There are estimated to be over 25,000 in existence in the United States. Most clubs work this way. There are a dozen to twenty members who meet once a month. Each member puts in a fixed amount of money, for example $10 or $20. The money is pooled and invested in some stock chosen by vote.

While these clubs have a social object, they are primarily educational. The members study the stock market, industry prospects and company records. Some clubs that have been in existence for several years have built up investments amounting to several thousand dollars per member. A later chapter will be devoted to investment clubs, giving examples and showing how to start one.

Do-it-Yourself. The course that most investors take is to worry out their own program, using such brains and ingenuity as they have, plus the advice that's always available from brokerage houses, market services and publications. To do this a person should cultivate his self-reliance and perspective and take time to study industries and companies.

Perhaps the person most in touch with the investor is his broker. While the broker's primary job is to execute orders, he inevitably is asked for a certain amount of advice. There are all kinds of brokers just as there are all kinds of doctors—some good, some mediocre. Try to pick a broker who has the long-term investment point of view rather than the short-term trading point of view and one with a proven good record.

Advisory Services. Once a person takes an interest in investing he will discover that a welter of published advice is available. He should be careful to separate out that which is realistic and useful from the miracle and crystal ball offers that are flamboyantly advertised in so many newspapers and magazines.

For example, how would you like to have the names of seven stocks likely to triple in value? Or a list of low-priced blue chips? Or 37 candidates for stock splits? Or a set of charts to tell you which way the market will go? All of this enticing information and more is offered for a few dollars—some of it even for free—in the ads that appear on the financial pages of newspapers. Probably you've wondered, though, just how good this information is. If the people who peddle the advice know so much, how come they aren't lolling on their yachts off the Riviera?

A realistic answer might be that no one can foretell the actions of the market as a whole, or of an individual stock. About the best you can expect from any investment advisory service is a conscientious job of research, good factual material and sober recommendations. As to the services that offer tips for quick profits or charts that are supposed to foretell price actions—be wary. If that sort of information were reliable, it would be worth much more than a few dollars or even a few hundred. In fact, it would not be for sale. So if you do feel the need for some kind of investment advice, don't grab the service with the most exciting ad. First take a look at the whole field. It may save you money and disillusionment.

The Big Financial Services. Moody's, Standard & Poor's, United Business Service, Babson's, Fitch's, Value Line and Argus are examples of the experienced organizations that have been in business for many years. Each provides a weekly report or survey covering business conditions in general and according to industry. Facts, figures and recommendations are presented on the stocks of selected companies. One issue of such a report may present a group of growth stocks thought to be attractive, another a list of stocks yielding good income, and so on. From time to time reviews are made of stocks previously recommended. Some of these services also provide for personalized consultation by mail. In some cases this privilege is included in the subscription price. In others it is not. Annual subscriptions range from $50 to $160 for the five services.

More-specialized Services. Next consider a kind of hodgepodge group of services that generally play up a special angle or treat a particular group of stocks. Here's a sample of subject matter covered by various specialized services: low-priced shares; "special situations"; mining and metal stocks; charts or indexes that supposedly give clues as to coming movements of the market as a whole.

Generally speaking, these specialized services present the theories and research of one man or a small group. They give a more individualistic approach than the larger services such as Moody's or Standard & Poor's.

How good are these specialized services? It's impossible to generalize. They range from good to useless. The worst are the tip sheets that breezily offer to give the names of a few stocks that, by implication, are bound to rise in price. These are sometimes known as fair-weather services because they make their money during booms in the market when everything is going up. When conditions change and their predictions turn sour, these services sometimes start doing business under a different name. Before subscribing to any specialized service, check with a reliable broker or investment counselor. Usually you can see samples of the more widely used services in a broker's office.

Brokers' Market Letters. Many brokerage houses send free to their clients a periodical market letter or survey. Some can be subscribed to for a fee by noncustomers.

To mention a few, Merrill Lynch, Pierce, Fenner & Smith, send customers a quarterly survey that discusses business conditions, industry by industry, and recommends particular stocks in each. Bache & Co. publishes a weekly one-page letter, which usually discusses a particular stock. Arthur Wiesenberger & Co.'s twice-monthly investment report, usually predicting the trend of the market and discussing several special situations, is sent to selected clients but also may be subscribed to. Clark, Dodge & Co. reviews companies and industries.

Some brokerage houses will analyze your securities holdings without obligation. Merrill Lynch, for example, will send anyone, including noncustomers, a form to be filled out with personal and financial information, investment objectives and securities owned. The firm will then send back an analysis and recommendations.

Financial Magazines. Some general information on industries and individual companies is given by certain financial magazines. Examples are *Financial World,* published weekly; *Forbes,* twice monthly; *Barron's National Business and Financial Weekly.*

As you can see, all kinds of investment advice are available.

It should be noted, also, that the cost of the advice is no sure measure of its worth.

The best procedure probably is this: First, decide on a long-term investment program for yourself. For many people this means buying steadily into good quality companies that show promise of growth, and holding patiently for the growth to materialize. Second, decide which kind of help will best complement your own abilities and temperament.

If you are basically self-reliant and have the time to study, perhaps you can utilize the material that's available from market letters, investment services and the like, and be your own adviser. For many people this method is satisfying, but it could be expensive for someone who didn't have the knack.

If you want to turn the job completely over to someone else, and you don't have the $100,000 needed for individual investment counseling, buy into good investment companies. This gives professional management at the lowest cost. But remember that cost is not the most important consideration. What's most important is the result.

investment companies— how to duck part of the investment decision

Now what if you want to duck the difficult investment decisions? You turn your car over to the auto mechanic for repairs; your health problems to a doctor; your legal problems to a lawyer. Why shouldn't you turn your investment problems over to professionals and let them put your money to work? Maybe you should. And one way to do it is to buy shares in an investment company. Instead of owning stock in one or two companies such as Eastman Kodak or Standard Oil of New Jersey, you own a tiny cross-section slice of several dozen companies. You get automatic diversification and all the while, the managers of the trust are weeding out stocks that they feel are doing poorly and substituting stocks that they believe have more promise.

Fine and good. But shopping for an investment trust is like shopping for anything else. There are many types and many brand names on the market. One investment company may differ from another fully as much as a 1955 Pontiac station wagon differs from a 1962 Volkswagen sedan. Some investment trusts are sold aggressively by energetic salesmen knocking on doors.

Others are available only if you learn about them and seek them out. Some are available at a discount; others strictly at the pro-rata value of their assets. Some try for growth; others for income. Some invest in blue chips; others in lesser known companies. Some are cautiously managed; others tend to shoot the works for big gains. Some have a splendid record of competent management going back over the years. And unfortunately, others seem to have been thrown together to give would-be managers something to manage and hungry salesmen something to sell. As in every other kind of purchase, it's well to know the field before you begin to narrow down your choice. Start with a few definitions and characteristics.

Net Asset Value per Share. This is the net dollar value of the securities the fund owns divided by the number of its shares outstanding in the hands of the public. Thus on a given day a certain fund might own securities having a market value of $10,-000,000. If it had outstanding in the hands of the public one million of its own shares, then the net asset value per share would be $10.

Capital Structure. The two types here are the closed-end trust, which is the older and less publicized, and the open-end or mutual fund, which is newer, almost always aggressively sold, and the kind you are more likely to hear about. Closed-end means that at some time in the past the trust sold a block of shares to the public but makes no continuous offering of additional shares. Thus the number of shares outstanding is constant. Most closed-end shares are traded on the New York Stock Exchange, just as are shares of large corporations such as Du Pont or Standard Oil of New Jersey, or else over-the-counter as are most bank and insurance company stocks.

Examples of closed-end trusts are Lehman Corporation and Tri-Continental Corporation, traded on the New York Stock Exchange, and Consolidated Investment Trust, traded over-the-counter. If you want to buy into a closed-end trust you get in touch with a broker and through him buy shares from another investor who already owns shares and wants to sell. The price the buyer pays, or the seller receives, depends to some extent on supply and demand. It may be above or below the pro-rata net asset value. If the price is above the net asset value the stock is said to be selling at a premium; if below, at a discount.

Open-end trusts, or mutual funds, which have become very popular, are based on a different idea. Open-end means that the trust stands ready at all times to sell new shares or redeem old ones. Thus the number of outstanding shares of an open-end fund is always changing. While these transactions usually are done through a broker, there is no public trading. Thus the law of supply and demand does not affect the price. Examples of open-end trusts are Massachusetts Investors Trust, Chemical Fund, Aberdeen Fund, and so on.

As you can see, in one major respect, closed-end and open-end trusts are the same—that is, they are in the business of investing money entrusted to them by the shareholders. In most other ways, however, they differ. As to performance, studies tend to show that the closed-end companies have done the best for the investors in the past twenty years.

Closed-end Funds. This is the traditional type, popular in Great Britain as early as 1880. A closed-end trust might be started somewhat in this manner. The sponsors decide to incorporate and sell, say, 100,000 shares to the public at, say, $10 a share. The one million dollars of capital thus raised would be invested in selected stocks or stocks and bonds. After the public offering, some of the original buyers of the shares would decide to sell them. Thus the shares would begin to be traded over-the-counter or, if the shares were listed, then through the medium of a stock exchange. In the beginning, of course, each share would be considered to be worth $10, the original offering price. But as shares were traded, investor psychology would begin to play its part. If investors were optimistic about the prospects of the trust, they might be willing to pay more than $10 a share, say, $11, to get their hands on a block of stock. In such a case, the going price of the shares would be 10% more than the pro-rata underlying asset value (assuming it had not changed in the meantime) and the shares would be selling at a 10% premium. Or, take the other extreme. Suppose public enthusiasm for the shares waned. Buyers might be reluctant to pay more than $9 a share. The shares thus would be selling at a 10% discount. In each case the stock broker would charge a commission for finding the buyer (or seller) and handling the transaction.

This tendency to sell either at a premium or discount from net asset value is a distinctive characteristic of closed-end trusts. It so happens that in recent years many closed-end trusts have been available in the market place at a discount. Think what this means. In many cases it enables you to buy part ownership in a list of stocks, for example Du Pont, Union Carbide, Minneapolis-Honeywell and IBM at, say, 10%, 15% or 25% less than their market value. There's no particular gimmick about this except that if you later sold your shares, you probably—but not necessarily—would have to sell at a discount. In the meantime, however, for every 75, 85 or 90 cents you had invested, you would have a dollar's worth of capital working for you. Also the discount could narrow, which would be an advantage.

There are several explanations for this discount. First, there are no salesmen aggressively pushing the shares and creating a demand. When you buy, you buy from some other investor, the transaction going through a broker. The commission generally is the regular New York Stock Exchange commission, which on a transaction of $2,500 down to $500 amounts to 1% to 2%. There is less incentive for brokers to try to sell you shares of a closed-end trust than shares in other companies whose stock is traded over-the-counter or on exchanges. In fact brokers have very little interest in selling you closed-end shares since money put in a trust is likely to stay there rather than move into and out of various stocks, thereby providing brokerage commissions.

The second possible reason for the discount is that the shareholder can't count on getting full net asset value (as he can for open-end shares). Therefore the buyer figures he may get less than liquidating value when he sells.

In the third place, most investment companies, both open-end and closed-end, carry a certain built-in tax liability. This consists of their accumulated but unrealized capital gains. Suppose, for example, you buy into an investment company that holds stock now worth $10,000,000 but that was originally bought for $6,-000,000. There is an unrealized gain of $4,000,000. If the company should sell all of its holdings and realize this gain, you would receive a return of almost 40% of your capital, on which you would be liable for a capital gains tax. In an open-end investment company, or mutual fund, where the selling price is pegged to net asset value, the buyer is unable to offset this liability by paying a discounted price. He, nevertheless, is at times able to buy some closed-end shares at a discount.

Discounts generally narrow during booms or rising markets and widen during declines. A few very popular closed-end companies traditionally sell at small premiums. When you sell closed-end shares, you sell on the open market, going through a broker who charges another commission of 1% or 2%. It is amusing to note that in some cases the same sponsor manages two funds, a closed-end trust selling in the open market at less than liquidating value, and a mutual fund sold by salesmen at a premium of, say 8%, above liquidating value.

Leverage. This is another distinctive characteristic of closed-end trusts. Most of them, Lehman Corporation, for example, have outstanding only one class of capital stock; that is, common stock. Some, however, have in addition to common stock preferred stock or warrants. Thus Tri-Continental Corporation, a big and successful closed-end company, has outstanding common stock, preferred stock, debentures and warrants. Each warrant entitles the holder to buy 1.27 shares of the trust's common stock at $17.76 per share. You can see that when Tri-Continental common was selling below $17.76, the warrants had only a potential value. But whenever the common stock has gone above the warrant price, the warrants have jumped sharply. This causes the warrants to rise and fall more rapidly than the common stock. The debentures and preferred stock would provide leverage except that the management usually keeps an equivalent amount invested in bonds or preferreds in its own portfolio.

Here is how the preferred stock and bonds of a closed-end trust can give leverage to the common. Suppose a closed-end trust is organized with assets of $100,000,000, of which half is represented by preferred stock and bonds and half by common. The holders of the preferred stock and bonds have a fixed $50,000,000 interest. What's left belongs to the owners of the common stock.

Suppose the stock market declines 20% and the value of the securities owned by the trust also declines 20%. The trust is then worth only $80,000,000, of which the holders of the preferred stock and bonds still lay claim to $50,000,000, leaving only $30,-000,000 as the equity of the owners of the common. Thus on a general market decline of 20%, leverage has caused the common stock of this closed-end trust to decline 40%, from $50,-000,000 to $30,000,000.

Similarly, suppose the stock market as a whole and the assets of the trust rise 20% to $120,000,000. The equity of the holders of the preferred stock and bonds remains at $50,000,000, leaving $70,000,000 for the common. Thus leverage has caused the common stock to rise 40% in value on a stock market rise of only 20%.

You can see that the best time to purchase and hold common stock or warrants of a leverage trust is just before or during a stock market rise. Unfortunately, few investors are able to spot such a rise in advance.

Why do managers of closed-end investment companies spend their time trying to make money for the public? For one thing, of course, a closed-end investment company is much like a tremendously wealthy client of an investment counselor. The management fee, which usually is ½ of 1% of the total assets, is a very good source of income. In some cases, too, the sponsors are brokers and handle the investment trust's brokerage business, receiving a commission on all purchases and sales. This could be a strong temptation to churn the investment company's portfolio, although in the best companies there is no evidence of this.

More important, perhaps, is the fact that many investment counselors and investment bankers consider an investment company as a kind of show window where they can display their astuteness. Managers of many companies take pride in the record they have made. The competition among funds grows rapidly.

The fact that most closed-end investment trusts sell at a discount does not prove that they are necessarily less well managed or less desirable than mutual funds. The American Institute for Economic Research has found from a study they made that the performance of closed-end companies is generally better than the performance of open-end companies. This is a controversial matter and certainly the open-end companies would make every effort to prove otherwise. However, it does seem reasonable that where a closed-end fund has 100 cents of each dollar to invest rather than only 92 cents or 92.5 cents as in the case of an open-end fund (investor's payment minus the usual load) the results of the closed-end fund over the years could be better. Also, since such funds are not continually selling new shares, they are not constantly faced with the problem of investing large sums of additional cash. It takes time for an open-end fund to get this cash invested and in the meantime, if the market is rising, older shareholders must face the fact that the value of their shares is diluted by these additional uninvested funds. But once again, the best measure is the performance of the fund, whether closed- or open-end, over a period of years.

Open-end Funds. These make up a very fast growing type of security. Investors buy more shares each month than they cash in. This increase in ownership seems to go on month in and month out regardless of whether the stock market is going up or down. Why such popularity? There are several explanations. Perhaps the most logical is that salesmen have a greater incentive to sell mutual funds than almost any other type of investment.

All mutual funds have only one kind of stock outstanding, common stock. The mutual fund itself supplies new shares, through salesmen or brokers, to all who wish to buy. It also takes back old shares from those who wish to sell. (There is some over-the-counter trading in shares of the larger mutual funds, but dealers who habitually sell mutual funds generally sign an agreement not to trade in this market.) Except in the case of the limited trading just mentioned, the price the investor pays when he buys a mutual fund is the exact net asset value per share at the time plus a sales commission.

This sales commission, or load, is not usually stated as a percentage of the net asset value. It is stated as a percentage of the offering price; that is, the net asset value plus the commission. If you wanted to buy one share of a mutual fund having a net asset value of $10 and the load was 8½%, you would pay $10.93. (The 93 cents is 8½% of $10.93.) Actually you pay 9.3% of net asset value.

Thus the sales commission generally runs around 8½% or 9½% of the net asset value, and this is considerably larger than the 1%, 2%, or 3% of the market price you pay when you buy closed-end shares or other listed stocks. And the salesman who sells mutual fund shares receives about a third of the total sales commission. This generous return makes it well worth his while to seek out prospective buyers at office or home.

There has grown up a new type of security salesman who resembles the life insurance salesmen and who is trained to sell open-end funds exclusively. This differs from the usual concept of a broker as being one who stands ready to sell you stocks, bonds, listed or unlisted, traded anywhere in the world, you name it.

Most open-end trusts make no charge for redeeming shares. This is in contrast to closed-end shares where you do pay a selling commission of 1%, 2%, 3% or some other amount depending on the size of the transaction. Some open-end trusts charge a nominal fee for redeeming shares, usually ½ of 1%. Very often the trusts that charge this redemption fee are the ones that charge no load.

No-load Mutual Funds. These are a strange breed of cat because they are not sold by salesmen. In fact, a no-load fund is one of the few things in this world that you can buy without paying a sales commission, directly or indirectly. The reason you don't hear much about no-load funds is that no salesman knocks at your door trying to persuade you to buy one. Why should he? He wouldn't get any commission. Yet, except for the lack of a sales charge, these no-load funds are run just the way the others are. You might wonder, then, What's the gimmick? Why should a mutual fund be willing to offer its shares at cost? And if it does, why doesn't everyone buy the no-load funds and save the commission?

Tackle these questions in order. How can a mutual fund exist and grow if it doesn't charge a sales commission?

For the answer, note that all mutual funds, open-end as well as closed-end, whether a sales commission is involved or not, charge a management fee for handling the shareholders' money. In most cases, this fee is ½ of 1% per year of the capital under the fund's management, although it can be higher or lower. Thus the managers of a fund having assets of $100,000,000 might receive an annual management fee of $500,000. Though this would be only a small percentage of the total assets, it could amount to 15% to 20% in terms of the fund's annual income.

Now while the managers of a no-load mutual fund receive no part of any sales commission, they still receive the management fee and thus are compensated for investing the stockholders' money. In addition, most managers of no-load mutual funds are investment counseling firms who handle large sums for private investors. For such firms the mutual fund may just be a side line, although a useful one, as the following example will show.

An investment counseling firm ordinarily accepts only wealthy clients, charging a management fee, usually ½ of 1% of the money at risk. The smallness of the fee makes it uneconomical for such a firm to accept amounts of less than, say $100,000, and it avoids the problem by charging a minimum fee of $500 or more a year. Such a firm may still want to accommodate the son of a good client or perhaps a young executive who promises to be a customer in the future. In many cases, too, wealthy clients want to establish small accounts for minor children or grandchildren.

One way to take care of the younger and non-wealthy investor is to set up a mutual fund. To such potential clients the firm can say, "Our mutual fund is managed in the same way as our big accounts. Put your money into the fund and you'll get the same treatment. There is no sales charge." Once such a fund gets started and begins to grow, it generally is offered publicly so that anyone may buy in.

This sounds like a good deal. Naturally, however, there are a few ifs and buts. You do have a larger choice among the funds with loads because there are more of them. Maybe a particular fund with a load would serve your purposes better because it would be easier to fit it into your holdings. However, the important thing is performance. A fund with a load, over the years, may perform so much better than one without a load that you would be foolish to buy the no-load fund merely to save the commission. It is like buying a suit of clothes or a pair of shoes. The cheapest in price may be, but are not necessarily, the best buys.

Here are some of the no-load funds whose performance you should check against others before you make your choice. De-Vegh Mutual Fund; Energy Fund, Inc.; Johnston Mutual Fund; Loomis-Sayles Mutual Fund; T. Rowe Price Growth Stock Fund; Scudder, Stevens & Clark Fund, Inc.; Scudder, Stevens & Clark

Common Stock Fund, Inc.; Stein Roe & Farnham Stock Fund, Inc.

Investment Objectives. Are you cautious or daring? Do you want to have extra spending money coming in all the time, or are you more interested in leaving your capital alone and letting it increase over the years? Are you a bargain hunter, or are you willing to pay for goods of proven quality? Whatever your inclinations, there are investment trusts, open-end or closed, with characteristics to match.

Here are typical objectives:

• *Long-term growth of both capital and income. Current income not stressed.*
• *Long-term growth of capital through use of smaller, younger and more speculative companies, ignoring income entirely.*
• *High current income. Capital growth not stressed.*
• *Concentration on a particular industry or geographical area.*
• *Concentration on a particular type of security other than common stocks, such as bonds or preferred stocks.*
• *Heavy investment in a few special situations; that is, companies whose stock is thought to be particularly undervalued for some special reason.*
• *Concentration on foreign securities; e.g. the various Canadian funds.*

Common Stock Funds keep nearly all of their capital invested in common stocks although they may switch some stocks into cash or bonds when a defensive position seems appropriate.

Balanced Funds generally keep a quarter to a half of their capital in cash, bonds or preferred stocks. The objective is to obtain protection against declining stock prices.

Bond and Preferred Stock Funds seek diversification among various types of fixed income obligations. There is some specialization; that is, some funds stick to high grade bonds, others to speculative bonds and so on.

Income Funds try to invest in high yielding securities, generally common stocks.

Specialized Funds concentrate on some particular segment of the investment field. Some funds confine themselves to one industry or a group of industries. Others buy into companies in one part of the country, or abroad. Some hunt for companies that are in trouble and that could be improved in one way or another. These last are known as special situations.

Altogether there are some 350 investment trusts to choose from. While the choice is wide, it may be narrowed down by sticking to two objectives: first, pick a trust whose investment objectives correspond to your own; second, pick the best management you can find.

how to pick an investment trust

Because the investment trust field is such a desirable place for the man with, say, $500 to $25,000 to put his money (and even professional investors such as pension fund managers are increasingly using this medium), the investment community has developed many types of funds to provide an appeal to the large mass market and also, to give salesmen for each fund something a little different to sell. There are, for example, balanced funds which generally keep a quarter or more of their capital in cash, bonds or preferred stocks. There are funds that invest only in bonds, and others that try to provide the largest possible income to their shareholders. But the funds that will be recommended in this book are primarily common stock funds whose objective is ownership of a broad selection of common stock in well-managed, aggressive corporations.

The reason for this recommendation is explained in the chapter on "Balance" (Chapter 6). Remember that investment trusts were used in each sample portfolio and their purpose was to give the investor common stocks to balance his cash savings, bonds and preferred stocks. In the case of the investor aged 30, investment trusts were the only common stock holdings shown. In the case of older investors, some investment trusts still were included, notably funds concentrating on more speculative growth stocks, in order to give participation in newer, fast growing fields of industry.

Balanced Funds. The investors referred to in the examples, striving for balance within their own portfolios, would not need a balanced investment trust. Such a balanced fund, however, might be useful to a person who wanted complete management of all his funds including fixed-income investments. It would relieve him of the necessity of choosing both stocks and bonds and also would remove the psychological pressures that bear on the investor and sometimes warp his judgment in favor of speculation or high yield.

One disadvantage to the balanced fund, and also to the bond and income fund, is that the management fee of $\frac{1}{2}$ of 1% takes a considerable slice of the income from bonds and preferreds. For example, if such income were $3\frac{1}{2}$%, the management fee would take around 15%. This 15% would be saved if the investor bought his own bonds and preferreds which, generally speaking, are more easily selected than common stocks. In some funds, it should be noted, the management fee drops to, say, $\frac{3}{8}$ of 1% when the size of the fund exceeds $100,000,000.

But the main objection to the balanced fund is that it does not provide as big an opportunity for gain as does the stock fund. And this limitation shows up in the performance records which generally show that over the past five, ten, or fifteen years, balanced funds have not done as well as those concentrating on common stocks.

Bond and Preferred Stock Funds. These are a means of securing diversification in fixed-income obligations. Since there is no growth in straight bonds or preferreds, and since the income is fixed, the management charge could be rather substantial in relation to total income. Ordinarily several "A" grade preferreds or utility bonds would be just as desirable as a slice of a good many, and there would be no management fee or other expense charged against the income.

Income Funds. These strive for a high yield for their shareholders. They invest largely in companies that pay out a major part of their earnings. Such companies show little growth, and risks in a free economy being what they are, a company that is not growing is in danger of declining. In particular, a company paying a high dividend, which is not secure, probably offers no more yield over the long run than a good bond or preferred stock. And these latter are of course far less risky since they have claims ahead of the common as to both dividend and position in case of liquidation.

Industry Funds. These spread their money over many companies in one industry. By buying into several such funds you could obtain tremendous diversification. You would not only be diversified over industries, but over many companies in each industry. However, diversification simply for diversification's sake is not always advisable or profitable. It probably is better to buy into a common stock fund which attempts to pick out a few of the most desirable companies in numerous industries.

Geographical Funds. These concentrate their investment in one state, such as Florida, or one area, such as the Southwest. Since the managers are confined to one area, and yet must obtain diversification, they may be forced to buy stocks not as promising as others they could buy if they were operating nationally. On the other hand, an unrestricted common stock fund could buy into any promising company in any state or area.

In the case of some funds concentrating their investments in Canada, there is a certain tax advantage. Preferential treatment is offered to investment companies operating in Canada but owned by non-Canadians. Such companies pay no capital gains tax and by paying a 15% tax on income from interest and dividends, can relieve their foreign shareholders of payment of any other Canadian tax. Nonresident-owned Canadian trusts, then, give American investors the opportunity to invest in growth stocks, allow the income and profits to accumulate and pay only the U.S. capital gains tax at the time they sell their shares. This is in contrast to American tax procedures where the investor in an investment company must pay capital gains tax whenever the trust realizes a gain.

Special Situation Funds. While the managers of most investment trusts avoid any participation in the affairs of the companies whose stock they may own, the reverse is true in the case of funds that invest in special situations. The managers of such funds seek out companies in trouble financially, whose stock is available cheap. When the trust finds such a company it buys into it and then strives to help with management advice or new financing, the object, of course, being to increase the value of the stock. Results of this type of investment can be very good or very bad. Since these funds are so speculative, they would not seem to be desirable for the average investor.

Foreign Securities Funds. Western Europe's growth in post-World War II years has been greater than ours. Particularly in recent years, European, Japanese and Australian stocks have risen. But there is often more risk in foreign securities than in those of American companies. One risk is the political instability and the unpredictable taxing policies of the country concerned. In one country an extra tax was imposed on corporations just before Christmas one year on the grounds that it seemed like a good way to raise additional funds.

The investor who wants a stake in foreign operations can obtain it by buying into leading American corporations that have interests abroad. In some cases 40% of the profits come from foreign operations. Goodyear, Pfizer and IBM are among those that do a large foreign business. For the average investor this is the safest way to invest abroad.

Common Stock Funds. These make up, by far, the largest category. Stock funds used to be separated into run-of-mill stock funds and so-called growth funds. More recently, however, almost all common stock funds own growth stocks. In fact they are all competing vigorously for the higher grade companies that give promise of the greatest growth. The records of these funds are publicized and the pressure is on them to show performance. Thus they offer an excellent place for the common stock money of those investors who perhaps do not have the knack or the interest or the resources to produce good results by investing directly in the stock of operating companies.

And the truth is that most investors operating on their own are not likely to show as good results as the better managed investment trusts. Look at it this way. The Dow-Jones Industrial

Average went from a level of 165 in 1949 to over 700 in 1961. But consider that there are thirty stocks that comprise the Dow-Jones Industrial Average. Of these thirty, some have gone up a great deal faster than others. Think how well off the investor would be if he could consistently have kept invested in the ten stocks out of the average that did the best. Yet this would be no simple matter. Investment trust managers spend hundreds of thousands of dollars a year on research. They have at hand the wealth of detailed information that modern corporations make available, plus computers to do the figuring. Yet most investment trusts do well if they beat the Dow-Jones Average. How much harder, then, is the task of the individual investor operating on his own? Too often he lives in a dream world where he hopes that a few hours of work, combined with tips and recommendations from brokers, will enable him to do the job that experts can do only with the greatest difficulty.

Newer Growth Funds. This is one group that probably should be separated from the main category of common stock funds. It is composed of funds that concentrate on new fields where there are thought to be the greatest chances of growth, and probably more than average risk. Since fast growing companies plow back most of their earnings, they pay out very little in dividends. So these newer growth funds yield very little.

The industries in which these newer growth funds have invested are publishing, cosmetics, electronics, atomic products, microwave transmission and so on. Such companies are young and have less stability than older companies. They also are smaller and therefore a small dollar amount of growth can show a large increase in earnings. Beginning around the spring of 1961 there grew up a tremendous craving on the part of the public for this type of company. How these young companies will do in the future is unknown. Some of them may not survive. But the object of the newer growth funds is to pick the best and hope that, by diversification, the success of some will outweigh the failure of others. As these newer growth funds grow, they will find it increasingly difficult to acquire or to sell large blocks of stock in small companies that have a limited amount of stock outstanding.

While these newer growth funds may serve a purpose and might well be a part of the investor's portfolio, it is questionable whether they should be given a major role.

Selection. There are two main criteria in selecting an investment trust. First, are the managers of the trust trying to invest the money entrusted to them the way you would invest it yourself? For most investors this means putting the money into common stocks of good quality and aggressive companies. Second, are the managers of the trust doing a bang-up job? In other words, is their investment record better than the average record of trusts with similar objectives?

Once these tests are met, there are other measures to apply. Is the sales charge reasonable? Is the annual management fee a modest one? Can shares be purchased in convenient amounts, assuming you do not wish to make a large lump sum investment? Does the trust permit reinvestment of dividends and capital gains distributions conveniently and inexpensively?

Here are other points to watch for. The biggest and most widely known trusts are not necessarily the best. The managers of the very largest open-end funds with the hardest hitting salesmen cannot confine their investments to a relatively few outstanding stocks. They have so much money coming in from shareholders that they feel forced to spread it throughout the stock market. The largest open-end funds get so heavily invested in so many companies that they become, as it were, musclebound and cannot buy and sell with any freedom. Too often the diversification is so broad that the results are mediocre. This underscores the fact that only the best companies can equal or beat the stock market averages.

Acquisition costs, while not as important as performance, do enter into the selection.

Sponsorship is important. Who manages the trust and why? Selling shares in mutual funds has been a good business over the past few years. The principle of investing through trusts has been sound, but unfortunately there is reason to feel that a few are more interested in the sales commissions and management fees than in providing the best possible results for the shareholders. Several such trusts have tangled with the United States Securities and Exchange Commission in connection with excessive management fees and collusion between sponsors and the investment advisory services hired to do the portfolio managing.

An outstanding long-term performance record is important. In addition, the investor may feel better about putting in his money if he knows that the managers have thought enough of the trust to put their own money in also. Of course, no one person could own a substantial interest in an investment trust with assets of hundreds of millions of dollars. However, a few could be mentioned, such as Lehman Corporation, Chemical Fund, State Street Investment Corporation and Tri-Continental Corporation, in which the managers and their families do have substantial holdings.

Which companies have done the best? This is the most important question and one on which many investors go astray. It is important because when you buy shares in an investment trust, you are paying someone to manage your money. If you don't get good management, you get nothing. Some investors go wrong because they buy the first trust they hear of. Or they may fall for some salesman's spiel without realizing that alternative and, perhaps, better investments are available. Other investors unwittingly buy a poorly managed trust because they see that it has made money during the past ten years. As a matter of fact, nearly all trusts have made some money during a particular period because the stock market itself has gone up. It is advisable to check on what the managers did over longer periods.

There are, in fact, several tests that should be applied to the management record of an investment trust. Ideally, the net asset value per share should go up with, or faster than, the stock market as a whole and decline more slowly. So one measure is to compare changes in net asset value per share with stock market averages during periods of rising prices and also during periods of declining prices. In addition to the rise and decline in the value of the shares, you naturally must take account of the amount of capital gains paid out. Most investors should reinvest these capital gains but in some compilations of investment trust records, these gains are listed separately. Dividends should be considered of less importance by most investors.

Several books will help you investigate various funds.
Investment Companies by Arthur Wiesenberger. Each year for

many years Arthur Wiesenberger & Co., 61 Broadway, New York 6, N.Y., has published a monumental book called *Investment Companies*. Its nearly 400 pages, plus supplements, are crammed with information on the theory of investment trusts in general as well as detailed information on all open-end and closed-end trusts. The book costs $25 and would be well worth that to many serious investors. Also, it may be examined in almost every brokerage house in the country and in almost every library.

Wiesenberger compares management of open-end trusts by listing in a table the percentage change in net asset value per share, plus dividends and distributions for each of the past 10 years and for the over-all period of 10, 9, 8, 7, etc., years. He also provides a transparent overlay of the Dow-Jones Industrial Average which may be applied to a similar chart of the performance of each open-end trust. A slightly different arrangement makes it possible to compare the Dow-Jones Average with the performance of closed-end trusts. If you are in the market for investment trust shares, be sure to study these tables in the Wiesenberger book.

Investment Trusts and Funds from the Investor's Point of View. This is another valuable publication on investment trusts put out each year by the American Institute for Economic Research, Great Barrington, Mass., price $1. The authors select a small number of funds, some open-end and some closed-end. These funds are then compared with their composite average. The assumption is that all dividends and disbursements were reinvested when paid. Recommendations are made in three categories: for investment, for speculative investment and for speculation. Read the book if you plan to buy open- or closed-end shares.

Johnson's Charts. Perhaps the most intriguing gadget for judging the largest open-end funds (but not the closed-end type) is a loose-leaf book called *Johnson's Investment Company Charts*, published annually by Hugh A. Johnson, Rand Building, Buffalo 3, N.Y. The book costs $35 and could, once again, repay the serious investor with valuable information. Most investment dealers and libraries would have a copy.

In *Johnson's Charts* each fund gets a page. Its management record is measured by a line on a chart showing how much your shares would be worth today (including all capital gains distributions) if you had invested $10,000 in the fund ten years ago. Dividends paid from income are shown separately. In a pocket in the back of the book are transparent overlays giving exactly comparable line charts of the Dow-Jones Industrial Average, Standard & Poor's Stock Index, the cost-of-living index and the stock market records of various companies such as Standard Oil of New Jersey, General Motors, A T & T, and so on. By placing these overlays on the chart of any open-end trust, you can see at a glance whether it did better or worse than, say, the Dow-Jones Industrial Average, A T & T or the cost-of-living index. Each chart is adjusted to allow for the commission or load.

Johnson's book also is a storehouse of other information on open-end trusts. A section called "tablistics" gives 20 pertinent facts about the trusts including type, size, offering price, periodic payment plan, reinvestment plan, selling charge, management fee and so on. Other tables rank the largest trusts showing which had the greatest capital appreciation and which best resisted general stock market declines over the past 10 years. You should refer to this book if you plan to buy open-end shares.

Barron's. Every three months *Barron's National Business and Financial Weekly*, 40 New Street, New York 4, N.Y., $15 a year, prints its mutual fund record, which gives the following information on each open-end trust: net asset value per share at the end of the last quarter, dividends from income for the preceding 12 months, distributions from capital gains for the preceding 12 months. Comparable figures are also shown for the preceding 10 years.

Barron's once published a percentage-type performance gauge of open-end trusts but discontinued it because overzealous dealers and salesmen were making misleading reprints which emphasized good short-term results where long-term results were not so favorable.

This points up one big pitfall in all statistics on investment trusts. Smart salesmen can sometimes juggle the figures or the periods to make mediocre records look good. Remember, in judging performance, use as long periods as possible, although more weight should be given to the past 10 years. And don't forget to include at least one period when the market was declining. You will often find that the trusts that look the best when the market is going up, look the worst when it is going down.

EXAMPLES OF COMMON STOCK FUNDS
LISTED ALPHABETICALLY

Aberdeen Fund, 15 William Street, New York 5, N.Y., an open-end trust managed and counseled by the Boston investment counseling firm of David L. Babson & Co. Policy is to invest only in stocks which the management regards as having above-average opportunity for long-range growth of capital and income. Primary emphasis is given to companies active in research and product development. Selling charge is 8½%. Annual expenses usually run around 0.8% of net assets.

Carriers & General Corp., 1 Wall Street, New York 5, N.Y., is a closed-end fund traded on the New York Stock Exchange. It was organized in 1929 by Calvin Bullock, Ltd., which has provided continuous management. Policy is one of wide industrial diversification, with emphasis on common stocks representing large and well-managed corporate enterprises. Annual expenses usually run around 0.7% of net assets. From time to time this trust has been available at a 12% to 13% discount.

Chemical Fund, 65 Broadway, New York 6, N.Y., is an open-end fund organized and managed by F. Eberstadt & Co. This trust is technically specialized but actually has interpreted the chemical field so broadly that it provides considerable diversification among industries as well as companies. Included are such new fields as atomic energy, missile propellants, special metals, electronic components as well as drugs, glass, rubber, paint, paper, photographic materials, plastics, etc. Selling charge is 7½%; annual expenses usually run around 0.5% of net assets. Management has a large interest in the shares.

Consolidated Investment Trust, 35 Congress Street, Boston 9, Mass., is a closed-end trust founded in 1933 and managed by its officers and trustees who include many distinguished businessmen. John P. Chase of the Chase Fund of Boston provides the investment advice. Policy is to emphasize issues with long-term investment characteristics. The stock is traded over-the-counter, often at a sizeable discount. Annual expense is one of the lowest in the business, usually running not much over 0.1%.

Lehman Corporation, 1 South William Street, New York 4, N.Y., is a closed-end fund founded in 1929 by the investment banking firm of Lehman Brothers who continue its management. This fund concentrates on equities promising long-term growth and satisfactory income return. Although most of its holdings consist of leading corporate issues, it has made a number of commitments in less well-known situations. The stock of Lehman Corporation is traded on the New York Stock Exchange and has been so popular that it has generally sold at a small premium. Annual expenses usually run around 0.4% of net assets.

Madison Fund, 660 Madison Avenue, New York 12, N.Y., is a closed-end trust which once upon a time was a railroad holding company known as the Pennroad Corporation. Its special situations have been eliminated, however, and today this fund follows a highly flexible investment policy, with the general objective of reasonable income combined with capital growth. Investments are concentrated in common stocks with emphasis varying from growth issues to defensive stocks according to the outlook. Its stock is traded on the New York Stock Exchange and has frequently sold at a discount. Annual expenses usually run around 0.6% of net assets.

Massachusetts Investors Trust, 200 Berkeley Street, Boston 16, Mass., frequently known as M.I.T., is the oldest open-end investment trust in the country, having been founded in 1924. The fund is managed by its trustees who have described their purpose as to "constitute a conservative medium for that portion of an investor's capital which he may wish to have invested in common stocks believed to be of high or improving investment quality." Selling charge is 8½%. Annual expenses usually run at the very low rate of under 0.2% of net assets.

Tri-Continental Corporation, 65 Broadway, New York 6, N.Y., is the country's largest closed-end investment company and one of the few remaining diversified companies with capital leverage. It has outstanding in addition to common stock, debentures, preferred stock and perpetual warrants for purchase of the common. The debentures and preferred stock were used originally to give leverage to the common and may do so again in the future. In recent years, however, Tri-Continental has kept bonds and preferred stocks in its investment portfolio at about the same amounts as the bonds and preferred stocks in its capital structure. This has neutralized the leverage of the company's common stock. The warrants do have leverage and move up and down faster than the common. Its investment policy emphasizes future growth of both capital and income, together with current income. The stock is traded on the New York Stock Exchange and has usually sold at a discount. Annual expenses usually have been very low running around ¼ of 1% of net assets. Management owns an important interest in the company.

EXAMPLES OF BALANCED FUNDS
LISTED ALPHABETICALLY

Eaton and Howard Balanced Fund, 24 Federal Street, Boston 10, Mass., was organized as an open-end trust in 1932. It is managed as if it were "the entire investment program of a prudent investor." Current income is an important objective as well as some growth of principal and income. Selling charge is 6%. Annual expenses usually run around 0.6% of net assets.

Loomis-Sayles Mutual Fund, Inc., 140 Federal Street, Boston 10, Mass., was organized in 1929 and was originally regarded as a common stock fund. In recent years, however, the fund has shown more of the characteristics of a balanced fund. The policy is a flexible one and the fund is not required to hold any particular proportion of fixed-income securities. There is no selling charge on this open-end fund. Annual expenses usually run a little over 0.6% of net assets.

George Putnam Fund of Boston, 60 Congress Street, Boston 9, Mass., is an open-end trust managed by seven trustees including the former dean of Harvard Business School, the former Treasurer of Massachusetts Institute of Technology and other prominent businessmen. The fund is conservative and at least 25% of assets must at all times be kept in bonds, preferred stocks or cash. Generally this proportion has not dropped below 30%.

Offering price is 8%. Annual expenses are approximately 0.5% of net assets.

Stein Roe & Farnham Balanced Fund, 135 South LaSalle Street, Chicago 3, Illinois, is a no-load open-end trust. The policy of this fund is to provide "substantially the equivalent of an individually managed investment account." Annual expenses usually run around 0.6% of net assets.

Wellington Fund, 3001 Philadelphia Pike, Claymont, Delaware, was organized in 1928. This open-end fund diversifies its investments among bonds, preferred stocks and common stocks without restriction as to the percentage of assets to be invested in any one type. Objectives of the fund are stated as conservation of principal, reasonable income and profits without undue risk. Selling charge is 8%. Annual expenses are about 0.4% of net assets.

EXAMPLES OF NEWER GROWTH FUNDS
LISTED ALPHABETICALLY

DeVegh Mutual Fund, 26 Broadway, New York 4, N.Y., has as its primary objective long-term growth of principal. Assets of this open-end fund are invested in a diversified list of common stocks of both the blue chip and the more aggressive types. There is no selling charge but a redemption fee of 1%. Annual expenses usually run around 1.4% of net assets.

Fidelity Capital Fund, Inc., 35 Congress Street, Boston 9, Mass., an open-end fund, was offered to the public in 1958. Selection of securities for the portfolio is based almost entirely on their potential capital appreciation possibilities. Many of the securities pay little, if any, income. The rate of turnover is high. Selling charge is 8%. Annual expenses usually run around 0.7% of net assets.

Keystone S-4, the lower-priced common stock fund of Keystone Custodian Funds, 50 Congress Street, Boston 9, Mass., provides a widely diversified holding in fast-moving, lower-priced common stocks. This type of security has frequently been subject to wide price movements in both rising and declining markets. This is an open-end fund and selling charge is 8.3%. Annual expenses are generally under 0.7% of net assets.

Massachusetts Investors Growth Stock Fund, 200 Berkeley Street, Boston 16, Mass., is not strictly a newer fund. It was organized in 1932 under the same management as Massachusetts Investors Trust and until 1952 was known as Massachusetts Investors Second Fund. Long-term growth of principal and future income are the objectives and assets are usually kept fully invested in the common stocks believed to have better than average prospects for long-term growth. These generally have been the larger and better known "growth stocks." Selling charge of this open-end fund is 8½%. Annual expenses usually run around 0.4% of net assets.

National Investors Corporation, 65 Broadway, New York 6, N.Y., began operations as an open-end fund in 1937 and in 1942 joined the Tri-Continental group sponsored by J. & W. Seligman & Co. Long-term appreciation and future dividends from income are its objectives. It was the first well-known investment company to espouse a complete "growth stock" philosophy. Selling charge is 7½%. Annual expenses usually run at the low figure of slightly over 0.2% of net assets.

Putnam Growth Fund, 60 Congress Street, Boston 9, Mass., is an open-end fund organized in 1957 and managed by approximately the same group that manages George Putnam Fund of Boston. Its policy is to strive for maximum long-term growth of capital, consistent with a prudent, yet aggressive approach. Assets may be switched from growth type securities to defensive securities as the outlook dictates. Selling charge is 8%. Annual expenses usually run around 0.7% of net assets.

T. Rowe Price Growth Stock Fund, 10 Light Street, Baltimore 2, Md., is a no-load open-end trust organized in 1950. Major objective is long-term growth of capital and income but the fund may, on occasion, switch part of its assets into bonds and cash if the occasion warrants. Annual expenses are roughly 0.8% of net assets.

Wellington Equity Fund, 3001 Philadelphia Pike, Claymont, Delaware, was organized in 1958 as an open-end trust. Management is Wellington Company which also manages Wellington Fund. Policy is to strive for long-term growth of capital and income through investments in common stocks. Offering price carries an 8% sales commission. Annual expenses usually run around 0.8% of net assets.

The funds listed above are examples that the investor might well consider. Their selection has been based on performance records, management costs and other factors. The fact that a given fund has not been included in the list does not mean that it is not a good investment. The individual should look over many funds before making his selection.

dollar cost averaging —a way to solve the problem of when to buy

Several years ago the partner of a large New York brokerage firm was scanning a table showing results of a hypothetical investment of $25 a month in General Motors stock. The figures showed that had anyone started such a program 25 years before and kept it up faithfully, reinvesting all dividends, he would own 2,354 shares worth over $100,000.

"It's amazing," this seasoned trader said. "I don't believe I've done that well myself." He went back and studied the results of his own investment program. It was a typical trading account in which for years he had been switching large sums of money from one promising stock to another. He had made some spectacular profits here and there, but taking the period as a whole, he found that if, instead of trading, he had plugged along putting a fixed amount into General Motors each month, he would have done better. He would, in fact, have increased his capital at a rate of more than 17% a year. Furthermore, many other stocks would have grown much faster.

The point of this story is that the investor who regularly invests a fixed amount in promising stocks and keeps the program going over the years often will make more money than the investor who tries to forecast the market's movements and to buy low and sell high.

Forecasting the major moves of the market, not to mention the moves of a few individual stocks, is much more difficult than most people imagine. Even the big banks and investment advisory services are lucky if they are right half the time, and when they are right, they may be right for the wrong reasons. For example, the trust departments of two large banking houses advised clients to sell stocks in 1945 on the theory that a bear market had begun. As it turned out, the market did decline for a short while but then turned up for the greatest sustained rise in history, leaving the sellers with fewer stocks.

Other prominent advisory services have suggested substantial reductions in stockholdings at times over the past 16 years. Clients who took this advice lost profits because, as it turned out, stocks continued to rise, the Dow-Jones Average going from around the 200 level to over 700 with no really serious major setback. If the hundreds of thousands of dollars spent on research didn't tell the professionals the right time to buy and sell, what chance has the individual?

So, in many ways, the safest method of investing is to diversify over time, as well as over stocks. That is, don't try to switch money into and out of the market. Just keep putting money in regularly and leave it there. This will average out the minor ups and downs and give you a reasonable cost. It is a method successfully used by College Retirement Equities Fund, the equity-holding half of the tremendous nonprofit retirement plan for teachers originally sponsored in 1905 by Andrew Carnegie.

The method offers these advantages:

• *It takes the guesswork out of timing.* You buy once a month, once a quarter, twice a year or once a year whether prices seem high or low.
• *It averages out your purchase price.* The fixed ssum automatically buys more shares at low prices and fewer at high prices.
• *It can be very profitable if you select stocks of leaders in grow-*

*ing fields, or well-managed investment trusts, and make it a point
to reinvest all your dividends.* (See *Charts*, 34, 35 and 36.)

• *The procedure is simple.* Brokers nowadays welcome small
regular purchases. And the New York Stock Exchange has sponsored a plan that permits the investor to buy as little as $40
worth of a Stock Exchange stock each month or $40 each quarter
and have this amount fully invested even though it means acquiring fractional shares.

• *Over a hundred mutual funds offer accumulation plans
whereby you may buy shares of $25, $50 or $100 worth at a
time, although in most cases the initial purchase must be considerably larger.*

• *You can join with others to form an investment club.* Each
member then contributes $10 or more each month. The com-
bined funds are invested periodically.

• *If you have a reasonable amount of self-discipline, you can
make regular deposits in a savings account and periodically withdraw a given amount and invest it.*

One of the intriguing aspects of this type of investing, known
as dollar cost averaging, is the way it averages out the cost of
your shares. Note the difference between buying a certain number of *shares* and investing a certain number of *dollars* in the
same stock no matter how many shares this sum will cover.

Several years ago two professors of the business school of the
University of Michigan set out to discover how an investor would
fare if he used this method to invest in run-of-the-mill stocks
listed on the New York Stock Exchange. The professors took the
period January 15, 1937 through January 15, 1950 and assumed
that the investor had put $1,000 a year into all New York Stock
Exchange stocks that had a trading volume of at least a million
shares in 1936. The results showed that if an investor had invested $1,000 a year in these 92 stocks for 14 years, reinvesting
all dividends, his money would have grown at the rate of over
12% a year, compounded, and wound up at $33,000. Even when
the professors assumed an investment in every second stock and
every third stock of the 92, the results were not far different.

It should be noted that in 1950 when the study ended, the
stock market was the highest it had been during any of the pre-

ceding 13 years. In other words, the bulk of the purchases were made at relatively low prices compared with the price level at the end. Just the same, the results probably would have been similar had the professors redone their study 10 years later. And there is reason to think that the stock market will be higher in the future. The period covering the next dozen years is expected to be one of impressive national growth and spectacular industrial change.

As further evidence of the worth of this method of investing, look at *Charts 34, 35,* and *36,* which show the results of investing $500 every six months in a leading growth stock, a leading closed-end investment trust and a leading mutual fund.

The following table shows the result of a ten-year hypothetical investment program in the common stock of Standard Oil of New

CHART 34

Results of a
$500 Semi-Annual Investment Program
in
Standard Oil Company (New Jersey)
with Dividends Reinvested

		Total Invested	Shares Owned	Market Value
1952	June	$ 513	6.60	$ 534
	Dec.	1,042	12.99	1,010
1953	June	1,580	19.77	1,411
	Dec.	2,147	27.51	1,981
1954	June	2,722	35.13	3,025
	Dec.	3,320	41.75	4,619
1955	June	3,937	47.16	6,061
	Dec.	4,578	51.91	7,922
1956	June	5,244	168.16	9,606
	Dec.	5,939	179.95	10,572
1957	June	6,647	191.53	12,641
	Dec.	7,406	203.50	10,149
1958	June	8,141	217.64	11,997
	Dec.	8,903	230.84	13,302
1959	June	9,668	244.18	12,606
	Dec.	10,461	258.88	12,847
1960	June	11,258	275.11	11,142
	Dec.	12,090	295.11	12,136
1961	June	12,930	314.32	13,830
	Dec.	13,823	333.38	16,919

Courtesy of Merrill Lynch, Pierce, Fenner & Smith.

Jersey. The assumptions were that $500 was invested on the first business day of January and the first business day of July beginning in 1952 and ending in 1961. In all, $10,000 was put into this program in the form of twenty payments of $500 each. Dividends were assumed reinvested on the day following the assumed date of receipt. Full allowance for brokerage commissions and odd lot differentials was made. In fact, the whole program was handled just as if it had been a Monthly Investment Plan on a semi-annual basis.

CHART 35

TRI-CONTINENTAL CORPORATION

Results of investing $500 on June 1 and December 1 in each year during the ten year period ending December 31, 1961, with investment of all regular and extra dividends.

Dec. 31	Total Semi-Annual Investments* (Cumulative)	Dividends	Invested*	Total Cost (Cumulative)	Shares Owned (Cumulative)	Market Value
		Annual	Cumulative			
1952	$ 1,000	$ 44	$ 44	$ 1,044	64	$ 1,125
1953	2,000	116	160	2,160	132	2,029
1954	3,000	207	367	3,367	183	5,009
1955	4,000	314	681	4,681	231	5,957
1956	5,000	509**	1,190	6,190	286	7,797
1957	6,000	539**	1,729	7,729	335	9,206
1958	7,000	864**	2,593	9,593	386	15,587
1959	8,000	596	3,189	11,189	425	16,693
1960	9,000	659	3,848	12,848	470	17,691
1961	$10,000	$733	$4,581	$14,581	506	$25,933

* All amounts invested at regular New York Stock Exchange commissions.
** Includes non-recurring extra dividends of $.50 per share in 1956, $.25 per share in 1958, and $.97 per share in 1959.
No adjustment has been made for any income taxes payable.

The mechanics of buying stocks in regular instalments are not difficult. Perhaps the cheapest way is to make one or two purchases a year. For example, you could deposit in the bank each week or month a sum that would amount to $500 on June 30 and $500 on December 31 of each year. Then on those dates you could order through a broker the number of shares of your chosen stock that $500 would cover. The New York Stock Exchange commission on a purchase of $500 would be around $12. If the purchase were an odd lot, you would pay only about $10 commission but you would be charged the odd lot price which would

CHART 36

MASSACHUSETTS INVESTORS GROWTH STOCK FUND

REGULAR INVESTMENTS OF $1,000 PER YEAR INVESTED SEMI-ANNUALLY FOR TEN YEARS

```
                                                                SUMMARY
Total of $500 Semi-Annual Investments Beginning 1/1/52.......... $10,000
Income Dividends For Period - Invested.........................   1,616
Total Investment Cost Including Invested Dividends             $11,616
```

Value of Investment December 31, 1961 Including Capital Gain Distributions..$24,497

Year Ended 12/31	COST				Through Semi-Annual Investments	CUMULATIVE VALUE OF SHARES ACQUIRED			
	Cumulative Semi-Annual Investments	Annual Dividends Invested	Cumulative Dividends Invested	Total Cost Including Invested Dividends		As Capital Gain Distributions	Sub-Total	From Investment of Dividends	Total Value
1952	$ 1,000	$ 19	$ 19	$ 1,019	$ 920	$ 19	$ 939	$ 18	$ 957
1953	2,000	48	67	2,067	1,743	45	1,788	61	1,849
1954	3,000	80	147	3,147	3,813	164	3,977	175	4,152
1955	4,000	114	261	4,261	5,328	541	5,869	307	6,176
1956	5,000	151	412	5,412	6,874	980	7,854	480	8,334
1957	6,000	179	591	6,591	6,512	999	7,511	548	8,059
1958	7,000	206	797	7,797	10,697	1,567	12,264	1,022	13,286
1959	8,000	227	1,024	9,024	12,857	2,144	15,001	1,351	16,352
1960	9,000	298	1,322	10,322	14,501	2,491	16,992	1,710	18,702
1961	10,000	294	1,616	11,616	18,527	3,628	22,155	2,342	24,497

The total cost figure represents the cumulative total of semi-annual investments of $ 500 plus the cumulative amount of dividends invested and includes a distribution charge on all shares so purchased of 8¾%, as described in the Prospectus. No adjustment has been made for any income taxes payable by shareholders on capital gain distributions accepted in shares and income dividends invested. The dollar amounts of the capital gain distributions accepted in shares were as follows: 1952--$18; 1953--$28; 1954--$92; 1955--$352; 1956--$373; 1957--$185; 1958--$111; 1959--$397; 1960--$418; 1961--$637; Total--$2,411.

be an eighth of a point above the last round lot sale price on stocks selling below $40 a share, and a quarter of a point more on stocks selling above $40.

Note the smallness of the commission—not much over 2%. It shows how you can keep costs down by accumulating the money yourself and buying direct through a broker. If, instead, you had joined an accumulation plan and put a small amount into a stock each month, the commission might have been nearly three times as much. If you had bought the most common type of mutual fund, the commission might have been four times as great.

There are some advantages, however, to joining a formal accumulation plan.

• *You usually make a cancellable agreement to invest so much a month or a quarter, and each time you invest, you receive a statement of account and often a reminder of the next payment due.* For many people the agreement and reminders help keep the program going.

• *In many plans the amount of each purchase, minus commission, is fully invested down to the fourth decimal place.* This purchase of fractional shares is not possible in ordinary purchases of stock made through a broker.

• *You may specify that your dividends automatically be reinvested in stock.* In this way you never see the dividend checks and are not tempted to spend them.

The most widely available plan for regular purchases of stocks is the Monthly Investment Plan of the New York Stock Exchange offered by its broker members. Here is how it works. Go to a broker who is a member of the New York Stock Exchange with the name of your stock picked from among the more than 1,500 listed on the Exchange. Decide how much you can afford to invest per month or per quarter. It can be as little as $40 or as much as $999. If you want more than one stock, you can split or alternate your payments.

When you decide what you want to do, you sign a cancellable agreement whereby you undertake to make the payments regularly. There is no penalty, financial or otherwise, if you miss a couple of payments, although the broker reserves the right to terminate the plan if you miss four payments in a row. The commission you pay will be 6% on amounts under $100; 2% plus $1 on amounts from $100 to $399 (with a minimum of $6) and 1% plus $5 on amounts above. Remember, also, the odd-lot differential. Each payment you make, minus the commission, will be invested in full and fractional shares of your stock to the fourth decimal place. Thus if your payment is $50 and the odd-lot price of the stock is $18, the commission will be $3 and your account will be credited with $47 worth of stock or 2.6111 shares.

You probably will want to leave your stock in the broker's custody until you complete your plan or purchase the desired number of shares. Or you can get free delivery after you have acquired 50 shares. If you want delivery beforehand, there will be a $1 mailing fee per delivery. If you decide to quit the plan, you will receive the number of full shares in your account without delivery charge. Any fractional shares will be sold and a check sent to you for the proceeds.

If you work in a company that will make payroll deductions for this type of investment, you can have as little as $4 a week deducted from your pay check and sent in to buy stock.

For more information on this plan see the nearest broker who is a member of the New York Stock Exchange or write to the Exchange at 11 Wall Street, New York 5, N.Y., for a free copy of The Story of MIP.

Over 100 open-end mutual funds offer some kind of plan whereby their shares may be acquired by small, regular purchases. Of the funds offering accumulation plans, most require that the initial purchase be at least $100 or $250 and that subsequent purchases be $25 or $50. Some plans, however, have no minimums and investors may put in any amount.

One important detail about an accumulation plan is whether it is of the level-charge or the prepaid-charge type. In the level-charge type the sales commission is a fixed percentage, say 8½% on every purchase. If you make 100 payments, the commission is the same on the first as on the last. In the prepaid-charge type, also known as the contractual or penalty plan, you agree to make to the firm sponsoring the plan a specified number of monthly payments. The sponsor will deduct sales commissions and other fees and invest the remainder. But most of the sales commissions and other fees for the whole series of payments will be lumped together and loaded onto the first few payments. Hence the prepaid-charge plan has what is known as a "front-end load."

In most cases of the front-end load, less than half of your first year's payment actually is invested. The rest goes to the sponsor. If you continue the plan to its completion, the commissions and fees will average down. But if you stop in the early months, you get back less than half of what you paid in because the sales commissions and sponsor's fees are not refundable. You are thus "penalized." There is nothing new about the principle. Life insurance traditionally is sold with a front-end load, half or more of the total sales commission usually coming out of the first year's premium. In life insurance, however, there seldom is an alternative available, while in the case of mutual funds, you have the choice of starting either a front-end load plan or a level-load plan.

In the frantic Twenties, many investment companies were sold with a front-end load, but the practice fell into disuse. Recently, however, it has been revived with tremendous vigor. A growing number of open-end funds have discovered that if a salesman can count on a big chunk of commission right at the start, he will push the plan much harder than if he must get his money in little bites over a period of years.

Open-end funds that have taken up the contractual plan claim that it is also good for the investor on the grounds that he needs to be "sold" on investing and the harder the sell, the better. Another reason given is that the penalty feature forces the investor to keep investing regularly.

Opponents of the front-end load point out that almost all open-end funds offer voluntary, or level-load, plans in which the sales commission is the same percentage of every purchase no matter when it is made. Member firms of the New York Stock Exchange also offer their Monthly Investment Plan, which permits level-load purchases of stocks, including shares of closed-end investment companies. Why, these critics ask, should an investor choose a plan that would cost him over half his investment if he discontinued in the first year or so, when he could adopt a plan in which an early drop-out would cost only the regular sales commission of 6%, 8% or 8½%?

Chart 37 illustrates the mechanics of the two methods. One reason why the over-all results look so good is that during most of the fifteen-year period the whole stock market was in a long and vigorous rise. The table compares results of investing $100 a month in a mutual fund via a level-load plan and via a contractual plan. Aberdeen Fund, used as an illustration, has been managed since 1953 by the investment counseling firm of David L. Babson Management Corporation.

CHART 37

TWO WAYS TO INVEST $100 A MONTH FOR 15 YEARS IN ABERDEEN FUND

via the contractual plan

	1946	1947	1948	1950	1952	1954	1956	1958	1960
cumulative monthly payments	$1,300	$2,500	$3,700	$6,100	$ 8,500	$10,900	$13,300	$15,700	$18,000
cumulative sales & custodian fees	666	738	810	954	1,098	1,242	1,386	1,530	1,668
year-end liquidating value	591	1,762	2,778	6,717	11,206	19,899	31,403	42,873	52,491

via the voluntary plan

	1946	1947	1948	1950	1952	1954	1956	1958	1960
cumulative monthly payments	$1,200	$2,400	$3,600	$6,000	$ 8,400	$10,800	$13,200	$15,600	$18,000
cumulative sales fees	102	204	306	510	714	918	1,122	1,326	1,530
year-end liquidating value	1,006	2,149	3,127	7,122	11,658	20,489	32,184	43,783	53,592

The figures in the table give the nub of the argument. Opponents of the front-end load point to the situation at the end of the first year. In the contractual plan, $1,300 would have been invested but would be worth only $591 if the plan were abandoned; and the investor would stand to lose the difference, $709. Advocates of the front-end load use the same figures to make a very different argument; the prospect of losing $709, they say, would tend to force the investor NOT to quit.

Although most contractual plans involve purchase of open-end funds, you can use this method to buy certain common stocks. In 1938, H. Dean Quinby of Rochester, N.Y., worked out an investment contract plan with Lincoln Rochester Trust Co. whereby investors could purchase stock in Eastman Kodak Co. Later he added plans for acquiring Du Pont, General Motors, General Electric, Standard Oil of New Jersey and AT&T.

The arguments for and against contractual plans are very bitter within the financial community. One argument against it perhaps should be noted. It is made by Robert E. Clark, executive vice-president of Calvin Bullock, Ltd., one of the oldest and most respected mutual-fund sponsors. "The person of moderate means should put his money into life insurance, savings and stocks in that order of importance. If circumstances force him to suspend one part of the program temporarily, it should be the purchase of common stocks. But the contractual plan tends to make the stock purchase compulsory when it should be flexible."

Another point to consider when checking on accumulation plans: most open-end funds will reinvest capital gains distributions at net asset value, that is, without charging a sales commission. But not all funds will reinvest dividends at net asset value. Some charge the regular sales commission. Under the New York Stock Exchange's Monthly Investment Plan, a sales commission of 6% is charged for reinvestment of dividends. One large closed-end fund, Tri-Continental Corp., has worked out a plan where distributions may be reinvested automatically with no sales commission and only a small service charge of 70 cents for each transaction. This is unusual in the closed-end field.

Of course the kind of plan available for accumulating shares of stock is not so important as the quality of the company's management. The most fascinating plan in the world would be a delusion if it were used to acquire shares in a mediocre stock or an investment trust with indifferent management. Nevertheless, if used to purchase securities of good quality, accumulation plans have their merit. Not many years ago only the wealthy invested in stocks, and they usually bought in big chunks. Today anyone who can save $15 a month can be a stockholder. The change is perhaps not surprising when you consider that so much down and so much a month is becoming a part of the American way of life. And purchasing stocks in that manner has certain peculiar advantages.

It takes the guesswork out of timing. It gives the investor his shares at an average cost. And if he selects a sound and growing company and reinvests his dividends, his money tends to snowball at a surprising rate. Start putting as little as $25 a month, or $300 a year, into good growth stocks today and in 25 years you should have many thousands of dollars. Invest $1,000 a year and you should end up with a small fortune. The trader who is in and out of the market probably won't do as well.

investment clubs are fun —and can be profitable

There's a maxim in Wall Street that says the public is always wrong. But there's one form of amateur investing to which this old saw doesn't seem to apply—the investment club. An investment club is a group of men or women, or both, who meet once a month partly for social reasons but mainly to learn about investing by doing. Each month the members pay in $10, $20 or some other amount and invest it as a group.

There are estimated to be well over 25,000 of these clubs in existence, and new ones are starting every day. In fact the idea has become so popular that the clubs have their own national organization, the National Association of Investment Clubs, or NAIC. This organization has published a set of three basic rules to which the typical investment club adheres. These are,

- *Invest regularly each month regardless of the market outlook.*
- *Invest only in growth stocks.*
- *Reinvest all earnings.*

By surveying its membership the NAIC has determined that the clubs that have followed these rules have, on the average, been able to show a capital appreciation. A poll conducted in July, 1960 showed an average gain of 8% a year compounded, (including reinvestment of all dividends). Where clubs had kept up their program for at least five years they showed an average gain of over 11%. This is not a bad record and is one worth examining.

Note first the advantages and disadvantages of the investment club as a method of investing. Among the advantages are, first, an investment club does not require a lot of money at any one time. In most clubs each member contributes $10 to $20 a month. Ten or twenty dollars, of course, seems like a small amount to invest, but over the years it snowballs. Back in 1940 a few young men in Detroit started what became the first modern investment club on record. Members put in amounts ranging from $20 to $40 a month but averaging about $30. Twenty-one years later the club's twelve members had a kitty of $156,000.

Second, if you want to invest more than the monthly amount the club decides on, you can take advantage of the club's research program and buy extra shares for your own account.

Third, an investment club is educational. Members take turns serving on the research committee. Thus, eventually, everyone gets a chance to dig up facts and figures and decide which stocks in a given industry look most attractive.

Fourth, starting a club is not difficult. There are standardized procedures and model bylaws available. Most brokers will accept a club account and give some organizational help. Once under way, however, a club ought to do its own stock selecting to gain experience. Very often the only way to become a member of a club is to help start one. Many established clubs want to stay small and will take in new members only when there is a vacancy.

There are several possible disadvantages to the investment club idea, of course. Looking at it purely from an investment standpoint, buying shares of a well-managed investment trust might be safer and more profitable (although not as educational). The managers of the trust are professionals; those of the club, amateurs. Also, unless members are congenial, a club could be wrecked by disagreement and wrangling.

A third danger an investment club faces is the possibility of some members becoming lazy and falling back on tips and rumors from brokers and trying to make a fast profit jumping in and out of the market. Clubs that have done this generally have not been successful. Remember that belonging to a serious club that adheres to proven principles takes at least one evening of real work each month, and probably several evenings for those who make the stock recommendations.

For thousands of people, however, the advantages have outweighed the drawbacks and clubs have been started in every part of the country.

It's an open question as to just how successful all these clubs have been. Most of them do not belong to any national organization or make public their investment philosophy or results. There are studies, however, based on the thousands of clubs that belong to the NAIC and presumably use the NAIC's methods of investing. These clubs have been polled by questionnaire and the replies tabulated by computer. The sample, while a relatively small percentage of the total NAIC membership, has been checked and found to be pretty well distributed geographically and by age of club. So it probably can be considered representative of clubs that belong to the NAIC and follow its standards. The following conclusions are based on the results of the clubs who answered the NAIC questionnaire.

One lesson learned is that the first two years of investing are the hardest. This appears to be because initial purchases are necessarily small and commissions, at least percentagewise, are large, usually amounting to 6%. Eventually a backlog of investments is built up and dividend income offsets the cost of commissions. But this takes time. Figures show that most clubs with a net worth less than the amount members have paid in were under two years old. And over half of clubs under one year old had this kind of paper loss.

Almost as difficult as the first two years is the period between the second and fifth year. During this time the club should be making a fairly good percentage return, somewhere between 8% and 11%, (according to the July, 1960 poll) but the dollar amount of each individual's stake still looks pretty small. Then, too, the novelty and fun of starting the club have worn off while the work of selecting stocks goes on and on. This period, therefore, is the one in which members are most likely to lose interest and allow the club to fall apart.

If a club can last through the fifth year—and, even better, the seventh year—the outlook brightens. The advantages of compounding become apparent, and the individual's stake begins to appear worthwhile. The average annual income plus appreciation in clubs that had been in existence seven years or more in 1960 was 14% compounded. And it should be noted that $10 a month invested for seven years at that rate amounts to around $1,400; $20 a month, to around $2,800; $30 a month, to around $4,200, and so on.

Remember, though, that these rates of growth—11% after five years and 14% after seven—didn't come automatically. All of the tabulated clubs were members of the NAIC and may be presumed to have been following the association's rules for investing. And the clubs that showed these gains did so during a strong bull market.

Let's take a look at this NAIC investment formula because it seems to work. It was worked out many years ago, shortly after the pioneer Detroit club was started. It happened this way. Two Detroiters, Fred C. Russell, purchasing clerk with the Aluminum Company of America, and John Biscomb, a clerk with the Ford Motor Company, wanted to accumulate enough money to go into business for themselves. They discussed the idea with a friend, George A. Nicholson, Jr., who worked for a Detroit brokerage firm. Nicholson suggested the basic guiding principles that subsequently were expanded and now constitute the philosophy of the investment club movement.

The NAIC itself was set up, with Nicholson's assistance, by Thomas E. O'Hara, a charter member of the original Detroit club, in order to handle requests that had begun to flow in from groups that wanted to start similar clubs. Nicholson became the chairman of the NAIC's Advisory Committee.

The Association publishes a news letter in which various growth stocks are analyzed and in which the portfolios of various member clubs are reviewed.

Since selecting good stocks is probably the hardest and the most important job that a club has, the NAIC has done considerable work on growth stock selection methods. It recommends first that a club take up an industry each month. Ideally, an industry should be selected from among those that are growing faster than the economy as a whole. A two- or three-man investment committee is appointed to build up a list of the leading companies in the industry, along with pertinent facts and figures on prices, earnings, etc. The committee reports to the full membership at the next meeting, and one stock is selected for purchase.

There are several ways in which the investment committee can get its information. The brokerage house where the club has its account will make available statistical market services. Often it will allow club members to take out pertinent material overnight. The investment committee may also write direct to the president of any company in which it is interested and ask for the annual report and whatever other material is available. Such letters will usually bring in a raft of information, sometimes direct from the president of the company himself.

To select the stock that comes closest to the ideal requires that all stocks under consideration be listed uniformly so as to show sales, earnings, dividends, price, etc. When a club is new a simplified form can be made up that will show these figures. Later a club may want to tackle the NAIC's chart technique. The principle involves plotting a company's sales, earnings and market price on a "ratio" or "semi-log" chart. On such a chart a compound rate of growth appears as a straight line. Once the figures for past earnings are plotted, a trend line may be drawn projecting them into the future.

Investment clubs have other problems besides the techniques of buying and selling. The first one, of course, is how to get organized. The way this usually works is that some imaginative person gets the idea and puts it up to two or three friends. All then sit down and suggest names of four or five others who might be interested. When the group reaches six or eight, it meets again to round out the membership to about fifteen. In this rounding-out process, it is advantageous, although not necessary, to add a lawyer and an accountant. The more different interests and professions represented, the better.

Next step might be to join the National Association of Investment Clubs and get an organization kit. Membership is $1 per club member per year. The cost of the kit is $5 which may be applied to the first year's dues. The kit covers the following ground: articles of agreement or bylaws, with an explanation of how to operate the club; investment policy; record keeping;

reporting for income tax; stock study aids with a blank form; model agent-agreement to be made with the broker handling the club's account. The address of the NAIC is 1246 First National Building, Detroit 26, Michigan.

When the club holds its first organization meeting, it may invite a competent investment man to discuss the mechanics of investing and methods of selecting growth stocks. Two members generally are appointed as agents. They open a two-name account with a brokerage house, put in the actual buy and sell orders and handle the money. The club's broker provides a safe-keeping account, holds the club securities, collects dividends and provides monthly statements.

The club should be organized so as to minimize taxes (usually by insuring that it is a partnership) and to provide for possible resignation or death of a member. If a member wants to resign the usual procedure is to require 30 days notice, then pay him his pro-rata share of the market value of the club's securities minus a 1% penalty and any commissions the club incurs to sell securities and raise cash.

Books must be meticulously kept. The treasurer and president should be bonded. Several unbonded clubs have had unfortunate experiences. The president of a Chicago club walked out with $20,000 of the members' money. The treasurer of another Chicago club sold $10,000 of the club's securities and accepted the proceeds without bothering to keep the other members informed. Clubs that belong to the NAIC are automatically bonded.

Almost every club has its favorite broker with whom it does business. Usually this is the broker who originally helped the club get organized. It should be remembered that a broker in this position gets very little direct benefit from handling the account of the typical investment club, particularly in the early years. His time is largely donated on a good will basis. Not until the club's portfolio reaches $10,000 does it begin to pay its own way in commissions. From then on, however, the broker-club relationship can be strictly on a business basis. One broker who advises over a hundred clubs makes commissions from that source alone of $1,100 a month—a third from the clubs and two-thirds from club members investing on their own.

Many clubs, especially in their formative years, fall by the wayside. Here are some reasons why, given by Thomas E. O'Hara, chairman of NAIC's Board of Trustees.

When a club starts out, interest is high. And if it can stay in business for a few years, it will be successful. But if the club hits a declining market, such as that of 1962, members may begin to doubt the soundness of their investing principles. An outside speaker at meetings can help keep a club on its toes.

A club is more likely to last if there are two or three founders each of whom brings in friends. A club started by one person alone is vulnerable.

Many clubs have foundered because all members worked for one company having nationwide offices and a policy of rotating personnel. One club made up of Du Pont employes lost 16 members in one year because of transfers.

Although one of the purposes of an investment club is to give the members an opportunity to learn investing firsthand, experience shows that not everyone has a talent or a desire for analyzing and selecting securities. The club will do best if it lets people follow their bent—those who are social-minded doing the programming, those who have a flair for business doing the analyzing, and those who are good at figures doing the bookkeeping.

There is no doubt that the investment club idea is intriguing. Ten dollars a month, or even twenty, is not a costly rate of investment. If the club sticks to sound precepts it can accomplish a variety of things: have fun, learn something about investing, make some money—8% and more later if the years just prior to 1960 are any criteria—and in so doing, disprove the old Wall Street maxim that the public is always wrong.

a guide to the stock market

You can't very well buy and own stocks without being attracted by the fascinating phenomenon known as the stock market. For anyone who doesn't haunt brokerage offices and pore over the daily financial pages, this stock market is a mysterious place. It has a glamor all its own, somewhat akin to the romance of buried treasure. Everyone knows that fortunes have been made in the market. Who hasn't read about the theoretical results of having invested $500 in General Motors in 1932? Who hasn't heard of the man or woman who bought the glamorous space-age stock just before it had its big rise?

Actually, of course, the stock market is a segment of the vast financial mechanism of the country where hard-headed businessmen are pitting their brains and experience against each other and where romantic dream boats only too often are crushed by the ebb and flow of irresistible economic forces. The nonprofessional investor probably can make money over the long run. But to do it, he must treat the stock market with all the respect that an experienced seaman holds for the sea.

To understand the stock market, think of it in another way—as a great department store. The goods on display consist of part ownership in some manufacturing company, a railroad or an enterprise engaged in any one of a thousand different kinds of business. For a given number of dollars you can become part owner of the company that produces your electricity, or that made your auto, your television set or the popcorn vending machine at the neighborhood movie. But unlike the goods in the department store, those in the stock market have price tags that aren't fixed. They change every day. And you can't return them and get back exactly the amount you paid. You may get less or you may get more.

This is because once a company has sold a big block of stock to the public, the stock keeps circulating around. People buy shares, hold them for a while, then sell them to someone else at whatever happens to be the going price. The amount of this buying and selling is almost unbelievable. In one day, 50,000 shares of one company's stock can change hands. And remember that there are thousands of these stocks being traded every day.

Who does all this buying and selling? If everyone simply bought a few shares now and again and tucked them away in a safe deposit box, the stock market would be a slow and dull affair. But small, serious investors who buy for the long pull furnish only a small part of the market's activity. Investment counselors, managers of big investment trusts and endowment funds, officers who handle trust company and insurance company portfolios, all are continually evaluating and re-evaluating the trend of business and the prospects of each industry and each large company within it. Since the country's economy is so complex and full of crosscurrents, these investment managers are always coming to different conclusions. On any given day, some investment managers may be selling thousands of shares of a particular stock, while equally experienced managers, having come to a different conclusion, are buying.

This big buying and selling causes much of the surging and churning in the market. But in addition, there are thousands of traders who try to catch a trend by jumping in and out of the market for short periods of time. Floor traders operating on the floor of the Stock Exchange itself, are particularly skittish, and it is said that many of them take positions for a few hours only, reluctant even to own stocks overnight or over the weekend.

All these forces working on the supply of stocks available for purchase and sale, cause prices to move up and down in what seems to be an erratic fashion. A great deal of the machinery of the stock market is devoted to keeping track of these prices that are ever changing. In fact, the common meaning of the term "stock market" simply is the general level of stock prices and the direction these prices seem to be moving. If the price trend is up, the market is strong; if the price trend is down, the market is weak; if not many shares are changing hands, the market is dull; or, if interest is high, the market is active.

At all times, of course, some stocks are rising while others are falling. Nevertheless, the buyers and sellers are somewhat like sheep and tend to surge in one direction or another. Thus, if a big account sells a big block of an auto stock, other stockholders may begin to worry. Owners of stock in other auto companies also may begin to fear that there is something wrong with the auto industry that they haven't heard about. So maybe they decide they should sell, too. If enough people decide to sell, they may set off a trend. Or, in a likelier case, bad sales figures or threat of a strike, may reach the ears of traders who may jump in and sell auto stocks in an attempt to anticipate selling by the general public. Conversely, favorable rumors may send the traders on a buying expedition in hopes that the public will come in and push prices up.

Because the market is so changeable, literally millions of people are interested in the general price trend. But discerning and measuring the over-all trend of thousands of fluctuating prices is not easy. Here is how it is done and how the results are published so that you or anyone else can keep track.

THE MARKETPLACES

First, note that there are several places where stock trading is concentrated. There are two large ones in New York, one in Chicago, one in San Francisco and others scattered around. The two that set the pace for all the others, however, are in New York—the New York Stock Exchange and the American Stock Exchange.

Of these, the New York Stock Exchange is by far the larger. On its floor, which is two-thirds the size of a football field, about a thousand men mill about all day buying and selling, to some extent for their own accounts but mostly for customers all over the country who have sent in orders via brokerage houses. Another thousand men on the floor are busily engaged in keeping track of the transactions and seeing that a record of each is kept and the price put into the ticker tape for everyone to see.

Not just any old stock can be bought or sold through the New York Stock Exchange. It limits its trading to the stocks of about 1,150 of the largest and most widely owned companies. Nevertheless, each weekday except Saturday, some 3,000,000 to 5,000,000 shares of these stocks ordinarily change hands on the floor of the Exchange.

You can imagine how hard it is to detect the trend in the turmoil of this rapid-fire buying and selling. Several publishing firms have made up lists of stocks they consider to be typical. Dow-Jones & Co., publishers of the *Wall Street Journal*, for example, uses a list of 30 industrial stocks. Every day when the stock exchange opens for business at 10 A.M., and each hour thereafter until it closes at 3:30 P.M., Dow-Jones statisticians take from the ticker the price of each of these 30 stocks, add them up and divide by a weighted divisor. The result is the well-known Dow-Jones Industrial Average.

There are other averages that attempt to measure the actions of the market. The New York *Times* computes one; so do *The New York Herald Tribune*, the Associated Press, Barron's and two investment services, Standard & Poor's and Moody's. Dow-Jones & Co. itself also computes a railroad stock average and a utility average. But the Dow-Jones Industrial Average (sometimes called merely the Dow-Jones Average) is far and away the most popular. If someone tells you that the stock market was up three points yesterday, the Dow-Jones Average is what he is referring to.

Other statistics besides the averages are used to measure and classify each session of the stock market. Every day, of course, some stocks rise in price while others fall. The ratio between the number that went up and the number that went down is significant. Sometimes you may find a disparity here. The Dow-Jones Average can go up while a majority of the stocks traded on the Exchange on that day can go down. If this seems baffling to you, don't worry. It baffles everyone.

Another measure is the ratio between new highs and new

lows. The price action of every stock is plotted day by day. As its price moves erratically up and down, it establishes a temporary range. Starting in January a stock might move up and down in a range from 25 to 30. Then one day it might go to 30¼. That would be a new high for the year and would be so listed by the analysts. At some other point it might drop to 24¾, which would be a new low.

Every day some stocks are making new highs while others are making new lows. The *Wall Street Journal* and other newspapers publish the list. On a bad day there might be a hundred new lows and only a dozen new highs. On an exceptionally good day the ratio might be reversed. The range between high and low for each year for every listed stock is published by Standard & Poor's and other services and is an excellent measure of a stock's past performance.

Note two other measures, the daily volume and the list of most-active stocks. The volume of the New York Stock Exchange generally ranges from 3,000,000 to 5,000,000 shares. On dull days it may be little more than 2,000,000; on very exciting days it might go over 5,000,000. If the volume dries up when the market is declining, that is an optimistic or "bullish," sign. But if volume increases as stock prices fall, that is bad, or "bearish." Conversely, a rise on expanding volume is good, while a rise on a smaller volume is suspect.

Each day the newspapers also list the 10 or 15 stocks most actively traded at the latest session. The list indicates the current fads among traders or the trend in thinking of big investors. And some traders make serious use of the list.

COPING WITH THE FINANCIAL PAGE

Here is a good daily routine for checking up on these and other market angles. Turn to the financial page of your newspaper and glance at the article that tells what the market did at its latest session. Most of the space will be devoted to the New York Stock Exchange; somewhere near the beginning you'll find a figure showing the level of the Dow-Jones Average and the amount by which it rose or fell. (The *Wall Street Journal* also lists this as a percentage; that is, up 0.75% or down 1.20%.) For perspective keep in mind that in recent years it has ranged from a low of 165 in June 1949 to well above 700 in 1961. It did not rise steadily from its low to the higher levels but wandered up and down and will continue to do so. You'll also see mention of new highs and lows and of the number of advances and declines.

Within the stock market are certain groups of stocks that tend to move up and down together, and these probably will be mentioned next. They are the motors, the domestic oils, the international oils, the steels, the drugs, the chemicals, the utilities, the rails and so on.

You might wonder why many domestic oil stocks should move in unison, considering that each company has its own management, which may be good or bad. While it is true that in the long run the best-managed companies will forge ahead, at the same time there are certain national and international events that affect the oil business everywhere. Several years ago, for example, oil consumption seemed destined to expand forever and the oils were in high favor. But after a while a world-wide glut of oil drove prices down, and oil stocks were in the doghouse. During that time, many a good oil stock was selling for two-thirds its former price.

The utilities, on the other hand, used to be scorned because they seemed too stable, with too little prospect of growth. Then later investors found that the utility companies were showing steady year to year growth in earnings. Hence, utilities became popular and some were bid up to prices 50% over what they had been only a year or two earlier.

In the course of a newspaper article you'll find a good bit of discussion of "why." Why did the market go up, or down, as the case may be? Why did the motors do what they did, and the oils? The writer of the article may discuss these questions himself or, more likely, he'll quote brokers and market analysts. This always makes good reading, especially if you can remember what is said from week to week.

Last week, perhaps, the market was strong and everyone was bullish, seeing a rising market ahead and giving convincing arguments in favor of the same. This week, the bottom falls out and the same people, without batting an eye, will give a brand-new set of explanations showing why the decline was inevitable.

As a matter of fact, the analysts can always find an explanation of what is going on but sometimes they have to reach halfway around the world to get it. On one particular day international tension may be rising and the world may seem to be coming apart at the seams, but the market may blithely move into new high ground. A few days later, the averages may plunge and the blame will be put on that same international tension.

"Chartists" are a particular breed. Day by day they plot prices on graph paper. They plot the Dow-Jones Average, for example, or the price of an individual stock, then draw lines through the points and project them into the future. Theirs is a fascinating world full of things known as resistance points, supply areas, double bottoms and triple tops.

Chartists do not claim to know when you or any other individual will buy or sell. But they do claim to be able to forecast the points at which investors en masse will move into or out of the market or into or out of an individual stock. The theory of charts and charting will be discussed in a later chapter.

WHAT THE WORDS MEAN

Here is some more jargon you'll run into. The stocks of the biggest and best-managed companies are known as blue chips, while the newer companies are said to be unseasoned. The most speculative and risky stocks are referred to as cats and dogs. The singular of cats and dogs, however, is dog, never cat.

If a broker thinks poorly of a certain speculative stock, he may call it a dog, but an equally speculative stock that he rather fancies, he may call a businessman's risk. By this he means he might recommend it to a businessman who had enough spare cash to take the gamble but would not recommend it to a widow who ought to conserve her nest egg.

Cyclical stocks are those that supposedly keep in step with the business cycle and go up when business is improving and down when business slackens off. Examples are steels, railroads and motors. You might think that a good way to make money would be to buy cyclical stocks during recessions and sell them during booms. This would be a good trick except that experience shows that something always goes wrong with the timing.

Growth stocks are stocks of companies in fast-growing industries, such as chemicals, drugs, electronics, business machines. While they also fluctuate, their ups and downs have an upward slant. Theoretically, you can buy good growth stocks and make money simply by holding on to them. The only fly in the ointment is that what was a growth stock once, may not be so considered two or three years later.

Defensive stocks are those that are thought to be able to resist any downward trend and hold up better than the average in case of a business recession. Utilities, finance companies, food chains and variety stores are defensive since they offer goods that are needed by everyone all the time. Utilities have traditionally been labeled defensive, but recently, lo and behold, some of them operating in fast growing parts of the country, have turned out to be growth stocks.

Then there are specialties—groups of somewhat obscure stocks that burst into prominence from time to time. Some time ago, for example, a company invented a vending machine that could change a dollar bill. This set off a craze for the stocks of all vending machine companies. A similar fad boosted the prices of stocks of boat builders.

THOSE PRICE QUOTATIONS

It is human nature to read the price of quotations of stocks you own, or are interested in, even though you may be (and probably should be) a long-term investor. But you should insulate yourself as much as possible against the temptations that the short-term fluctuations induce.

Most metropolitan newspapers give quotations for the New York Stock Exchange and the American Exchange. These show the range of prices at which the "listed" stocks changed hands during the last trading session. There also may be selected quotations from the "unlisted," or over-the-counter, market, which is maintained by thousands of dealers scattered over the country and loosely connected by private telephone and teletype. They deal in stocks of a great many companies that either have very few shares outstanding, or are too obscure to warrant listing on the big exchanges. In this market, quotations are not based on actual transactions but are bid-and-asked prices; that is, what would-be buyers are willing to pay and what potential sellers are willing to accept. In the case of mutual funds, the bid price is the net asset value per share—the amount a shareholder would receive if he cashed in his holdings. The asked price is the net asset value per share plus the sales commission—the price an investor would pay to acquire the shares.

The stock market quotations, like The World Almanac, attempt to crowd as much information as possible into the smallest space. Hence the tables are full of abbreviations and footnotes. Most newspapers print the name of each company and immediately after it a figure, which is the annual dividend in dollars. Then comes the day's volume, the highest price during the day, the lowest, the closing price, and the net change from the previous day's close. There also may appear, in front of the stock's name, the high and low so far during the year.

OTHER ITEMS OF INTEREST

After combing through the quotations and spotting the stocks that you own or are watching, glance through the rest of the financial pages for any special articles on industries or companies in which you might be interested. If you own an auto stock, note any statistics showing comparative sales of the various makes. If you own an oil stock, note any changes in oil or gasoline prices, supply statistics and so on.

Of particular interest is any article about an individual company showing its sales and earnings for the most recent quarter. Occasionally, a company will decide to raise or lower its dividend, or split its shares, or acquire or merge with another company. Of course this is all vital news to an investor.

When a company splits its stock, it merely replaces every share with two or more new shares. It's as though each child at a birthday party had one piece of cake and someone went around and cut each piece of cake in two.

Theoretically, a split does not change the value of what each stockholder owns, but as a practical matter, a split is thought of as bullish. The reason is that generally a split is a sign that a company is prospering and growing. If the stock gets up to, say, $150 a share, a three-for-one split will bring the price back down to around $50 a share, where people will be more likely to buy in. And most companies like a good broad ownership. Thus, while a split in itself is not bullish, it is an indication of growth and traditionally accompanied by an increase in the dividend. Also, the stockholder who once owned, say, ten shares, thereafter owns 30 shares, and even though each share is worth only a third as much, it makes him feel more prosperous.

Note the significance of earnings. Let's say that a company earned $1 per share last year. If it were to earn $1.20 this year, a 20% increase, that would be very encouraging. To spot the trend, compare each quarter's earning with those of the year before.

A company seldom pays out all it earns in the form of dividends. A company earning $1 per share might pay out 40 cents to stockholders, retaining the other 60 cents in the business. Thus the owner of 100 shares would receive 100 times 40 cents, or $40 a year. This would be paid in four quarterly instalments of $10 each.

After you have read an article about a company and noted its current earnings, dividend, and so on, it is customary to glance again at the stock market quotations in order to relate these figures to the current price of the stock. This is because the price of a stock in dollars is more meaningful when it is related to the company's operations.

If a company earns $1 per share and is selling at $8, its price is said to be eight times earnings. If the dividend were 40 cents a year, the stock, at a price of $8, would be yielding 5% (40 cents divided by $8). Eight times earnings has been rather a low ratio for a stock in recent years, and 5% is a high yield. These figures would indicate that for some reason investors were pretty chary of owning this particular company.

Another more popular company earning $1 and paying out 40 cents might sell for $20 a share. In this case investors probably expect the company to do very well since they are willing to pay a price of 20 times one year's earnings and accept a yield of 2% (40 cents divided by $20).

The growth stocks traditionally sell at high prices in relation to current earnings. But the theory is that earnings will grow, so that today's prices are reasonable in relation to what earnings will be a few years hence. Super-growth stocks may sell for 30 to 50 times earnings and pay no dividends or, at best, dividends in stock. Take an electronics stock that is selling for $50 a share and earning $1. If its earnings grow at the rate of 25% a year compounded (and this is quite possible), it will earn $1.25 next year, then $1.56, $1.95, $2.44 and $3.05 five years hence. Thus while it is selling for 50 times current earnings, it is selling for only a little over 16 times projected earnings five years from now.

BUT WHICH STOCKS ARE GOOD?

Now in all this welter of prices, earnings, dividends and so on, how in the world does the run-of-the-mill investor pick out the particular stocks he buys? He gets advice, of course. Chances are he gets most of it from his broker. Actually, a broker is a salesman and an expert in the mechanics of the market. In addition, he is supposed to know something about the wares he sells. But the advice he provides is free. And although it is said that the best things in life are free, the advice that some brokers are able to provide does not, unfortunately, fall into this category. Brokers feel impelled to give advice, however, partly because they are asked for it and partly to encourage purchases and sales. They make money only when their customers buy and sell.

Advice also is available from the stock market advisory services described in Chapter 10. The best of these are technically sound bulletins that analyze stocks and recommend for or against certain ones. If the investor will study the best information of this type available and adopt and stick to a sound, long-range investment philosophy such as the one outlined in this book, he may be able to handle his investments successfully. Otherwise, he should be ready to pay out money to get responsible financial judgment from an investment counselor or through purchase of a good investment trust.

The big danger is that the stock market is so glamorous. It's a great place for making money on paper. It draws men and women to it as the gold fields of California drew the Forty-niners. To invest successfully you must, of course, understand the stock market and follow it. But it is hard to study it and follow its vagaries without being drawn into the business of trying to beat it. And that, for most people, simply is not possible.

the mechanics of investing

It's as easy to buy a stock as it is to call up the department store where you have a charge account and ask them to send out an item you have seen advertised in the paper. Call your broker and order five shares of Standard Oil of New Jersey or ten shares of Eastman Kodak or any given number of shares of any listed stock and within a very few minutes you can be sure you will have acquired the stock at a reasonable commission and paid the going price that everyone else was paying at the time.

This is very amazing when you think about it. If stocks were bought and sold the way real estate is, for example, the process would be costly, time-consuming and frustrating. To buy a few shares of even a widely held stock you would have to advertise in the papers or go from broker to broker in hopes of hearing of someone who had just that amount of that particular stock for sale. Even after you found a seller, you might want to continue the search until you had lined up several offers for comparison.

Behind the simple telephone call that enables you to buy or sell shares within minutes, is a complicated network of communications and a code of conduct that permits very large, as well as very small, financial transactions to be made verbally and hurriedly by two parties, each knowing that the commitment will be honored to the "t" by the other.

It is interesting to understand how this business works and who are the people you deal with, directly, or at the far end of the transaction.

The particular brokerage firm you deal with is strictly a matter of personal choice. If you were seeking one you might do well to ask your bank, or a businessman whose judgment you trust, for a recommendation. In most towns there is a choice among several. There may be one or more branches of large New York houses, such as Merrill Lynch or Bache, and there undoubtedly will be local firms who may, or may not, have membership in the New York Stock Exchange. Even if a local firm does not belong to the Exchange it will have a New York correspondent that handles its stock exchange business.

Unless you know your way around among the local firms, you may want to choose one belonging to the New York Stock Exchange. The salesmen or customers' men employed by NYSE member firms must be registered representatives of the Exchange which means that they have served an apprenticeship and passed an examination given by the Exchange. Also the NYSE does a tough policing job on its member firms, requiring them to maintain certain minimum liquid capital and restricting the trading and borrowing that the firm's partners may do. Each member firm receives one examination a year from the Exchange's accountants and also one surprise audit from an independent accountant. In addition to the NYSE member firms in your town, there may, of course, be old, established houses with fine reputations who are nonmembers. When in doubt, however, choose a member firm, at least for a starter.

The man you deal with in the firm you choose will be a salesman. His title used to be customer's man. Today it is the more dignified "account executive." After you have dealt with him awhile you simply refer to him as your "broker." But regardless of these titles, remember that his main job is to sell the services of his firm. And these services consist largely of handling buy and sell orders. Like any other salesman, a broker will give advice, if requested to, or often whether requested to or not. But that is not his real business. His real business is simply to provide the machinery for converting cash into securities and vice versa. And his income is pretty closely tied to the amount of this business he does.

No matter how fancy or simple it looks, a broker's office consists essentially of salesmen, a ticker tape usually blown up and projected onto a screen so that anyone may see prices at which transactions on the New York and American Exchanges are occurring, and a teletype for sending orders rapidly to the floor of the Exchange for execution.

The older brokerage houses generally have a board, like the scoreboard at a ball park, where prices of leading stocks are posted and kept current and also the hourly level of the Dow-Jones Averages. Opposite the board may be chairs for the professional traders and speculators, or the professional "watchers" who like to follow the continual fluctuations of the market.

Anyone can walk into a brokerage house and check the prices or sit for a while and watch. In many offices an electronic gadget is available on which are lettered buttons. Punch in a symbol of a listed stock and you will immediately get the latest quotation.

Opening an account with a brokerage house is the simplest part of investing. (The hardest part, of course, is to make money at it.) If you walk into a brokerage house absolutely cold, the receptionist will introduce you to a salesman or "account executive." When he learns which stock you are interested in, he will get you a quotation, or current price. At the same time he will give you a "new account" form to fill out, plus a signature card. The account form calls for your name, address, occupation, employer and bank reference, roughly the same information you would give in opening a charge account anywhere.

Several decisions are required at this point. Do you want a joint account with right of survivorship, similar to the joint account you and your spouse might have at your bank? Also, do you want the stock certificate put in your name, or names, and delivered to you, or do you want to leave it with the broker in what is called "street name"? In the latter case, you will not receive dividends, annual reports, etc., direct. The broker will receive them for you and credit the dividends to your account, sending you a statement periodically.

If you plan to hold your stock as a long-term investment, it will save the brokerage house a lot of bookkeeping if you have certificates put in your own name. But if you plan to do quite a bit of buying and selling, it will be more convenient to leave your stocks in street name.

If you open a margin account, you will automatically leave your stock in street name. Under present rules, you can buy stock only by putting up a sizeable hunk of the purchase price. The rest you borrow from the broker, usually at interest of 5% to 6%. After you once own your stock, it can decline until your loan is about two-thirds of the price before you have to put up more margin. Incidentally, to open a margin account with most brokers requires at least $1,000, which is applied to your initial purchase.

When you give your order to buy, you must decide whether you want to buy "at the market," in other words, pay the going price, or put in a "limit order" specifying that you will pay a certain price and no more. Such an order may be "open"; in other words, you can leave it with the broker indefinitely so that if the stock ever comes down to your price, you'll get it. Most orders by individual investors, however, are put in at the market. If you give such an order, you will, if you request it, receive confirmation of your purchase, along with the exact price paid and the commission, within a matter of minutes. A written confirmation will come along later.

Below we have shown how the commission is figured on a round lot (ordinarily 100 shares):

New York Stock Exchange Commissions
money involved

under $100	minimum $6
$100 to $399	2% plus $3
$400 to $2,399	1% plus $7
$2,400 to $4,999	½% plus $19
$5,000 and over	$\frac{1}{10}$% plus $39

On odd lots (less than 100 shares) the commissions are the same as the above less $2. On odd lots, also, an eighth of a point is added to the price when it is under $40 a share and a quarter of a point when it is $40 or over.

Once you get your confirmation, payment is not legally due until the fourth business day after the purchase. A few brokerage houses make it a practice to suggest immediate payment of all or perhaps half the amount. But you can be sure that when you sell, they will wait until the fourth business day before giving you your money.

What happens to your order once it is sent on its way? If you are in some city other than New York, the order goes via teletype to your broker's New York office, where it is immediately phoned to a clerk on duty at a booth along the side of the Stock Exchange itself.

The floor of the Exchange is a big, crowded expanse, resembling a great ballroom except that scattered across the floor are small horseshoe-shaped islands. Each island is a trading post, the headquarters for approximately 75 stocks. Along the edge of the floor are large open-sided phone booths, each phone connected by direct wire to some brokerage house.

Normally a couple of thousand men mill around the floor. About half of them are members who own seats or whose firms own seats for them. The other half are messengers, pages and clerks. If you stand in the visitors' gallery above one end of the floor, and watch these 2,000 men, shouting and writing hurriedly on scraps of paper, you might think they were wandering around aimlessly. But pick out one man and watch him for a while, and you will see him start from a phone booth and eventually end up at a particular trading post. There he exchanges a few brief shouts with one or two men standing about and writes on a pad; then he threads his way back to the same booth.

The process you have observed is this: a floor member has received a customer's order for purchase or sale of a particular stock via his phone clerk at one side of the floor. He has gone to the proper trading post, bought or sold the required stock verbally, made a record of the transaction on a slip of paper, and brought the paper to the telephone booth so that the clerk can phone back a report to the brokerage house.

Now let's say that the order is to buy 100 shares of Socony Mobil at the market. Here is how it is executed. The clerk who receives it by phone in one of the side booths of the Exchange, pushes a button that causes a number to turn up on a big annunciator board high up on the wall. Each member keeps an eye on the part of the board where his number is located. When the member representing your broker sees that "his number is up," he hurries from wherever he is to the telephone booth to pick up the order, which in this case is "Buy 100 Socony at the market."

The member threads his way to the spot where Socony is traded, Section A of Post 10. This is the place, approximately six feet square, where practically all Socony stock changes hands, no matter in what part of the world the buyers and sellers live. Trading in Socony amounts to nearly three million shares a year. In similar spots around the Exchange are traded millions of shares of other stocks. This is the secret of the ready and continuous market available to investors. As the member with your order approaches post 10A, he sees several other members standing there, so he calls out "How's Socony?" Note that he gives no hint as to whether he wants to buy or sell. Someone answers "52-to-a quarter," meaning that $52 a share is the highest price that anyone is willing to pay for Socony at the moment and that $52.25 a share is the lowest price at which anyone is willing to sell.

At this point the member begins to bargain, saying "52⅛ for 100." Note that if he could buy 100 for that price, he would better the market by an eighth of a point and save the purchaser $12.50. Suppose at this point another member arrives asking "How's Socony?" He has an order from one of his firm's clients to sell 100 at the market, although he does not reveal this detail. He is told "52⅛-to-a quarter." The newcomer says, "Sold 100 at 52⅛." A Stock Exchange employee called a reporter at once jots this information down and sends it by pneumatic tube to the ticker room so that in a few minutes the transaction will appear on the high-speed tape, which is duplicated almost immediately in member-firm offices all over the country.

Each member involved then makes a written notation to send back to his own firm, showing the name of the stock, the number of shares bought or sold and the name of the firm on the other end of the deal. No written communication is exchanged between the members. They have made a verbal contract, and in all the history of the Exchange no member has ever reneged.

From that example you can see that the Stock Exchange is an auction market. The highest bidder, the member representing the buyer, bought from the lowest offerer, the member representing the seller. The deal was arrived at openly and audibly so that all members in the vicinity had an equal chance to interpose by making better bids or offers. Had two bid the same price simultaneously, the matter would have been decided by matching coins.

Not all transactions on the Exchange are quite as simple as the one outlined above. Suppose that the member wanting to buy

100 shares of Socony arrives at Post 10 and finds the lowest offer is 52¼. He offers to pay 52⅛ but no one steps up with 100 shares to sell. What does the member do? Since he has an order to buy at the market, the best he can do, obviously, is to buy at the offered price of 52¼. If he does so, from whom does he buy?

Chances are in this case that he buys from the person who originally informed him that the market was 52-to-a quarter. This person is the specialist, a member whose main job is to maintain a fair and orderly market in certain stocks assigned to him by the Board of Governors. He stands at his post all day, furnishing current quotations and holding himself ready to buy and sell as required. Each section of each trading post has its own specialist. Sometimes there are several who specialize in the same stocks. From time to time the specialist writes out current quotations on a slip and a reporter phones them up to the Stock Exchange quotation room, where current bids and offers on all stocks are instantly available by telephone to inquiring member firms.

One reason for the specialist is that most large orders from professional money managers are not put in at the market but at a particular price. Thus a trust fund officer, instead of ordering his broker to buy at the market might have ordered him to buy 100 Socony at 51½. He would have realized that this was three-quarters of a point below the lowest offer, but he would have hoped to get his 100 shares during a dip in the price. He could make his order good for just one day, or good for one week, a month, or until cancelled. Similarly, another investor, instead of ordering his broker to sell at the market, could have instructed him to sell at 53. Such orders at a particular price are known as limit orders.

Now when a member comes to the post with a limit order, say an order to buy Socony at 51½, he can't stand around waiting for the market to dip to that level. That might take a day, a week or a month. And in the meantime he has other orders to fill at other posts. But the specialist, who is always standing at Post 10, will take the order for him and agree to execute it if and when Socony dips to 51½. In return for this service the specialist receives part of the member's brokerage commission. In this type of transaction he is a broker's broker.

Thus the specialist may have various orders to buy Socony from 52 all the way down through 51, 50, 49 and even down to

40 if some investor is optimistic enough to think that someday he can get it for that price. On the other side of the specialist's book might be orders to sell starting at 52¼ and going up through 53, 54, 55 and so on, perhaps to 60.

As it turns out, then, the specialist has a book full of all kinds of orders "away from the market," that is, either higher or lower than the current trading level. Remember that a large percentage of all orders placed are limit orders. This may be hard to realize if you are a person why buys or sells stocks only occasionally, because you probably do so "at the market." But professional investors and traders often prefer orders at a specific price.

So ordinarily, even if there is no great activity in a stock, there are still plenty of actual bids and offers on the specialist's book and even though there may be no other members around, the specialist is ready to give a bid and offer. The bid will be the highest bid he has in his book, which in the case of Socony might be 52, and the offer will be the lowest offer, which might be 52¼.

But what if there were so little interest in Socony and so few limit orders in the book that the highest bid was only 51 and the lowest offer 54? That would seldom happen in a widely traded stock like Socony, but it might in an issue that was less active. Such a three-point spread would be undesirable in the view of the Board of Governors of the Exchange. The Board prides itself on "close markets" and "continuity" in price movements. Thus under ideal conditions there should be small fluctuations between successive trades. An investor hates to think that a stock he has just bought for $54 a share would, if sold back a few minutes later, bring only $51.

So if it happens that the highest bid on the specialist's book is 51 and the lowest offer 54, the specialist is expected to do something about it. Specifically, he is supposed to "improve" the market by certain judicious buying and selling for his own account. Thus he can arbitrarily narrow the 51–54 gap by offering to buy for his own account at 52 or sell at 53. Any customer will thereby be saved a point, or $100 per round lot (100 shares).

This combined role of the specialist as broker for others and dealer for himself caused considerable criticism in the years following the stock market crash of 1929. In the heyday of the boom, specialists had participated in pools and helped rig markets.

Today, however, the specialist works under stringent rules and the strict scrutiny of the Board of Governors of the Stock Exchange. He is supposed to trade "against the trend" most of the time. In other words, he is supposed to slow rapidly declining markets by buying stock for his own account even if he doesn't particularly want it. He also is supposed to slow rapidly rising markets by supplying stock, selling short if necessary. That means selling stock he does not own but which he borrows to deliver to the buyer. Later he must buy an equivalent amount to return to the lender. If the price goes up in the meantime, he is in the position of having to pay more for the stock than he originally sold it for.

Where, you might ask, does a specialist borrow as much as 10,000 shares of stock when he has to sell that much short? Officers, directors and large stockholders of a given company usually make large blocks of stock available for lending to specialists and other members.

Here are a few of the rules that a specialist must observe.

He may not, under pain of expulsion, buy or sell stock for his own account at a price at which he holds an order to buy or sell for a customer. He must pay an eighth of a point more or sell for an eighth less.

A specialist must be able to buy and hold at least 400 shares of each of the stocks in which he is a specialist. In actual practice he has capital to buy or sell a good deal more than 400 shares. This is a precaution to enable him to slow down runaway markets should they occur.

When a specialist wants to fill a limit order entrusted to his care by buying from or selling to himself, he must first send for and get the approval of the floor member from whom he got the order. Thus if the broker doesn't think the price fair, no trade is consummated.

A specialist may not show his book to other members.

A specialist makes money on commissions for executing limit orders and by trading for his own account. But he constantly runs the risk of losing back a slug of his profits in a very short time.

As you can see, the role of the specialist is vital. What makes it so is the size of the Exchange's business. Years ago specialists were not needed. The members originally sat around a table at their designated "seats" (a term still used to describe a membership) while the president read off the names of the stocks, one by one. If a member wanted to buy or sell, he shouted out his bid or offer. Gradually, this formal method broke down into a general auction at which brokers shouted their bids and offers at any time. Then, as volume grew, it became customary for members interested in particular stocks to congregate at certain definite points on the floor.

The first specialist is said to have been a member who broke his leg and who therefore had to sit in one place. He offered to hold and execute orders for brokers in one stock, Western Union. This turned out to be a convenient service, and the specialists gradually became the nerve centers of the Stock Exchange. Of the 800 to 1,000 members on the floor on an average day, probably 350, or over a third, are specialists. In an inactive stock from one half to three quarters of all trading may go through the specialist. In an active stock the specialist will handle a quarter to a third of all transactions.

As a group the specialists pride themselves on performing a public service by keeping a close, continuous and orderly market in their stocks. It is largely their doing that makes it possible for a man in Houston to buy stock in any one of 1,150 listed companies from a man in Jacksonville in five minutes' time, with no prior notice, at a price that is almost exactly the same as the one that a man in Portland, Ore., got from a man in Milwaukee ten minutes before.

Now suppose that you order not 100 shares but only 10, in other words, an odd lot. This order would come in the same way to a phone booth at the side of the floor, but then instead of being handed to the firm's floor trader, it would be placed in a pneumatic tube that would carry it directly to the inside of the proper trading post. There the order would be time stamped and placed on a hook.

At each post several odd-lot dealers are constantly on duty. They fill all buy and sell orders themselves, occasionally running around to the outside of the post to obtain or get rid of round lots (100 shares) to balance their position. Odd-lot prices are not determined by the auction method directly. Rather they are tied to the prices of round lots.

Thus when you buy an odd lot, you pay an eighth or a quarter of a point more than the next succeeding round-lot sale after your order is in possession of the odd-lot dealer. When you sell, you get an eighth or a quarter less. The differential is an eighth on stocks selling under $40 a share, a quarter on stocks selling at $40 or over. There is a slight compensation to the odd-lot investor in that his brokerage commission is $2 less than it would be on a round lot.

In the case of a 10-share order for Socony, assume that the next round lot sale after your order arrived, was at 52½. At that moment you would be credited with a purchase of 10 shares at 52¾. But your brokerage commission would be $2 less than if you had bought a round lot. Specifically, it would be 1% plus $7, or $12.28 minus $2, or $10.28.

There are two odd-lot houses on the New York Stock Exchange. Carlisle & Jacquelin and De Coppet & Doremus. Each workday evening they plunge into the mountainous problem of sorting out thousands of transactions of various sizes. To arrange for delivery of odd lots sold to customers, these firms must send round lots to the transfer agents of hundreds of companies and obtain stock certificates in various smaller sizes, including fractions. On the other side of the picture, they must assemble all the odd lots bought from other customers, arrange them in round-lot sizes and get the little certificates transferred into big ones. If you don't think this keeps the clerks busy, remember that on an average day nearly a quarter of a million shares are bought in odd lots and an additional quarter of a million different shares are sold.

Incidentally, the question is sometimes asked, can you buy one share of stock on the Stock Exchange? The answer is Yes. The brokerage commission is figured on the dollar value of the purchase. So the commission on one share of a stock costing $250 a share is the same as that on five shares of a stock costing $50 a share. Of course, if you buy one share each of five different stocks, that means five transactions with all the incidental paper work. Even so, if that is your considered decision as to how to invest, you should go ahead and do it. Many of today's fortunes were founded years ago on the purchase of a few shares of good stock here, others there. It's not the quantity you buy each time so much as what you pick.

the over-the-counter market

There are roughly 25,000 corporations whose shares are traded in America today. Of these, only about 2,200 companies have their shares listed on any stock exchange. Of the approximately 23,000 corporations remaining, another 3,600 are widely enough held to be considered publicly owned. Their shares are traded outside the exchanges in what is known as the over-the-counter market.

What is this over-the-counter market and how does it differ from the markets made by the exchanges?

Actually, the over-the-counter market is the oldest form of securities market we have. Over-the-counter trading began during the earliest days of the Republic when the Continental Congress and canal and turnpike companies raised capital by offering their stock and bonds to the public. The actual offerings were made through banks. Thus a bank generally kept a supply of securities on hand and when a customer wanted to buy a particular stock or bond, he would pay the banker by check or cash and the banker, in turn, would hand the security over the counter. The price would be a matter of negotiation between the bank and the buyer.

In those early days, too, certain issues became very much in demand. It was natural that what the English called "stock jobbers" would begin buying and selling these popular issues as a full time business. The first organized market sprang up under a buttonwood tree on lower Wall Street. In the street and on the sidewalk, robust traders sold stocks to each other and to the public, rain or shine, by shouting their bids and offers and making hand signals. There are people alive today who can remember when the American Stock Exchange, then called the Curb, operated outdoors. It was a colorful sight, the brokers wearing different colored hats for identification, and buying and selling by sheer lung power, all the while sending secret wigwagging, headscratching or hat tipping signals to their clerks leaning out of office windows above.

Eventually, around 1920, the Curb moved indoors. In the meantime the New York Stock Exchange had developed in a more dignified way, the members meeting in the morning and sitting around a table while the head of the Exchange read off a list of stocks and listened for bids or offers.

The auction trading of the exchanges and the negotiated trading engaged in first by banks, and later by "dealers," grew up side by side. Their early differences persist to this day. The most obvious difference is that trading on an exchange is concentrated in one place—the floor. But the approximately 3,000 dealers who handle the over-the-counter business are spread all over the country. They do their trading by means of an intricate network of private telephone and teletype hook-ups. If you put in an order for an over-the-counter stock, the order does not go to any central place. Rather, it will be shopped around by phone or teletype to several dealers, perhaps in different cities.

There is a difference, too, in the kind of security traded. For purposes of illustration, compare securities traded over-the-counter with those traded on the New York Stock Exchange. The New York Stock Exchange tends to list securities of large and well-established companies that appeal to large numbers of investors and therefore are heavily traded. In the over-the-counter market you find almost every kind of security, including those of large, well-established companies right down to the smallest and newest local company.

A company that wishes to have its stock listed on the New

York Stock Exchange must meet rather stiff initial requirements. The Exchange generally requires the following:

1. Demonstrated earning power under competitive conditions of over $1 million annually, after all charges and taxes.

2. Net tangible assets of over $8 million, but greater emphasis will be placed on the aggregate market value of the common stock, where $8 million at the time of listing is looked for.

3. At least 400,000 common shares outstanding (exclusive of concentrated or family holdings) among not less than 1,500 shareholders, after substantially discounting odd lots.

4. The company must be a going concern, or be the successor of a going concern.

As you can see, only the largest, best known companies can qualify for NYSE listing.

Over-the-counter dealers, on the other hand, will handle almost any kind of stock or bond in which the public expresses even a mild interest. The range is wide. At the top are many large and well-established companies whose stock is traded both on exchanges and over-the-counter. At the lower end are the stocks of small obscure companies hardly known beyond their own home towns. In the middle are all kinds of companies, some fairly large but not well enough known to be listed by exchanges.

In addition, the over-the-counter dealers handle much of the business in government, state and municipal bonds; most corporate bonds; large numbers of preferred stocks, and almost all bank and insurance company stocks.

The over-the-counter market performs another very important function. It makes available to investors new issues—stocks and bonds that heretofore have had no public market. This function is known as underwriting and will be discussed in the next chapter.

The manner in which securities are priced in the over-the-counter market and the way in which customers are charged for purchases or sales is much less uniform than it is on the New York Stock Exchange. Buyers and sellers for any NYSE listed stock are always available and commissions can be, and are, standardized. Over-the-counter dealers, however, undertake to handle a wide variety of securities, many of which are sparsely held and thinly traded. The problems of finding a buyer or seller, often are unpredictable.

As an example, assume an investor wants to buy an over-the-counter stock known as First Consolidated (name fictitious). He asks for a quote from his broker. The broker looks up the stock in the quotation sheets and finds that half a dozen over-the-counter dealers make a market in this particular stock; in other words, they stand ready to buy or sell it at any time. The broker may then call two or three of these dealers to get a quote. He does not reveal whether his customer is a buyer or seller. Let us say that the quote is, in one case, 25½ bid, 26⅜ offered, in another, 25½ bid, 26¼ offered. The stock, then, can be bought by the broker for 26¼. But in order to pay his overhead and make a profit on the deal, he will have to charge the investor somewhat more. Perhaps he will quote his customer a price of 27. If this is agreeable, the broker will buy the stock at 26¼, resell it to the investor for 27, and make a mark-up of ¾ of a point or roughly 2¾% of the purchase price.

However, instead of marking up the stock, the broker in the above example could have resold it to his customer at the 26¼ price, and charged a commission. Some brokers who are members of the New York Stock Exchange, and who do most of their business in listed stocks, do charge the NYSE commission rate no matter whether a stock is listed or over-the-counter.

When you purchase or sell stock in the over-the-counter market, the mark-up or commission will depend on a number of factors: the kind of broker you are dealing with, (big house, small house); the kind of security; how widely it is traded; the size of the transaction in dollars (the smaller the transaction the larger the mark-up or commission will be percentagewise), and so on.

The way the over-the-counter dealers keep track of the prices of the thousands of securities they deal in, is rather intricate. Unlike New York Stock Exchange prices, which are prices at which transactions actually took place, over-the-counter quoted prices are bids and offers. The bid is what you might expect to receive if you sold the security, while the offer is what you might expect to pay if you bought it. The difference represents the dealer's mark-up or charge for handling the transaction.

Here is how these bids and offers are ascertained and published. There is a central organization known as the National Quotation Bureau. Traditionally, between 2 o'clock and 4 o'clock each afternoon, each over-the-counter dealer who makes a market in any given security, sends in the bid and offered prices at which he is willing to buy or sell. The information is then tabulated on what are known as the "pink sheets." These are simply legal-sized sheets of pink paper on which are printed alphabetically the names of the most widely traded over-the-counter stocks. After each stock appear the names of the dealers who make a market in it, along with their current bid and offer. These pink sheets are available in every brokerage house and may be inspected.

Over-the-counter corporate bonds are quoted in a similar way in the "yellow sheets," while government and municipal bond quotations appear on what is known as "the blue list."

Now, should you buy over-the-counter stocks, or stick to those listed on exchanges? This question cannot be answered categorically because, although many over-the-counter stocks are obscure and speculative, others are of the highest grade. For example, many preferred stocks are issued in quantities too small to warrant listing on the New York Stock Exchange. Yet these stocks may be very desirable. Bank stocks, insurance company stocks, some investment trusts and many other issues that may well be attractive, also are available only in the over-the-counter market. Or the investor may want to buy into a local company about which he has some personal knowledge. Therefore, most investors will inevitably find themselves in this market at one time or another.

Nevertheless, except where the investor desires a specific over-the-counter security for a particular reason, he might well make it a practice to stick to stocks listed on the New York Stock Exchange. For one thing, the New York Stock Exchange admits to listing only large, seasoned companies. Of course, such companies can deteriorate and their stocks can decline. Nevertheless, they must initially conform to certain standards of size and quality. Also, the Exchange requires its listed companies to conform to certain practices that benefit shareholders. And similar requirements are not applied to companies whose shares are traded over-the-counter.

For example, companies listed on the Exchange (except in a few special cases) must submit to their stockholders complete annual reports audited by independent certified public accountants, and also quarterly reports of earnings. In contrast, some unlisted companies do not issue regular or complete reports and may even refuse to disclose pertinent information to stockholders.

The New York Stock Exchange also insists that a common stock, in order to be listed, must carry voting rights. Preferred stockholders must also have the right to elect two directors if a company defaults on six quarterly preferred dividends.

Another advantage to listed stocks: they are policed by the U. S. Securities and Exchange Commission. The SEC cannot, however, do the same job on the vast, unorganized over-the-counter market. For example, the SEC requires a listed company to send out proxies to stockholders so prepared that motions to be made at stockholder meetings are known in advance and can be voted on Yes or No. Blanket proxies, whereby the managements of unlisted companies sometimes perpetuate themselves in office, are prohibited.

Of course, many unlisted companies are as scrupulous about these matters as listed companies. The point we make is that there are no rules or regulations to require it, other than state corporation laws which in many cases are neither strict nor strictly enforced.

When you do buy stocks over-the-counter, which, as we have said, every investor does at one time or another, there are certain precautions you might consider. It is proper and desirable to know whether the firm you employ in a transaction is acting as dealer (principal) or as broker. If the firm is acting as dealer, his mark-up will come out of the price at which the security changes hands. If he is acting as broker, he will charge you a percentage commission. In either case, an ethical broker will be glad to tell you the amount of the charge if you ask. The exception might be where a dealer sold you a security he had had in his own inventory for some time. In that case he would not be required to tell you how much he had paid for it originally.

The over-the-counter market, while not directly regulated by the Securities and Exchange Commission, is self-policed under the general direction of the SEC. The policing body is known as the National Association of Securities Dealers. This organization

new issues

Somewhere along the line every investor is faced with a question: should he buy stock freshly issued, either by a publicly held company that needs additional capital, or by a newly formed company offering its stock, or by a company that has heretofore been privately owned and never had stock in the hands of the public before.

The underwriter is the middleman in the transaction whereby such companies sell securities to the public. He buys the securities from the issuing company, holds them for the account of his own firm, at least temporarily, then resells them to the public. A broker, on the other hand, merely acts as agent for the buyer and seller. Many firms that do a day-to-day brokerage business also underwrite new issues from time to time.

The biggest part of the underwriting business consists of the selling of new securities of established companies that need additional capital for modernization or expansion. These issues are often so large that no single investment banker can handle the whole job. Syndicates are formed in which a dozen houses may join together, each buying a portion of the securities and reselling its share to its customers at a mark-up. This mark-up pays the overhead and provides the profit to the underwriter. The average mark-up in the case of shares sold by companies listed on the New York Stock Exchange is less than 4%. The financial pages of the newspapers carry ads every day for such newly issued securities—bonds, debentures, preferred stock, common stock, convertible debentures or preferred and so on. An expanding utility company, for example, may offer a large issue of bonds to finance new power lines or generators. A large finance company may sell debentures to raise money to re-lend to auto buyers.

Very often, existing stockholders of established companies are given the first opportunity to buy these additional shares. This opportunity is given via the issuance of "rights." As an example, suppose you own 25 shares of the ABC Co. and you get a letter from the president saying the company is issuing additional stock and enclosed are 25 rights entitling you to buy 2½ more shares.

Here is how such rights come to be issued. Say the ABC Co. wants to expand and needs more capital. It decides to sell additional stock, increasing its outstanding shares from 100,000 to 110,000. This decision affects you and every other stockholder because it threatens to decrease slightly your share of ownership and profits unless—and here is the crux of the matter—unless you buy your pro-rata share of the new stock. In that case you will maintain your original position.

For this reason many states require companies to offer new stock to their stockholders before they offer it to the public. Go back to your 25 shares of ABC. You have received 25 rights, one right for every share you own. Since the company is increasing its capitalization by 10%, you now have the privilege of increasing your holdings by the same amount, or of buying 2½ more shares. Your 25 rights will come in the form of two certificates. One will be a full certificate, or a "warrant" (not to be confused with another type of warrant to be described later), representing 20 rights and entitling you to buy 2 shares of new stock. The other will be a fractional certificate representing 5 rights and theoretically entitling you to buy half a share. As a matter of practice, you generally can't buy half a share. Your fractional certificate must be combined with others to make up a full certificate. Either you buy enough additional fractional certificates from someone else to make up a full share, or you sell your fractional certificates for cash.

On each certificate there are instructions. If you want to sell the certificate for cash, you sign in one place. If you want to subscribe to new shares, you sign in another and make out a check based on the subscription price. If you have a fractional certificate and want to buy additional fractions to make up a full certificate, you can do that, too. You will be billed later for the cost. In all cases you send your certificates back to the ABC Co.'s transfer agent, which is probably a New York bank.

How much are stock rights worth? In actual practice they are worth what other investors are willing to pay for them on the open market. But there is a formula by which their theoretical value can be judged. Assume the ABC is currently traded at $25 a share. The rights entitle you to buy 2½ new shares at $22 a share. The company has set this low price to encourage you to buy. But if you don't care to buy, what can you get for your rights?

To get the theoretical answer, write down the market price of the old stock, $25; subtract the subscription price of the new stock, $22; then divide by 1 plus the number of shares you must own to buy one new share, which in the example is 10 shares.

The theoretical value of ABC rights, then, would be—

$$\frac{\$25 - \$22}{1 + 10} = 27\frac{1}{3} \text{ cents}$$

Since you have 25 such rights, their total theoretical value is $6.83. If you decide to sell them, you may get a bit more or less, depending on how brisk the demand is and what is happening to the price of ABC stock on the market.

Whatever you do about your rights must be done promptly. When the ABC Co. offers to sell new stock at $22 a share, or $3 under the market price, it is highly vulnerable. Suppose the stock market dropped suddenly, carrying the price of ABC down to $20. The right to buy new shares at $22 would be worthless, and the new issue would not get sold. Naturally, then, the ABC Co. wants its stockholders to make up their minds in a hurry. Still, they must have time to read and understand the proposal, fill out the forms and mail them. The New York Stock Exchange therefore requires listed companies to give stockholders 16 days to use or sell their rights. Companies not listed on the Exchange generally allow a comparable period. The Stock Exchange also sets a date at which the stock will sell "ex-rights." This ex-rights date is the date after which the stock no longer carries the right with it.

Whether you should exercise rights or sell them depends on how you feel about the stock in question and whether or not you should be buying more of the same or diversifying into other stocks. Don't be swayed too much by the appearance of a bargain. The price of the stock will be automatically reduced, as of the ex-right date, by the value of one right. So in the end you are about even with the board if you sell the right and take the money instead of subscribing to the new stock offering.

Warrants are long-lived rights. Some have expiration dates; others are perpetual. They generally come into being as a "sweetener" to make an issue of stock or bonds more attractive. Usually the price at which a warrant entitles the holder to buy a specified number of shares of common stock is considerably above the market price of the stock at the time. But there is always a chance that the market will rise to a point where exercise of the warrant will be profitable. This gives it a speculative appeal.

Another part of the underwriting business is offering for sale the securities of new, or privately-owned companies that have decided to "go public." Such new issues, being smaller than offerings by established companies, require fewer underwriters and the underwriting mark-up is likely to be higher, 6% or 7%. When a small company offers securities to the public for the first time, it generally issues common stock. Its future, in all likelihood, is too uncertain for it to attract the type of investor likely to buy bonds. However, capital can be raised by making a bond convertible into common, which gives the bondholders the first claim against the company's assets and a chance to buy the common stock if the company does well.

In the case of a very small, new, speculative company, one underwriter alone may handle the whole issue. And the underwriter may do it on what is known as a "best efforts" basis. In other words, instead of buying the whole issue and taking the responsibility for reselling it to investors, the underwriter may undertake only to sell as much of the issue as he can. If he fails to sell it all, the balance is left in the hands of the issuing company. When stock is offered on a "best efforts" basis it often indicates that the underwriter is not too confident that he can place the whole issue, or that he does not have enough capital to swing the deal on the usual basis.

Now what are the obligations of the underwriting house when it offers securities to the public? It has a certain obligation to the issuing company. The job there is first to advise the issuer as to timing, price, terms, etc., of the issue, then to get the issue sold and the proceeds into the hands of the issuer at the least cost. The underwriting firm also has obligations to its customers for it is to them, largely, that it expects to sell the securities. A reputable broker or investment banker doesn't want to recommend purchase of securities and then have them go sour and decline in price. That would be an excellent way to lose customers and go out of business. Finally, of course, the underwriting firm has a responsibility to its own partners and this simply is to meet expenses and make a profit so that the business can prosper.

An underwriting firm with years of experience and a reputation to maintain will make every effort to offer its customers only sound securities reasonably priced with respect to the issuer's underlying assets and prospective earnings. Large issues of the securities of nationally known companies generally are offered by syndicates headed by large New York underwriters. Even so, there can be no guarantee that the securities so offered will turn out to be good investments.

When it comes to local issues, the prospective investor must be even more careful. In most cities there are local firms that have been in business for years and that exercise the greatest care in choosing which issues they will underwrite. However, in addition to outstanding and reputable local underwriters, there are also those who are less choosy about what they will do. The worst of these are simply looking for stock that they can unload on the public at as high a profit as the traffic will bear. Unfortunately, the space age has provided a label that apparently can be stuck on to almost any small company to give it glamor. The most prosaic small companies have gone public and at the same time have changed their names to include such words as missiles, electronics and the like, whether or not they were actually in the missile or electronic business.

Here are a couple of notorious gimmicks designed to take your money. One is known in the trade as a bail-out. The following is an actual case with names omitted. A group of mining promoters organized a company having 6,000,000 shares of common stock. They put in $10,000 in cash and 115 claims covering 2,260,-000 acres in Utah which had cost them $30,000. In return for their investment of $40,000 in the company they received 3,000,-

ooo shares of stock and offered the other 3,000,000 shares for sale to the public at 10 cents a share.

Right there you can see that if all went as planned and the public paid 10 cents a share for the stock, the promoters' own stock would have a market value of 10 cents a share or $300,000. Not only that, but they would be in control of a company having a quarter of a million dollars of capital (the $300,000 from the public sale of stock minus selling expenses). This is known as a bail-out because the public would have "bailed out" the promoters and acquired assets of dubious value.

Now how about the underwriters? In this case they agreed to sell the stock on a best efforts basis. For this they received between 25% and 33% of the selling price. All they had to do was to ballyhoo the stock and every time they sold 1,000 shares they raked in $25 to $30. They owned no stock themselves, nor did they agree to buy any. Therefore they took no risk. The big risk, of course, was taken by those who paid 10 cents a share for stock that had a true worth of a good deal less than that.

The other notorious gimmick used by small and unscrupulous underwriters is known as a lock-up. In this case the underwriters bring out a new issue of a glamorous sounding stock and give it a big advance ballyhoo. They let it be known that this is going to be a "hot issue" and that the demand for it will be so great that the stock will have to be "allocated." In other words, eager customers who want 100 shares will be lucky if they get 10 or 25. To guarantee that the issue will be hot, the underwriters let their friends and relatives (although this is against the rules) sign up for large blocks of the issue in advance. This does, in fact, create an apparent scarcity. A would-be purchaser, finding that he cannot get any stock allocated to him on the day of the offering, starts bidding for the stock in the open market. This runs the price up. During the height of this price run-up, the insiders quietly begin leaking out their "locked-up" stock at perhaps double or triple the price they paid at the offering.

It is a well-known fact that many small underwriters have this reputation: if you are a good friend or customer and buy their new issues, they will get you in at the offering price and get you out at the top of the run-up. It's not hard to guess who is left holding the bag. It's the uninformed investor who buys at inflated prices and fails to get out in time.

Why is this sort of thing allowed to go on, you might ask. Actually, a great deal is being done to prevent it by both the Securities and Exchange Commission and the National Association of Securities Dealers. But it's a difficult job to police the 100,000 securities salesmen scattered over the country. And while the SEC requires the issuers of securities to make the most detailed advance disclosure of their assets, prospects, how the money is to be used and the risks involved, the unfortunate truth is that a great many investors simply won't bother to read registration statements but prefer to base their decisions on what they hear from a salesman or someone else supposedly in the know.

In regard to new issues, the basic SEC law is the Securities Act of 1933, sometimes known as the "truth in securities" act. When securities are first offered to the public, a summary of the company's business operations and its financial condition must be furnished to prospective buyers free. In the case of large issues of stock this summary is known as a propectus. When the amount of stock is less than $300,000, an abbreviated summary known as an offering circular may be used.

In either case, whether a salesman solicits an investor in person, by mail or by phone, a copy of the prospectus or offering circular must be furnished. If it is not, the nearest regional office of the SEC would like to hear about it. Sometimes the first written communication a prospect receives is the confirmation of an order he has given by telephone. Even at this late date, he may be able to cancel his purchase if the offering circular reveals information he was not given over the phone.

But the truth is, few purchasers of small new issues really study the offering circular or prospectus. In this case it's pretty hard to protect them from their own folly. However, the SEC and the NASD do have other rules designed to prevent the other form of skullduggery mentioned earlier in this chapter.

When a new issue comes out, the underwriter and members of his firm and his immediate family are not allowed to purchase any stock at the offering price unless such purchases are disclosed in the prospectus and conform to their past pattern of investing. And even if such persons have a history of investing in every new issue underwritten, they are supposed to receive only a reasonably small percentage of the issue and to buy it to hold for investment, not to sell for "a quick turn."

What is a reasonably small percentage and what is a pattern of investing? These are terms, of course, that are susceptible of different interpretations. In almost every large offering of a hot issue, the NASD or the SEC, or both, have required the underwriter to fill in exhaustive questionnaires showing the disposition of every share of stock. Fines have been levied against culprits who violate the spirit or the letter of the rules.

The same rules apply to broker-dealers who may not be members of the original underwriting group but who have received expressions of interest in the stock from their own customers. If they receive an allocation of stock from the underwriter as an "accommodation," they must accept it at the offering price, less a selling group concession, and sell it to their customers at the same price.

Despite all the pitfalls in the new issue market, there are bound to be attractive opportunities for investment. In recent years the breakthrough in research has peppered the land with new, exciting ventures. Engineers, chemists, physicists, advanced mathematicians and young men with energy and big ideas have splintered off from established companies and started up new businesses with glamorous names and space-age products that mystify, and yet intrigue, the layman. One company turns out quartz high-vibration frequency systems while another uses the latest electronic computers to solve complicated problems for business and government. A third develops atomic isotope application, radioactive analyses and nuclear power technology, while a fourth offers a revolutionary electronic teaching machine. A fifth has developed a ceramic coating for missile nose cones while a sixth sells a heat resistant paint to protect missile launching pads.

Many of these young companies have sold stock to the public and have achieved success so rapidly that their stock has skyrocketed. Naturally, the question arises in the mind of the investor, should he not try to participate in this space-age business and acquire shares in young companies that seem to be growing like Jack's beanstalk and outstripping even the old-established leaders in electronics and chemistry.

This is a hard question to advise on. Undeniably, many of these little companies will grow and prosper and pay off handsomely for those who get in on the ground floor. Many more, however, because of lack of capital, lack of management know-how or inability to compete with the larger groups, will eventually fall by the wayside. The most difficult problem is selection. One experienced investor, wanting to participate in the growth of these small companies, but despairing of being able to select those that would survive, walked into a brokerage office with the names of 20 and bought 100 shares of each. His idea was that if ten paid off, it might more than offset the failure of the other ten.

For the average person, however, such a program is not possible. On the other hand, selection of one or two promising companies is very difficult. The information is available to evaluate the prospects of a new enterprise. The U. S. Securities and Exchange Commission sees to that. But the average person hardly has time to read and compare the prospectuses of dozens of companies. And he probably should consider a good many before selecting even one. The large, reliable statistical services cannot evaluate the thousands of small new issues constantly appearing on the market. In the end, the investor is almost forced to ask for help. And chances are the person he will consult about a particular new issue will be the very underwriter who is trying to peddle it.

One is almost tempted to say that the average person should leave small new issues strictly alone. Yet the business of raising public money for small, enterprising companies is a legitimate one. Every company from General Motors on down had its humble beginnings. If it had not been for courageous investors willing to finance promising new ventures, we would not be a great industrial nation with a high standard of living. Think what a service the backers of Henry Ford performed, both for themselves, and for the public. They made themselves millionaires but also enabled Ford to begin mass production of automobiles.

If an investor is interested in trying to get in on the ground floor of small new companies, he should do everything possible to avoid the pitfalls and he should realize also that these are more numerous than in any other kind of investing.

Here are some ideas for the person who wants to invest in small new companies on his own.

Deal with a reputable underwriter. You can get names of good ones from your banker. Those houses that are members of the New York Stock Exchange generally fall into this category.

Learn everything you can about the company before you buy. Read the prospectus if the stock is already out. If it isn't, get what is called the "red herring." This is a preliminary prospectus containing what the company considers to be information required by the SEC. If the SEC does not raise any questions as to the adequacy or accuracy of the red herring, it becomes an effective prospectus. Otherwise, the underwriter revises it and resubmits it. All the facts about the company, and particularly all unfavorable facts and contingencies, are clearly set forth in the final prospectus. It would cost a potential investor thousands of dollars to buy such a complete and unbiased picture of a company's operations. The SEC makes the issuer and underwriter provide it to you free. So use it.

Now, here is another way to buy stock in new, small space-age companies and cut down somewhat on the risk. Buy stock in a "small-business investment company," which invests its capital in selected small growth companies.

These small-business investment companies, or SBIC's, are a fairly new phenomenon. They are privately organized but can borrow money at nominal rates from the government and also receive certain tax advantages. In return, SBIC's must agree to lend to or invest in businesses having limited assets and net profits. Such small businesses historically have had difficulty raising capital or obtaining long-term financing.

Since 1958, when Congress passed legislation fostering SBIC's, hundreds have been organized. Many are closely held and difficult to buy into, but many others have "gone public." Their stock is traded over-the-counter or on exchanges. So by buying into one of these, you indirectly invest your money in the small companies that the SBIC itself selects, finances and, in some cases, advises. If these small companies prosper and grow, so will your investment. If they do not, chances are you'll lose money. The risk is there, though it may be less than if you invested in some small company yourself.

Here are the most pertinent facts about this kind of investment.

Professional management. This probably is the most important single consideration. An SBIC may be organized by any group of people with capital. Many have been set up by banks. Others have been established by investment counselors or management men well versed in making large-scale investments. Many SBIC's, on the other hand, have been set up by obsure businessmen who operate on the local level. In such cases the ability of the management is unknown.

Management policy. If you are interested in small growth companies that may be on the verge of a large expansion, there are SBIC's that concentrate on this type of investment. Others, however, buy into run-of-the-mill concerns with little glamor. One SBIC, for example, invested in a chain of bowling alleys, a small iron and steel rolling mill, a clay-products company, a traprock company, a printing company and a string of motels.

Price. When SBIC's first began selling stock to the public in volume, there was not much investor interest, and many SBIC shares were selling below net asset value. Later, the public became enthusiastic about SBIC's, and in some cases their stock soared.

Any investor contemplating purchase of stock in an SBIC should ascertain the relation between the market price and the net asset value per share. All other things being equal, of course, it is better not to pay too high a premium.

Leverage. This is a characteristic of investment companies that use borrowed money. Suppose an SBIC has X dollars of invested capital, and borrows twice as much at a nominal rate of interest from the federal government. If it then makes a large profit on its total capital, this profit (after interest is paid) accrues to those who put up the original money. The advantage of leverage will not accrue, however, to those who buy into an SBIC later if the price has been bid way up.

Tax advantages. An SBIC and its stockholders receive preferential tax treatment. Dividends the company receives from investments are completely exempt from corporate income taxes. By comparison, ordinary corporations receive only an 85% exemption. Then, if the SBIC suffers losses on its stock investments, these losses may be deducted either from ordinary income or from capital gains. Also, if stockholders in an SBIC sell their shares at a loss, this loss, too, may be deducted from ordinary income.

Diversification and professional selection. SBIC's have many of the characteristics of ordinary investment trusts. In fact, Arthur Wiesenberger, in his "Investment Companies," devotes several pages to a discussion and a list of SBIC's. When an investor buys into an SBIC, his money is reinvested for him by professionals and is spread over many companies.

SBIC's differ from ordinary investment trusts in one important respect, however. An investment trust generally puts its money into well-established companies with a record of earnings extending back at least ten years. By contrast, an SBIC must confine its investments to small companies. And many companies that SBIC's invest in have never had any earnings at all and, at most, have what might be considered good prospects.

Also, while many SBIC's are heavily invested in the most glamorous kind of small electronics and space-age companies, others are providing capital to more prosaic small businesses—ones with less promise of growth. So the potential investor in an SBIC should check its investment policy and note the type of company it is buying into.

Management, of course, is most important, and good management is worth paying a premium for. A good many SBIC's are being run by businessmen with a long record of success in big enterprises. Be extra cautious before investing in an SBIC run by lesser men.

Finally, remember that there are on the market shares of investment trusts and mutual funds that also invest in glamorous growth companies. Massachusetts Investors Growth Stock Fund, Putnam Growth Fund, Fidelity Capital Fund and National Investors Corp. are some of the trusts that concentrate on this glamorous type of growth investments. Shares of these trusts are available at net asset value plus a 7½% to 8½% sales charge.

If an investor insists on putting his money into the stocks of new, small companies that may be the growth stocks of the future, perhaps an SBIC is the answer. But he also should consider the advisability of investing, directly or via an investment trust.

charting, puts and calls, margin buying, short selling, commodity trading —discussed but not recommended

Anyone who studies stocks, reads the financial page and deals with brokers is bound to hear a good deal about speculative gimmicks and supposed short cuts to making money. Today the search for an easy road to riches goes on as relentlessly as the old search for a touchstone that would turn baser metals into gold.

TECHNIQUES OF THE CHARTISTS

There are two basic ways of selecting stocks and gauging the course of the stock market. One is known as the fundamental approach. It calls for a study of business conditions and interest rates, of the relative position of industries, of the earnings of companies and quality of management. It attempts to evaluate, to discover merits, weaknesses, potentials. This is the approach that has been stressed by this book.

But there is another method known as the technical approach. Its premise is that stock prices themselves, as they move along from day to day, weave a pattern and tell a story of events to come. The technician, through his price charts, watches the interminable battle between buyers and sellers. He senses the rise and fall of investor confidence. From the actions of prices, he believes he can spot the time when supply or demand is winning out, and when a stock or the market as a whole is about to break out and go higher—or lower.

Use of the technical approach is not recommended for the individual. For one thing, it requires a great deal of statistical work, more than the ordinary person can handle or understand. And while the best professional technicians use their charts to forecast the longer-term price movements, most amateur technicians are prone to use charts to try for short-term profits. This calls for trading in and out of the market, which seldom works for the ordinary investor.

Nevertheless, the technical approach is of interest. At its best, and when combined with the fundamental approach, it can be revealing. And when stocks are relatively high and it is harder and harder to find bargains in the market, some big institutional investors, the managers of large funds, pay a good deal of attention to the charts and prognostications of the really competent technicians.

One of the tools most used by technicians is the point and figure chart. A point and figure chart shows only one thing, price movement. It neither shows volume of trading nor takes into account time in the usual sense. Time, says the chartist, is merely a measure of change. Therefore, unless the price of a stock changes by, say, one point, no entry is made on the chart even though weeks and months go by.

Look at *Chart 38*. It is based on one-point units and shows price movement of a stock that was first charted at 20. Once the chartist posted an X opposite the figure 20, he was interested in two things only—whether the stock sold at or above 21 or whether it sold at or below 19.

This stock subsequently sold at 19, so an X was made in the 19

CHART 38

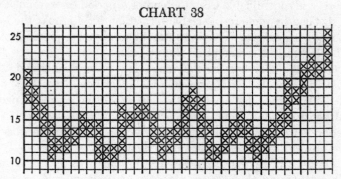

Courtesy Edmund W. Tabell of Walston & Co.

square just under the previous posting at 20. This X established a down trend and, as long as this down trend remained in effect, all subsequent postings were made in the same column. In this case the down trend continued until a price of 17 was reached. The stock then reversed one point by selling at 18 and the chartist moved over into the next column to post 18.

Once this 18 posting had been made, a sale at 19 or 17 would establish a trend. The next recordable sale was 17 and the trend carried down to 15 in the second column. Subsequent fluctuations produced the pattern shown.

There are variations of this method—for example, the one-point unit, three-point reversal chart. In this case a reversal in trend is posted only if it extends three boxes up from the previous low or down from the previous high.

What does the chartist learn from his intricate pattern of X's? Chiefly he pays attention to "congestion areas." These are irregular horizontal bands in which the X's waver up and down but their main direction is sideways. These areas represent periods of accumulation by investors (perhaps insiders) who have confidence that the stock will go up, or distribution by holders of the stock who have reason to believe that it will go down. Eventually, once the sideways movement is over, the stock will break out either up or down.

The technician often can identify these periods of accumulation or distribution, although congestion areas take many forms and it requires experience and reference to other technical data to tell whether a given area represents a top or a base. In the most easily identifiable case, the end of a period of accumulation is signaled by some recognizable formation; for example, the bottom of each column of X's is a little higher than the previous one. This indicates a breakout on the up side.

Once the direction of the move has been determined, the chartist attempts to estimate how far up or down the stock will go. This vertical movement is thought to depend on the horizontal width of the accumulation period. Thus if the accumulation period in a one-point unit chart had covered 15 horizontal squares, the upward movement might be estimated at 15 points.

As you can see, the technician uses his charts to try to measure the great intangible force of investor confidence that makes stocks sell at seven times earnings at one time and 20 times earnings at another. How do you measure the force that can push the price of a stock sharply up or down even though the company's financial situation would seem not to have changed?

For this purpose the technician uses many charts. One shows the breadth of the market, in other words, the share volume of advancing stocks and the share volume of declining stocks traded daily on the New York Stock Exchange. Another shows the number of stocks traded that advanced in price versus those that declined. When volume is increasing and advances exceed declines, the market presumably is in for a rise.

What is the true value of a stock? If the investor knew this, he would immediately know whether it was overpriced or underpriced. Of course, no two persons would agree on the true value. The wide differences in opinion are what makes the stock market. Nevertheless, the technician does try to measure approximate true values and gauge whether stocks are priced too high or too low.

Take a look at the next chart. It illustrates an appraisal of the "central value" theory of Benjamin Graham, the author of several well-known financial books. To arrive at the long-term central or normal value, this theory assumes that the stocks in the Dow-Jones Industrial Average should sell at a level where the ten-year average earnings are capitalized at twice the yield on high-grade bonds. The central value line on the chart shows where the Dow-Jones Average would be if it were at this theoretical norm. The shaded areas above and below the line give a 20% tolerance up and down to allow for periods of high and low investor confidence. When the actual Dow-Jones Average gets outside these shaded areas, in other words more than 20% above or below its theoretical central value, the assumption is that stock prices are way out of line.

CHART 39

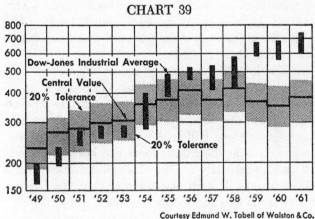

Courtesy Edmund W. Tabell of Walston & Co.

Another intriguing way by which technicians attempt to measure confidence is by means of Barron's *Confidence Index*, published each week by *Barron's National Business and Financial Weekly*. There is a school of thought that the upward and downward movements of this index precede those of the Dow-Jones Industrial Average by two to four months.

The index measures the shifts back and forth between demand for the highest grade, relatively safe bonds, and run-of-the-mill and hence more speculative bonds.

The great law of action and reaction says that things do not move up or down in a straight line. A movement starts, gains momentum and goes too far. Then a reaction sets in. When this reaction is completed, the primary movement starts again. Once more there is a reaction. Thus in a bull market stock prices seesaw upward. In a bear market they fluctuate downward. These wavelike motions are perhaps rough and irregular, but the technician attempts to gauge them.

One of the oldest attempts to interpret these undulating movements of the stock market was the Dow Theory, originated some

60 years ago by Charles H. Dow, first editor of the *Wall Street Journal,* and his successor, William P. Hamilton, and further developed by a financial writer, Robert Rhea. These observers of the Wall Street scene believed that the stock market was a relentless forecaster of business conditions. The market gives its bloodless verdict, say the Dow theorists, because businessmen are the chief buyers and sellers of stocks and each contributes what he knows about business. The market thus sifts and averages what all businessmen think about the future.

The Dow theorist, watching the continually moving lines of his industrial and railroad averages, thinks of himself as an observer standing on the beach watching the ocean. He measures the waves to determine whether the tide is coming in or going out.

The tides, or broad bull or bear movements, last several years. The ripples are the daily fluctuations and have no meaning. The waves that tell the tale are the short swings lasting for several weeks or months. If each new wave rolls up the beach a little higher than the last, and recedes not quite so far, there is a bull market. But at some point a wave will not go as high as the preceding one. It will also recede further. This might indicate that the tide had turned and a bear market begun.

The Dow theorist doesn't hope to catch the exact turn of the market. He knows that major trends run for several years. He expects to be late and doesn't mind as long as he's right. In October 1929, Hamilton wrote a famous editorial in the *Wall Street Journal* entitled "A Turn in the Tide." It stated that a bear market was definitely under way. Jeers came from Wall Street because the industrials had already fallen 75 points and the rails 21. But, by 1933, industrials had dropped another 264 points and rails another 154 points.

Today the Dow Theory is considered by many to be somewhat archaic. But the technicians believe that the great law of action and reaction still operates. A modern interpretation of the law, Elliott's Wave Principle, is founded on the theory that price movements from one point to another consist of a series of waves rather than a straight line. A major price movement goes through five waves before the move is completed. Three of the waves are in the direction of the main move. The other two are correctionary moves in an opposite direction.

Chart 40 indicates that over the past hundred years the stock market has moved upward in one great five-wave cycle, downward in another, and in 1949 started again on a long-term upward movement.

CHART 40

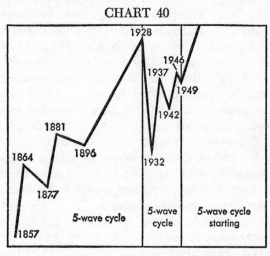

Courtesy Bolton, Tremblay & Co., Montreal

There are a great number of other indexes and charts that attempt to forecast price movements, measure intrinsic value and gauge investor confidence. Almost every brokerage house has a chartist on its staff.

The great danger in all these charts and theories, of course, is that the layman tends to see in them the open-sesame to riches, the lazy man's easy road to wealth. But they are far from that. Even the technicians handle these tricky tools with the greatest circumspection. They use their charts not in a vacuum, but as a check and a supplement to the fundamental approach to investment values.

The layman who makes investment decisions based on fifteen minutes of chart work a day is simply playing financial Russian roulette.

PUTS AND CALLS

Let's say that a speculative-minded person is told that a particular stock is "hot." In other words, some development, not generally known, is supposedly about to push up its price. The person who hears this rumor perhaps does not have enough money to buy a large amount of the stock but he would like to get in on the rise. One way he could try it would be to buy a "call."

Assume the stock was selling for 23½. One hundred shares would cost $2,350 plus commission. But a call on the stock (in other words an option to buy it for a given period at approximately the current price) would cost a great deal less. Specifically, a call good for six months and ten days, exercisable at a price of 23¾, would cost in the neighborhood of $350.

If a speculative-minded person bought such a call, his profit and loss prospects would be as follows. The most he could lose would be $350. And he would lose it only if the stock declined and did not recover to 23¾ during the life of the call. In that case, the call would be allowed to expire. But if the stock went up, he would stand to make $100 for every point it rose. However, the first 3½ points, or $350 of profit, would go to offset the cost of the call. Thus if the stock rose from 23¾ to 27¼, or say 28 to cover commissions also, he could count on breaking even. All he would have to do would be to sell 100 shares at 28, then exercise the call and buy 100 shares at 23¾. But if the stock went above 28, then he really would stand to make a clear profit of $100 for every point of rise.

This example shows one way of using a call. A "put" is the opposite of a call. When you buy a put, you acquire the right to sell 100 shares of stock at a fixed price at any time during a given period.

Suppose, for example, the speculative-minded person owned 100 shares of a stock that he had bought originally at 50 and that now was selling at 70. He might want to keep his stock in hopes it would go higher. On the other hand, he would like to put a floor under his profit. So he might buy a put for, say $500. If the stock continued on up, he would let the put expire and his ultimate profit would be reduced by $500. If the stock went down, he would exercise the put by requiring the man at the other end of the deal to buy the stock from him at 70. In effect, he would then have sold it at 65 (70 minus the five points for the put).

Puts and calls, as you can see, are simply options to buy or sell. They have been used by traders for hundreds of years, but non-professional investors seldom have taken the trouble to understand them. In recent years, however, the public has shown a growing interest, and dozens of put and call options are offered for sale each day in the financial pages of newspapers. In addition, put and call brokers stand ready to write puts or calls on any widely traded stock.

If a person wanted to buy a call on 100 shares of XYZ stock (puts and calls are seldom sold on less than 100 shares) he would not bother to shop through the newspaper ads but would go directly to his broker. The broker, in turn, would get in touch with a put and call broker in New York. There are only 15 of these, but each one has a stable of clients who own many stocks and who are ready to sell or "write" options on any of them at a price.

A typical option writer owns a large portfolio of the most commonly traded stocks. From experience he knows he can make money by standing ready at all times to sell any stock he owns for, say, three, four, or five points above the current price, or by buying more stock for, say, three, four, or five points below the current price. Therefore at any time he will write an option on any 100-share block of stock he owns, charging a price equivalent to three, four, or five points, depending on the length of the option, whether the stock is high-, low- or medium-priced and whether its price has been stable or volatile.

By shopping around, the broker eventually would be able to buy the speculator the kind of option he wanted, provided the stock was that of a large company, widely owned. In such a case he would be buying a newly written option, exercisable at the market price at time of purchase. It could be made to run for 30 days, 60 days, 90 days or six months and ten days, the extra ten days in the last case being to insure the buyer that any profit would be a long-term capital gain. To have the transaction count as a long-term gain, however, the owner of the option would have to sell the option itself, rather than exercise it.

Prices vary, but the average cost of a six-months, ten-day call, for example, would be 14% of the total value of the stock. If a person bought a call and some time later decided to exercise it, he could sell it back to the put and call dealer direct, or he could actually acquire the 100 shares and sell them in the market. The result would be the same, and in either case he would pay two regular New York Stock Exchange commissions on the 100 shares and have a short-term gain or loss.

Once a person owns a put or call, he can sell it at any time during its life. If he sold it well in advance of its expiration date, it might be resold by the dealer. The "special" put and call options advertised in the daily papers are such resales. While newly written puts and calls usually are exercisable at the then market price of the stock, those up for resale must carry the original price, which may be above or below the market price of the stock at the time of resale. The sale price of the option will have been adjusted to cover the difference.

Now for the crucial question. Can you make money trading in puts and calls? Theoretically, yes. But in actual practice, the chances are against the nonprofessional. The United States Securities and Exchange Commission has made an exhaustive study of puts and calls. Here are a few of its conclusions:

— *The buyers of puts and calls generally are individuals, mostly small investors. Calls are more commonly bought than puts.*

— *Approximately 43% of calls are exercised. The rest are allowed to expire.*

— *Of the 43% exercised, about one-half (21½% of the total) are exercised at a loss, the owner getting back, on the average, 40% of his cost and losing 60%.*

— *On the 21½% of calls exercised at a profit, the profit averages 150%.*

Translated into briefer language, the above would seem to say that if you are a small investor and are considering buying a call, the chances are about four to one against your making money at it.

BUYING STOCKS ON MARGIN

You can buy a house with 20% down, a car with 25% down, a washing machine with nothing down, but if you want to make an investment for the future by buying common stocks, you have to put 50% down. Is this necessary and fair? Or are the authorities still terrified by the spectre of 1929 when low stock margins admittedly gave impetus to the downward market spiral and the crash?

These questions have been asked by the president of the New York Stock Exchange. And to them, one or two others might be added. Should the ordinary person buy on margin? What are the advantages and disadvantages of this kind of purchase?

To cope with the subject, get firmly in mind the meaning of certain stock market jargon. The "initial margin" is the percentage of the purchase price that the customer pays when he buys a stock. If he buys a share at 100, he must put up under recent requirements 50%, or $50, and the broker can lend him $50. Once the stock is purchased, however, the margin begins to change as the market price of the stock goes up or down.

Suppose, for example, that the stock, purchased for $100, were to rise to 140. At this point the loan still would be $50, so the customer's equity would be $90 ($140 market value minus $50 loan) or 64% of the stock's value. The margin would then be 64%. On the other hand, suppose the price of the stock were to decline to 80. The loan still would be $50, so the customer's equity would be $30 ($80 market value minus $50 loan), or only 37½% of the stock's value. So the margin would be 37½%.

One reason it is important to keep these distinctions in mind is that the Federal Reserve Board regulates only the initial margin. Thereafter, the margin that the customer must maintain is determined by the brokerage house and the rules of the New York Stock Exchange. As a matter of fact, the maintenance margins that most brokerage houses and the New York Stock Exchange require are well below the 50% level required by the Federal Reserve Board at the time of purchase.

According to New York Stock Exchange rules, margins must be maintained at 25% or above. In other words, as far as the Stock Exchange is concerned, the customer's equity can decline to 25% of the market value of the stock.

Most brokerage houses, however, are a little stricter and insist that margins must not fall below 33⅓%. Thus in the example, the customer's stock, which he purchased at 100, putting up $50, could fall in price only to 75 before he would receive a "margin call." The value of the stock would be $75, the customer would owe $50 on it leaving his equity at $25, or 33⅓% of the market price.

To sum up—under recent Federal Reserve Board regulations, a customer can buy stock by putting up 50% of the purchase price. Thereafter, under most brokerage house rules, the stock can decline 25% before the customer will be called for more margin. The margin at any time may be computed by this formula:

$$\text{margin equals } \frac{\text{market value minus loan}}{\text{market value}}$$

So much for margin calls. Now take the more optimistic possibility. What if instead of going down, the price of the customer's stock goes up? In this case, his equity and margin rise, and he can actually buy more stock without putting up any more cash. This is known as pyramiding. Assume that when the stock reached 120, the customer sold out, took his larger equity and used it to repurchase on a 50% margin. After paying off his $50 loan, he would receive $70 (disregarding commissions). Using this as his 50% margin, he could buy $140 worth of stock ($70 is 50% of $140). He would then owe $70 (50% of $140).

In actual practice it is not necessary for the customer to sell, take out his equity and repurchase. He can acquire the additional $20 worth of stock by a paper transaction. If the customer pyramided once and the stock continued to rise, he could pyramid again.

The stock market crash of 1929 was not caused by margin trading, but low margins undoubtedly made it worse. After each of the awful days of the panic, Black Thursday (October 24, 1929), Black Tuesday (October 29) and the others, lights burned all night in Wall Street as clerks, fighting to catch up on their paper work, sent out thousands and thousands of telegrams calling for more margin. The customers who could not put up the cash were sold out forthwith, adding to the terrible downward pressure on prices.

The crash brought to light the two great perils of low margins. First, many a small trader, using margins as a means to speculate, suffered a total loss of his savings, whereas if he had bought stocks outright, he probably would have salvaged something. In fact, if he could have held on, he or his heirs might have done very well, as many stocks today are selling at several times their 1929 high. Second, the pressure of forced liquidation contributed to the panic, which had such a depressing effect on business as a whole.

After the crash Congress undertook to prevent a repetition. Some experts wanted to abolish margin trading altogether, but this was overruled on the grounds that it would impair the liquidity of the great securities markets. Others wanted to have the privilege of trading on margin reserved for investors with accounts of $10,000 or more. This idea also was rejected.

In the end, it was decided that the problem could be solved by regulating initial margins. The Federal Reserve Board, according to its discretion, can move the level upward or downward. From 1934 when it received this responsibility up to 1962, the Board changed the requirement 17 times, having set it as low as 40% in the late Thirties and as high as 100% during the short boom of 1946. The Board takes some satisfaction from the fact that no sudden drop in stock prices in recent years has developed into a downward spiral.

Brokerage houses themselves have a rule that to some extent deters the small investor from speculating on borrowed money. A margin account cannot be opened without a deposit of at least a thousand dollars. And the New York Stock Exchange reports that 80% of all margin accounts are held by people with incomes over $10,000.

If a man buys a house or a car or a washing machine with a small down payment, he gradually pays off the debt and eventually owns his purchase free and clear. Instalment buying actually is a way of saving. But the trader who buys on margin seldom pays off his debt in instalments. Whether he is ahead or behind, he is likely to liquidate his loan by selling the stock. And in either case he is a good prospect for another hot tip on a sure winner. Successful investors didn't make their fortunes in this way.

SHORT SELLING

In the old days many a fortune was made by selling short. Such famous figures as Joseph P. Kennedy, father of President Kennedy, and Bernard M. Baruch used the technique. After the excessive speculation of the Twenties, however, the New York Stock Exchange and the United States Securities and Exchange Commission, adopted regulations that wiped out the opportunities for "bear" raids on the market. Today, short selling is still possible but it is so hedged by restrictions that it is rather sparingly used, even by speculators on the floor of the Exchange. Nevertheless, anyone still can sell short if he wants to.

To most people short selling is a kind of upside down way of trying to make money. If a speculator bought 100 shares of stock at 20 and later sold it at 30, he would make $1,000 less commissions. But let's suppose, now, that he sells it first at 30, then buys it later at 20. He still would make $1,000 less commissions. In the second case, he would have borrowed the stock through his broker, sold the borrowed stock at 30, then later bought it back at 20 and returned it to the borrower.

In the old days when the stock market was much more volatile and when stocks surged up and down more rapidly, short selling was popular. In fact, speculators on the floor of the Exchange sometimes ganged up on a stock, sold it short, drove the price down and "covered" their short positions at much lower levels, making a pot of money in the process.

It is doubtful, however, whether the small individual investor ever consistently made money selling short. To do so he would have to guess correctly that the stock he borrowed and sold would, in fact, go down. If it went up, instead, he would be in a serious predicament. In the first place, when he borrowed the stock he would have had to put up as security to the lender all the proceeds from the sale. If the stock later went up, the short seller would have to increase his deposit with the lender by an amount equivalent to the increase in his stock's value. If the stock kept going up, the day might come when the lender would want his stock back. In this case, the borrower would have to buy shares in the open market, take a loss, and close out the deal.

Prudent short sellers, if there are any such people, sometimes hedge their short sales by use of a stop loss order. Thus if a speculator sold a stock short at 30, he might put in a stop loss buy order at 32. Thus if things went wrong and the stock began to rise, 100 shares would automatically be purchased for him at 32 and he would stand to lose only two points.

Short selling is a particular form of short-term trading that should be attempted only by the most sophisticated market operator. The ordinary investor cannot use it successfully.

COMMODITY FUTURES TRADING

Commodity futures markets have been described as "the fastest trading markets in the world—where you operate on as little as 10% margin—where fortunes have been made and lost in a matter of months."

Basically, this description is true. As a young man, John Maynard Keynes, author of the famous Keynesian theory of economics, was determined to be financially independent and never to "relapse into salaried drudgery." So shortly after World War I he began speculating, first in foreign exchange. He sold German marks and bought U.S. dollars. But early in 1920 the dollar began to decline in relation to the mark, and Keynes soon found he had lost £13,000.

He borrowed enough to keep going and plunged into the commodity futures market, trading heavily on very small margins in lead, tin, copper, zinc, rubber, wheat, sugar, linseed oil and jute futures. Within four years he had made £58,000. During most of his life he continued to speculate in commodities and stocks, finally accumulating a £500,000 fortune.

Keynes, of course, was a genius. Unfortunately, the ordinary speculator in commodity futures may well have the opposite experience. A Department of Agriculture study some years ago indicated that three times as many small speculators lost money as made it. Still, the lure of quick riches is strong. Every large brokerage house has its contingent of men, and even women, who are trying to outguess the weather and the professional commodity traders in New York, Chicago, Minneapolis and Kansas City. Here are the mechanics of it and the way the speculators figure their chances of success.

Suppose in early spring you overheard a wheat farmer say, "I've just planted my crop and I see that wheat is currently selling at $2 a bushel. I'd be happy to get that price for my crop when I harvest it next September."

At this point you might say to yourself, "This might be a good deal. The long-range weather forecast is for a hot, dry summer. Congress may raise the support price of wheat. By September the going price may be considerably above $2." So you say to the farmer, "Tell you what. I'll contract to take 5,000 bushels next September at $2 a bushel. And I'll give you 10% down to show good faith."

If you and the farmer made this kind of deal, you would in effect have bought a September wheat future and he would have sold one. Every day thousands of transactions of this kind are made. Only instead of farmers and speculators meeting face to face, they give their orders to brokers who send them by wire to traders on the floor of one of the commodity exchanges. There the orders are filled much as are orders to buy or sell stocks on the New York Stock Exchange.

Visit the Chicago Board of Trade and from the visitors' gallery you will see the pits, or trading areas, where contracts for wheat, corn, oats, rye, soybeans and lard are constantly being bought and sold by quick signals of hand and finger. In Minneapolis there is the Grain Exchange, in Kansas City, the Board of Trade. In New York and Chicago there are the two Mercantile Exchanges, where egg and potato futures are bought and sold. At the New York Commodity Exchange it's hides, lead, rubber, copper and zinc.

There are only two reasons why a person would buy or sell a commodity future. One is to speculate; the other is to avoid speculation. The farmer in the example just cited knew wheat was $2 a bushel right then, and he wanted to establish the price for his crop once and for all without having to worry about future fluctuations.

Traders in commodity futures, such as wheat, make possible what is known as "hedging." In January, for example, a chain of grocery stores decides it will need 100 carloads of flour to be delivered June 1. It asks a flour mill to quote a firm price. Now the miller does not want to buy all that wheat in January and store it until June. But in order to quote a firm price on the flour, he must know the cost of raw material, as well as overhead and profit. This means he must immediately establish the price he will pay for his wheat. He can do this by buying wheat futures. Who will sell them to him? Some speculator who thinks wheat is due to go down, so that by June he can buy the futures back for less and make a profit.

When a rubber manufacturer buys raw rubber, he may sell an equivalent amount of rubber futures. Since he thus buys rubber as a commodity and contracts to deliver finished rubber goods at a later date, he guards himself against a loss in case the price of rubber, and rubber goods, changes while his raw material is in inventory or in process of manufacture. Once the finished goods are sold, he will cancel his hedge by buying futures. If, in the meantime, rubber has gone up, he will pay more for his futures but he also will receive a higher price for his rubber products. Or, if rubber has gone down, he may have to sell his products for less than planned but also he will buy back his futures for less and hence make an offsetting profit.

You can see that the speculator, by taking the other end of the deal from the hedger, is providing a public service. But that, of course, is not why the speculator is in the market. He buys and sells for only one reason—to make a profit.

The larger and more conservative brokerage houses will accept as commodity trading customers only those who they think understand the risks and can afford to take them. And unless a new customer has a stock account (and on the average over half of them do), he usually must open his account with a deposit of at least $1,000.

Commodity futures trading may look pretty exciting on paper. But it is something that the prudent investor should stay far away from. Here's a true story to illustrate the point.

An unsophisticated speculator bought a couple of coffee futures contracts, putting up $1,500 margin. The market turned against him and he decided to sell, but he couldn't the first day because coffee was down the allowable daily limit on the first transaction and there were no more trades that day. He put his sell order in the next day, and again futures were down the limit on the first sale and trading stopped. This went on for five days. By the time his position was liquidated, he had lost his $1,500 plus nearly $10,000 more.

In fact, all the gimmicks and devices described in this chapter are things definitely not recommended for the readers of this book. Trying to predict the course of the market, or of an individual stock, by charts and graphs is very difficult even for the professional technician with a staff of analysts who keep current several thousand charts. Successful use of puts and calls, margin buying, short selling, commodity futures trading is predicated on the ability of the speculator to forecast short-term fluctuations in prices. Even the professional cannot do it consistently. And as for the ordinary person—any tendency on his part toward fooling around with this kind of dynamite amounts to a propensity for financial self-destruction.

invest in real estate?

"They are making more people, but they are not making any more land." This remark, attributed to an old Texan, explains why a growing number of people want to invest their money in real estate. They note the predictions that population will grow, business will boom, communities will expand and land will be eaten up by new houses, schools, offices, factories, shops, recreation areas and roads. And of course the one universal ingredient for all this expansion will be land and buildings—in other words, real estate. Why, then, isn't real estate a sure-fire investment?

The answer is that real estate as a whole undoubtedly will rise in value over the years. If you could buy all the land now for sale around your town and hold it for ten years, you probably would double or triple your money.

As a practical matter, though, you can't invest in "real estate as a whole." You have to select a particular deal involving a combination of location, price, terms, taxes, mortgage, seller, lender, agent and so on.

Start out with these thoughts:

Investing in real estate usually is more difficult than investing in stocks. In five minutes you can find out the history and earnings record of any stock listed on the New York or American Stock Exchange. To get comparable perspective on a piece of land or a building you may have to spend days digging out all the facts.

In most cases when you buy real estate, either individually or through a syndicate, you get more or less locked in. That is, there usually is not a continuous market in which you can sell your interest quickly for cash. (Real estate companies and real estate investment trusts having stock in the hands of the public are an exception; such stock may be readily saleable.)

Real estate investment very often is riskier than investment in the common stock of a strong growing company listed on the New York Stock Exchange. A building is a building, tied to one location. But a company like General Electric or Du Pont is flexible, diversified, with continuity of management.

Generally, an investment in real estate will require a large chunk of cash—in most cases at least $5,000 to $10,000. This makes it hard for the average investor to spread the risk over several situations or to make small, periodic investments. Again, an exception is the real estate company or investment trust offering stock to the public.

Set against these possible disadvantages is the fact that many real estate investments produce a large cash yield, some of which may be a return of capital in the form of pay-out of depreciation reserves and therefore tax-free. Cash yields of 7% to 12%, of which half is a return of capital and thus tax-free during the early years, are not uncommon.

YOUR OWN HOME

In considering the possibilities, start with the purchase of your own home. For most people, this investment is the safest and easiest. A soundly built house in a good location, kept modern and in good repair, should increase in value over the years about as fast as other prices. In the meantime you are living rent-free while paying down the mortgage, increasing your equity and getting an income tax deduction for interest and real estate taxes.

In recent years you could purchase a home with relatively small cash—10% to 25%—which gives you as much "leverage" as you would get in most professionally arranged real estate deals, and a lot more than you would get in the stock market. The leverage, of course, could work in the opposite way and cause a large loss.

Leverage is simply the amount of cash you put up in relation to the total value of the investment. Say you buy a $15,000 property for $5,000 down. Suppose during the succeeding year it increases 10% in value. You have a potential profit of $1,500 on your $5,000 investment, or 30%. A great many real estate deals depend on leverage for their high return.

DUPLEX OR SMALL APARTMENT

Going a step further, what about buying a duplex house or a small apartment? Going it alone this way is difficult. Even though you can get a professional appraisal, you must do most of your own thinking and judging. You are limited to small or inexpensive properties. And all your eggs are in one basket. In a duplex or four-unit apartment building, one vacancy cuts your gross by 50% or 25%.

SECOND MORTGAGES

Second mortgages are widely advertised in metropolitan newspapers. They offer a high but insecure yield and are extremely difficult to appraise. Here is an example of how a 12% second mortgage is created. A seller lists a house for sale, asking price $15,000. A buyer wants the house, but he has only $2,000 in cash and can borrow only $10,000 on a first mortgage. (For the purposes of this discussion the word "mortgage" will be used to cover both mortgage and trust.) The buyer thus needs an additional $3,000. The seller agrees to finance the balance himself by taking back a five-year second mortgage at 6% interest. But since in doing this he is foregoing an all-cash price for his house, he insists that the price will have to be $15,750 or $750 more than the price he had originally asked.

The deal then boils down to this. The seller gets $12,000 cash plus a $3,750 second mortgage for his $15,000 house. Now along comes the middleman. He has some capital and is looking for investments providing a big yield. He offers $3,000 cash for the $3,750 second mortgage. This is fine with the seller because he then will have received a total of $15,000 cash, which was what he originally wanted for his house. On the other hand, the middleman having bought this mortgage at a discount of $750, has invested $3,000 but is receiving 6% interest based on $3,750. In addition, he stands to make a profit of $750 over the life of the mortgage. All these factors combine to bring up his average yield on the $3,000 to a whopping 15.7%.

Now suppose this middleman becomes pretty good at finding second mortgages that can be bought at less than face value. He forms a mortgage company and buys up lots of second mortgages. Then he gets an even better idea. Why not resell these mortgages to small investors at a price that will yield them 12%? As explained below, this will give the mortgage company a capital gain of over 8% and in the meantime the new investors will have taken over the risk. In addition the company will charge for servicing the mortgages.

This is how the second mortgage investor gets involved. He sees the mortgage company's ad in the newspaper promising him 12% on his money. He writes in and discovers that he can buy a $3,750, 6%, five-year "guaranteed" second mortgage for $3,250, which will give him the 12% yield that was advertised. The word "guaranteed" sounds fine. So does the 12%. So the mortgage company transfers the mortgage to the investor thereby making an 8½% capital gain, but agrees to continue collecting the monthly payments. But the risk has been assumed by the investor.

The whole thing seems like a kind of fairyland where everybody picks money off the trees. The weak link, of course, is the buyer of the house, who to all intents and purposes is paying 15.7% on the extra $3,000 he needed to make the purchase. As long as he keeps up his payments everything is fine. But if at some point he decides he can't stand this heavy drain, things begin to happen. He might decide to let the house go. The house would be sold at auction and might bring only $12,000. The holder of the first mortgage would get $10,000, leaving $2,000 for the holder of the second mortgage. The investor's 12% investment would be gone. So would be $1,250 of his money. If perchance he complained to the mortgage company that his investment was supposed to be "guaranteed," he would receive the suave reply that the mortgage was guaranteed to be a second mortgage, which it was. Everyone knows, of course, that most second mortgages are risky.

RAW LAND

Raw land is jumping in price on the outskirts of many cities. But for the small investor, land has its problems. Generally speaking, a vacant lot is not a good investment. It may already have been marked up to its ultimate retail price. In buying lots by mail in Florida, Arizona or other exotic-sounding places, you are buying at the retail price after a big appreciation already has been realized by the promoter. Also, you may be buying in a remote area whose future you cannot measure.

Raw land that is in the path of development and can be bought by the acre is a better bet. You cannot borrow money on land from a bank, insurance company or savings and loan association. But in many cases the seller will take back a large purchase-money mortgage, which permits the buyer to acquire title for a small down payment. In Florida it is standard practice for the seller to take only 29% in cash, the balance in a purchase-money mortgage. There is an advantage to him in this arrangement because as long as he receives less than 30% down, he can spread his capital gain over the life of the mortgage and pay his tax at the long-term capital gains rate.

Of course, once you have bought land on this basis you must pay taxes, interest and usually amortization of the loan and, in the end, a 10% sales commission. You also lose the interest you would have received had you invested the money elsewhere. For these costs to be offset, the land must go up in value pretty fast. It might be that your land would have to appreciate 12% to 15% a year to give you a gain comparable to what you might get in other forms of investment.

SYNDICATES

A real estate syndicate has this advantage: when a number of investors pool their capital, larger deals can be tackled. And in the larger deals there are better chances for bargains.

Most syndicates are semiprivate affairs. A real estate broker will locate a piece of property that he deems attractive, then offer others a chance to participate in its purchase. He usually invites members of his family or firm, friends or those who have participated with him in previous ventures. In rare cases "participations" are offered directly to the public. The amount of money each member of a syndicate puts up generally runs into the thousands, $5,000 to $10,000 being most common. However, small syndicates are sometimes formed where participations run as low as $2,500, $1,000 or even $500.

The one big advantage a syndicate has over a corporation is that the syndicate itself pays no corporate income tax. Remember that the stockholder in an ordinary corporation is doubly taxed. The corporation itself pays a tax of 52%, or somewhat less in the case of small companies, on its profits. Then the stockholder is taxed again on his dividends. Members of a syndicate pay taxes only on their individual profits.

Syndicates also are great users of other special tax advantages, as are real estate corporations and real estate investment trusts. A real estate syndicate, corporation or investment trust often can provide a tax-free return to its members by using the depreciation allowance. Although this gimmick is important primarily to the person in the high tax bracket, it should be understood by all because it lies at the bottom of a great deal of real estate investing.

The key to it is the fact that as a building gets older it wears out and the Internal Revenue Service allows money to be put each year into a "depreciation reserve" tax-free. Theoretically, this reserve is built up so that eventually money will be available to replace the building.

In any event, use of the depreciation allowance for other purposes than replacing the building opens the door to the tax-free income. For instance, many wealthy people have bought real estate with a mortgage and allowed the depreciation money to pay the mortgage off.

Here is an example used by Mr. Sheldon B. Guren of U. S. Realty Investments in a speech to the New York Society of Security Analysts. It shows how depreciation money may be paid out to a building's owners.

Assume that property has been bought for $1,000,000: $900,-

000 for the building and $100,000 for the land. Cash payment was $400,000 and a 6% mortgage was secured for the balance, or $600,000. Annual payments on the mortgage are $45,000 including principal and interest. Rent comes in at $100,000 a year and operating expenses, including insurance, repairs, real estate taxes and management, are $19,000. Here are two statements showing how a tax-free payment of $36,000 a year could be made to the owners of the building.

Profit and loss for income tax purposes:

rent income		$100,000
expenses:		
mortgage interest	$36,000	
depreciation (5%)	45,000	
operating expenses	19,000	
total expenses		100,000

Cash flow:

rent		$100,000
cash disbursements:		
mortgage (principal and interest)	45,000	
operating expenses	19,000	
total expenses		64,000
balance for distribution		$36,000

As you can see, here is a property that made no profit and therefore paid no income tax, but was able to pay its owners 9% on the cash investment of $400,000.

This 9% actually was not income but a return of the investor's own money. Many times, however, the investor does not realize that he simply is taking money out of one pocket and putting it in the other.

This gimmick can be carried even further. If the depreciation allowance is large enough, the owners may not only get a tax-free distribution, but may receive a tax loss in addition, which they may use to reduce their other income.

Note that the cash return is tax-free to the owners because technically it is not a dividend but a return of capital. This has further tax implications. If you owned a $10 share in the deal described above, you would receive 90 cents the first year, which would be tax-free. But since it was a return of capital it would reduce the cost basis of your share to $9.10. So if at the end of the first year you sold your share for $10, you would have to report a capital gain of 90 cents. If you sold it for $11, you would have to report a capital gain of $1.90, and so on, even though you actually paid $10 for the share.

When you join a syndicate you are necessarily putting a great deal of reliance on the judgment and integrity of the manager. He is the one who locates the property, appraises its potential, determines the price and arranges for mortgages and leases.

You should, of course, study the details of the transaction. Many syndications, and most large ones, are registered with the Securities and Exchange Commission, so detailed facts and figures are available. But all the study in the world will not save your investment if you put it in the hands of a manager whose judgment or integrity is questionable.

How much should the syndicate manager receive for his knowledge and the time he puts into the deal? That is a touchy subject among syndicators. The ways in which a manager may be compensated include the following:

He may act as the sales agent through whom the property is sold to the syndicate. For this he receives a real estate commission.

He, or someone in his family, may get the contract to manage the property for an annual fee. His real estate firm may also write the insurance on the property.

He may belong to another syndicate that will hold a mortgage or lease on the property or deal with the main syndicate in some other way.

Sometimes the manager receives a free participation in the syndicate.

He may receive cash.

Naturally, a brilliant and experienced manager should be adequately compensated. On the other hand, the handing over of a relatively large interest, free, to the syndicate manager cuts down on the return of the members who are putting up the money. Whatever the arrangements, all details of the syndicate manager's compensation should be an open book.

Two disadvantages of investing through a syndicate are lack of liquidity and lack of diversification. A syndicate member who wants to convert his membership into cash may offer it to other members. If the syndicate is profitable, they probably will buy him out at cost. Otherwise, it may take considerable time and shopping around to make a sale. There is no organized market in syndicate memberships.

As to diversification, most syndicates own just one property. If that goes sour, the whole investment feels it. And since participation usually costs many thousand dollars, it is not the best type of investment for the unsophisticated investor.

REAL ESTATE COMPANIES

The incorporated real estate company is one answer to lack of liquidity and lack of diversification. Such a company usually owns several properties so that the risk is spread. And the company's stock is sold initially in small units, which are more easily traded than a large participation in a syndicate.

The obvious disadvantages of this kind of real estate company is that it is liable for the corporate income tax on its earnings. Stockholders, in turn, are taxed again on the dividends they receive. Use of "negative earnings," however, can reduce or even eliminate both taxes.

REAL ESTATE INVESTMENT TRUSTS

In 1961 it became possible for the real estate investor to avoid this double taxation in a new way, to achieve diversification and to maintain liquidity. Under a law amending the Internal Revenue Code, it became possible for a real estate investment trust to own real estate and pay no corporate income tax as long as it fulfills certain conditions, the main one being that it pay out to its shareholders at least 90% of its net income. This is the same kind of provision that applies to investment companies. Thus an investor may buy shares in a real estate investment trust, pay only one tax on his profits, have diversification and be able to sell his shares at any time in the open market.

Real estate investment trusts had their origin in Boston in the middle of the nineteenth century. The purpose was to permit small investors to pool their savings and participate in diversified real estate ownership under experienced management. Title to the real estate itself was vested in a Board of Trustees. According to John H. Gardiner, vice president of the Real Estate Investment Trust of America, these early Boston trusts supplied a great deal of the capital for the development of Boston during its great period of growth in the nineteenth and early twentieth centuries, and also for the growth of cities of the Middle West and West—Detroit, Chicago, Minneapolis, St. Paul, Kansas City, Omaha, Duluth and Seattle.

In 1936, however, real estate investment trusts were stopped dead in their tracks by a federal court decision that held them to be taxable as corporations. This meant that a trust had to pay the corporate income tax, now 52%, before paying dividends, and that the shareholders again had to pay the personal income tax on the dividends. It took 25 years for the trustees and shareholders of real estate investment trusts to get this double taxation eliminated.

To qualify for the corporate tax exemption, a real estate investment trust not only must pay out 90% of its net income but must meet these additional requirements. There must be 100 or more shareholders and not more than 50% of the shares may be owned by five or fewer persons. These provisions are designed to insure that every trust will have broad ownership and not be a personal holding company for a few people. At least 75% of the gross income must be from investments related to real estate and not over 25% of the total assets can be in non-real estate investments.

To insure that the tax advantages given to real estate investment trusts cannot be used by real estate operators in the pursuit of their usual business, the regulations prohibit a trust from directly managing any property it owns, or receiving income from a contractor who does such managing. Neither may the trust be in the business of developing or selling land. In other words, the role of the real estate investment trust must be "passive." It can hold real estate investments but cannot engage in the real estate business.

A good many groups around the country have taken advantage

of the new law to set up real estate investment trusts. Some are privately owned; that is, their shares have not been offered to the public at large. Others have registered with the SEC and their shares have been sold to the public and are traded in the over-the-counter market. The Real Estate Investment Trust of America, the largest and oldest real estate investment trust in the country, has its shares listed on the American Stock Exchange.

For the person who is interested in investing in real estate, a well-managed real estate investment trust has these advantages. First, it gives diversity to the small investor. A few hundred dollars can acquire a cross section slice of several big pieces of property. Second, it gives liquidity. The value of the shares is established each weekday and then can be converted into cash quickly and easily. Third, it gives professional management of the investor's real estate money. Fourth, it gives the shareholder a certain control over the activities of the trustees. This comes about because they are required to pay out 90% of the net income. They cannot let the income build up and then use it for new ventures over which the shareholders have no control. If the trustees want to expand, they must come back to the shareholders for additional capital. In this respect, the real estate investment trust differs from the real estate investment company which need not pay out any specified percentage of net income to its shareholders and in addition may borrow capital for new ventures.

While the real estate investment trust does offer many advantages, it by no means provides a foolproof vehicle to the non-professional investor. There are many possibilities of skullduggery. For example, there is nothing to prevent real estate operators from setting up a trust, selling shares to the public, and then unloading onto the trust parcels of real estate at inflated values. Suppose, for example, that a group owning various office buildings, apartment buildings or pieces of undeveloped land, sets up a real estate investment trust, and sells real estate to it. How are the shareholders going to know whether the prices paid are fair and reasonable?

In this respect, the operations of a real estate investment trust are much harder to evaluate than the operations of an investment company. When the managers of an investment company buy 1,000 shares of IBM or Standard Oil of New Jersey, their judgment may be questionable but at least the shareholders know that the price they pay is the going price of the stock. Real estate values are much harder to measure. When a real estate investment trust buys an office building, especially if it buys from one of its own trustees, the shareholders have no ready means of evaluating the transaction.

Put it this way. The real estate investment trust offers the potential investor several advantages over real estate syndicates and real estate investment companies. But in every one of these types of investment, the most important qualities that the potential investor should seek are integrity, competence and experience on the part of the trustees or managers.

Richard H. Swesnik, an experienced real estate operator and syndicator of Washington, D.C., has expressed the problem:

"A real estate investor seeking advice may very well weight his decision 25 per cent as to quality and location of the property and 75 per cent as to the men who must select and operate the property. If this formula appears lopsided and needs correction, let us do it now. Make it 10 per cent–90 per cent. In other words, invest in persons, not things . . . 'things' never make money."

estate planning

It's hard to earn money. It's hard to save it. It's hard to invest it and make it grow. And it's hard to pass any of it on to your family if anything should happen to you. Many people think of estate planning as something a man need do only when he approaches the end of his life. Not so. Today's tax and inheritance laws are such that young people as well as old are asking for trouble when they brush aside questions of estate planning, wills, marital deductions and the like. The truth is that even if you own nothing but an outboard motor, you have an estate problem in the sense that it must pass on to someone when you die. And of course, most people's estates are much more complicated than the mere ownership of an outboard motor.

A Washington, D.C. lawyer tells this story. A widow came to his office and asked for help in settling her husband's estate. The partner who took the case began a list of the husband's assets. There was no will. And although the husband had made a comfortable salary and at the same time had lived rather modestly, no record could be found that he owned anything except his personal effects and $900 in a checking account.

The lawyer conducted an extensive investigation. But such check stubs as could be found told nothing. Income tax returns revealed no income from rental property, stocks or bonds. Calls were made to all local banks but no hidden savings account or safe deposit box was turned up. The natural assumption would be that this man had squandered his money. Yet he had no expensive habits. He did not gamble, drink or run around with women.

What happened to the difference between what he made and what he spent? The lawyer still is convinced that somewhere, somehow, there are savings or investments. But where, no one knows.

Most estate problems are certainly not this baffling. But the truth is that most men do leave their affairs in a jumble. This is not because their lives are unduly complicated but simply because they can't seem to get around to the task of setting up a program for their families that would automatically go into operation upon their death. Death is unpleasant to think about and always seems remote. The tendency is to put the problem off and plan "to get to it one of these days."

Even when a man "gets to" the problem, he must be extremely careful to get good advice. Those who administer the tax and inheritance laws give no special concessions to amateurs. There is the case of a man who over a period of 22 years transferred securities to joint ownership with his wife. He did so with the idea that he would get the bulk of his fortune out of his estate and thus avoid estate and inheritance taxes. When he finally consulted a tax lawyer, he was informed that he should immediately go back and report all these transfers to the Internal Revenue Service as gifts, hoping that because he reported them voluntarily, the Service would not charge him a penalty but only the gift taxes he should have paid, plus interest.

Another case: a lady sat next to a lawyer at dinner and upon learning that he did a good deal of estate and tax work, she stated blandly, "Well, I am one of those fortunate people who do not need a will. My husband and I have no children so that if one of us dies, the other gets everything."

"Do you and your husband have any relatives?" the lawyer asked.

"Yes, but only nieces, nephews and cousins."

"Well," he replied, "I'm afraid that if either of you died a certain portion of the estate would go to relatives."

A horrified look appeared on the lady's face. "You don't mean that some of my money would go to that snooty daughter of Aunt Agnes?"

That, of course, is just what the lawyer meant.

Then there is the case of the couple who owned a farm in joint name. The husband never made a will, thinking that his wife would get the property. She did get the real estate but the court ruled that the livestock and machinery were part of the husband's estate and had to be divided among his wife and relatives.

It would be possible to go on indefinitely with this kind of example. The truth is that estate planning is about as mysterious to most people as bee keeping. And, of course, it's a great deal more important and, strangely enough, not really too complicated. Let us consider some of the major elements—wills, joint ownership, estate taxes, inheritance taxes, gift taxes, trusts and the like. Take federal estate taxes first, as they are responsible for a great deal of maneuvering and planning.

Estate taxes. For estate tax purposes a wife may be considered to own half of her husband's property and he may be considered to own half of hers. This law was adopted to make uniform a situation that used to exist only in the so-called "community property states." It means that a man can leave half of his estate to his wife without having estate taxes assessed on that amount. Then his exemption takes care of $60,000 of the balance. Here's an example that will clear up the point.

Suppose a man is planning his estate and figures that everything he owns comes to $200,000. He assumes that administrative expenses will be $20,000, which will leave a net estate of $180,000. Now he can leave half of that amount, or $90,000, to his wife tax-free. On the remaining $90,000, his own exemption of $60,000 will apply, leaving a taxable estate of only $30,000.

It is important that a man figure this kind of thing in advance. Here is the reason. Suppose in the case just mentioned the husband had planned to leave his wife only $50,000. This would be costly because he would not be taking full advantage of the marital deduction. The $50,000 to his wife would be subtracted from his $180,000 net estate, leaving $130,000. Of that his own exemption would take care of $60,000, leaving a taxable estate of $70,-000 instead of only $30,000 as under the first arrangement.

Just to give an idea of what the federal estate tax rate is, here is the schedule of the first few brackets:

CHART 41

Federal Estate Taxes

	Amount taxable	Tax rate
	First $5,000	3%
On the portion from	$ 5,000 - $10,000	7%
" " " "	10,000 - 20,000	11%
" " " "	20,000 - 30,000	14%
" " " "	30,000 - 40,000	18%
" " " "	40,000 - 50,000	22%
" " " "	50,000 - 60,000	25%
" " " "	60,000 - 100,000	28%

You can see that the tax on $30,000 under this schedule would be $3,000 (3% on the first $5,000, plus 7% on the next $5,000, plus 11% on the next $10,000, plus 14% on the last $10,000). The tax on $70,000 would be $12,300.

Inheritance tax rates vary from state to state and, in addition, are extremely complicated. Under New York law, for example, the rates after deductions and exemptions are 2% up to $50,000, 3% from $50,000 to $150,000, 4% from $150,000 to $300,000, etc.

The amount of estate and inheritance taxes and administration expenses will vary widely from case to case. A tax lawyer can make a pretty good estimate if he knows your detailed financial picture. If you want an idea of how much these expenses come to on the average, look at *Chart 42*. It is based on a recent compilation, "Your Estate," published by Estate Recording Company, 4331 Fairmount Ave., San Diego 5, California, price $6.50. The authors analyzed over 10,000 actual estates probated in all parts of the United States and show hundreds of examples.

Avoiding taxes and administrative costs. There are four ways in which property may be passed on to heirs. Number one is via a will. Number two is by right of inheritance in the absence of a valid will, in which case state law prevails and the wife usually receives a third, a half or, in some states, a child's share. Number three is by joint ownership, for example where husband and wife own property jointly or as tenants in the entirety. Number four is by contract; that is, for example, where a life insurance policy or a pension plan names a specific beneficiary.

By a judicious use of the first and last two of these methods, a person can direct the disposition of his estate and minimize

CHART 42

Average Settlement Costs in Estates of Various Sizes

Federal Estate Tax

Size of Average Estate	With Marital Deduction	Without Marital Deduction	Inheritance Tax	Administration Expense
10,000	——	——	2.0%	12.8%
25,000	——	——	2.2	8.0
50,000	——	——	2.4	6.9
100,000	——	5.3%	2.8	5.0
250,000	2.5%	14.3	3.2	4.9
500,000	5.9	18.3	3.4	4.8
1,000,000	10.6	24.6	4.4	4.4

fees and administrative costs. One way is to have your property pass to your heirs by contract or by joint ownership. Let's assume a man has a wife and children, a $20,000 house, $40,000 worth of life insurance, and $5,000 worth of savings, stocks and bonds.

Now, he can have his house in the joint names of himself and his wife. His wife can be the beneficiary of his insurance, which she may choose to get in the form of monthly income with the right to draw on the principal if necessary. Checking account, savings account and savings bonds also could be in joint name, which in most cases and most places would give the widow cash. In this situation there would be very little administrative cost.

Would this man need a will? It might appear not, but actually he should have one. He might inherit money unexpectedly and die suddenly right afterward. Or he and his wife might die simultaneously, in which case, if there were no wills, the court would have to appoint guardians for the children and their property. In fact, both man and wife should have wills even though most of their property is owned jointly, and especially where they have minor children. In this case the wills should appoint guardians for the children. Otherwise, guardians would be appointed by the courts. It is usual to state in wills that if husband

and wife die in a common accident, it is presumed that the husband died first. Thus under his will the wife would inherit from the husband under the marital deduction provisions, assuming the husband owned the major part of their assets, and had named his wife as beneficiary of at least half of his net estate.

Joint ownership will not, by itself, solve the estate tax problem. Even though a house, for example, is in joint name, the Internal Revenue Service presumes it to have been bought by and owned by the husband. If the wife could prove that she had paid for any part of the house with her own money, then only the balance would be included as part of the husband's estate. But lacking such proof, the house would be in his estate even though in joint name. All personal property, including household effects, are part of the husband's estate except for articles the wife can prove that she paid for or received as wedding gifts.

Holding property jointly does not affect estate taxes, but it can provide immediate benefit for the survivor and save on administrative costs. It should be borne in mind that putting property into joint ownership can at times incur gift taxes.

Another good thing about having a will: it enables a person to dispose of certain personal property that might have a sentimental as well as an actual value. Listing these items avoids the unpleasant squabbling that so often takes place in families. A woman, for example, may promise a ring to one of her daughters. In this case she should make a specific bequest. Disposition of heirlooms such as paintings, jewelry and antiques should be very specific. One old lady promised a fine antique sewing table to three different relatives. Naturally, when she died, there was a fight about who was going to get it.

Now any lawyer can draw a will, but as in everything else there are specialists. As a matter of fact, many lawyers prefer not to draw wills for their clients or even for themselves, but go to "will lawyers" who specialize in this business. It is particularly important to have a specialist when you get into the business of setting up trusts. If you wanted to set up a trust and named your bank as trustee, the trust officers of the bank would particularly like you to have the job done by an experienced will lawyer. And they may insist on checking it while you are alive. In many cases they will refuse to accept the administration of a trust that they feel is not properly drawn.

Trusts. Here is one way in which a husband can avoid having his estate taxed twice—that is, when he dies and then again when his wife dies. Suppose a man has a fairly large estate, or else suppose his wife has some money of her own. There are several reasons why, in either case, the man may not want to leave all his money to his wife. If his estate is large, the taxable amount may be well above their combined exemptions. On the other hand, if she has money of her own, additional money would increase her estate tax problem.

In such a situation the man could put some of his assets into a testamentary trust (one that begins upon his death), specifying that the wife should get the income during her lifetime and that the principal be distributed among their children after her death. The amount thus put into the trust would be taxable as part of the husband's estate but would not be taxable again as part of his wife's estate.

In the above case, the money in trust would become part of the children's estate and would eventually be taxable to their estates on their respective deaths. It is also possible to keep the trust out of the children's estate by setting it up so that the wife would get the income during her lifetime, then the children would get it during their lifetime, and the principal would go to the grandchildren. The trust also should provide that if there are no children or grandchildren left, the principal would go to other relatives or finally to a specified charity.

The common way to manage this kind of trust is to leave the money and securities in the hands of a bank to be managed by the bank's trust department, perhaps with instructions to hire investment counsel. The bank or trust company will live forever, as they say, and provide continuity of management. Individuals sometimes are made trustees, but there is the danger that one or all of them may die, whereupon the court would have to appoint someone to take their place. This calls for legal work, which costs money. Also, individuals get old and perhaps lose their capabilities. It is advisable, however, to name as co-trustee with the bank an individual such as a wife, son, daughter, close family friend or even the family lawyer.

In the case of small trusts, the funds may be put into the bank's common trust fund, which is a pool of small trusts. The common trust fund is managed by the bank in the same way as its larger trusts, and being relatively large itself, such a fund provides the advantages of diversification of investments and a relatively low administrative cost.

Here is an example of what can happen when individuals are named as trustees, rather than a bank. A man, supposedly astute in financial matters, died recently and left his insurance, about $38,000, to his wife. He left his securities in two trusts called a first and second. His wife was to get the income and if need arose could withdraw principal. The two trusts themselves were around $40,000 net. They were to be run by three trustees, one in California, one in New York and one in Virginia. Now really, this was ridiculous—three trustees in such widely scattered areas trying to administer such a small amount. Fortunately, the trustees all agreed to step aside and turn actual management over to a bank.

A living trust is one that a man sets up during his lifetime; it gets the trust established before he dies. If he makes it revocable, it will make for convenience but have no tax effects. But if he makes it irrevocable, then the assets put into it will not be included in his estate. They will, however, be subject to gift taxes. Either way, when the man dies, the trust will continue operations just as it did before his death. This eliminates delay and also cuts down on probate and other administrative expenses.

Payment of estate taxes. After a person dies the estate tax must be paid within fifteen months, although in certain circumstances the payment may be delayed or paid in instalments over periods up to as long as ten years. Assets such as securities or real estate may be valued at the market price at the time of death or twelve months later, whichever is lower. This privilege, incidentally, was not available in 1929. In those days, stocks and other assets were valued as of the date of death. Some widows whose husbands died at the peak of the stock market boom found that when the estate was settled the value of the securities had dropped but the tax still was levied on their value at the peak of the boom. This resulted in tragic situations where widows who should have been wealthy upon the death of their husbands ended up penniless.

This brings up another problem, the need for cash in the estate. It is needed for debts, funeral expenses, doctor's bills, court costs and, finally, for the widow and children pending settlement. In addition, of course, there is the payment of taxes. One way to provide immediate cash is to have a particular life insurance policy designated for the purpose. Another is to have at least some liquid assets in joint name of husband and wife. If this is not done, something may have to be liquidated at a disadvantage to give the widow living expenses pending final settlement. Every state stipulates that the widow is entitled to an allowance that will see her through this interim period.

Another point: a person should be careful how he leaves flat sums of money to charities or other beneficiaries. The dollar amount may seem reasonable at the time the will is drawn, but later, at time of settlement of the estate, such gifts may represent a much larger proportion of the total than had been contemplated. There have been cases where a widow got much less than her husband had intended because his total estate had shrunk but his cash bequests had not. It is better to make such bequests in terms of a percentage of the net value of the estate; say, 5% to this charity and 5% to that person.

Providing cash to pay the taxes is a matter of special importance where a large estate is composed primarily of non-liquid assets such as real estate or stock in a closely held or family-owned company. In this latter case, holdings may have to be sold at distress prices. Life insurance policies are often added to an estate specifically for the purpose of providing cash for taxes as well as for living expenses for the widow.

There is a relatively new law designed to help in cases where such stock represents at least 35% of a man's gross estate or 50% of his taxable estate. The provision permits a family-owned corporation to buy back enough of its own stock from the estate to pay the federal tax, funeral and administrative expenses. Another law allows the executor of such an estate, under certain conditions to pay the tax over a period of ten years. These could be ways for the estate to pay taxes without the necessity of selling a family corporation to outsiders.

In these family-held corporations, there is always a problem about the value of the stock for estate tax purposes. The Internal Revenue Service puts on its own valuation, which may be considerably higher than the owners or heirs think is fair. This often is a subject of dispute, arbitration or litigation. One way to minimize this is to have the husband enter into an agreement with the other stockholders or partners to buy his interest at a predetermined amount. Courts have upheld the validity of such agreements when made at arm's length. Insurance also may be bought and set up so that surviving partners, stockholders or the corporation itself will have cash to buy out any that die. Any lawyer retained to handle such matters should be a specialist.

One interesting way to provide cash to pay estate taxes is to purchase in advance certain government bonds, the 2½'s of 1967–72, which have at times sold for 82 to 86. Their value for paying estate taxes is 100. In other words, for $820 to $860 you may be able to buy a bond worth $1,000 if you die. And if you live, you will eventually receive par and a capital gain if you hold the bonds to maturity.

Gifts. A person with potential tax problems should give money away from year to year to those who someday will be his heirs. You can give any number of people up to $3,000 apiece in any one year without paying a gift tax. This can go on year after year.

Furthermore, you have an additional exemption above the $3,000 a year per person amounting to $30,000 over your lifetime. Your wife can join in giving, which raises the annual exclusion to $6,000 and the lifetime exclusion to $60,000. Once you've given money or assets to a son or daughter, a grandchild or some other relative or a friend, it's his, or hers, and there won't be any estate tax on it. In addition, you can set up a trust for a minor with instructions that the income be accumulated until he or she reaches 21. The trust pays the income taxes, generally at much lower rates than your own, so that when the minor receives the estate, which will include accumulated earnings, no tax will be due.

This subject of gift taxes is not very well understood. A certain lawyer who works for the federal government objected so strenuously to the idea of paying estate taxes that he transferred his home to one of his sons. The idea was to get it out of the estate but still keep it available for use by himself and his wife. This was a foolish move for several reasons. First, the transfer to the son was subject to gift taxes, although the lawyer never thought of that. Second, suppose the son dies while the parents are still living. The house may pass on to the grandchildren and may not be usable by the grandfather and grandmother.

Actually, this man's total estate was so small that the estate taxes, had he figured them out, would have been negligible. The trouble was, he acted without proper advice.

There are other precautions to take in setting up a program of gifts. Naturally, you don't want to give money to your wife if there's any likelihood that she plans to elope with the milkman. Also, you don't want to give away money or property that you might need. But for wealthy people, gifts made well in advance of death are the best way to avoid estate taxes. The words "well in advance of death" are used because the Internal Revenue Code presumes that any gift made within three years prior to death was given "in contemplation of death" and therefore is taxable as part of the estate. Sometimes, of course, this presumption can be overturned.

The federal gift tax is 2¼% on the first $5,000 above the exemptions; 5¼ on amounts from $5,000 to $10,000; 8¼ on amounts from $10,000 to $20,000 and so on. Note that the rates are lower than estate tax rates, about 15% lower.

Some states have gift taxes, but the tax rate is very low or even nonexistent if the gift is made to close relatives.

Gifts to charitable organizations, churches, schools, hospitals are generally free of gift tax. They are deductible up to 20% of gross income if given to charitable organizations in general. An additional 10% of gross income may be given tax-free if the gifts go to churches, hospitals or schools. They need not be made in cash. They may consist of such things as shares of stock or a part interest in real estate.

Note also that all states now have legislation permitting minors to own stock. You buy the stock, then fill out a form available at any brokerage house, giving the minor's name, address and the name and address of an adult member of the minor's family who will act as custodian. Of course, you also fill in the name of the stock, number of shares and so on, and the stock will be registered in the name of the custodian and the minor, and delivered to the custodian for safekeeping.

For more information on this subject, go to the nearest brokerage office and ask to look at a pamphlet called Gifts of Securities or Money to Minors, published by the Association of Stock Exchange Firms.

One kind of security that is suitable as a gift for a minor is stock in an investment company. Investment companies are in the business of managing their stockholders' money by reinvesting it in a diversified portfolio of carefully selected securities. Thus a minor who owns investment company shares receives professional management of his money.

Life insurance. It's a common delusion that life insurance is exempt from estate taxes. But under federal law the face value of an insurance policy can be and almost always is included in a man's gross estate even though the wife is the beneficiary. In most places, however, if life insurance is payable to the wife, it is not subject to attachment for debts. Also, a beneficiary of an insurance policy often receives payments over a period of time, taking part of the principal each time and leaving the rest at interest. Such a beneficiary need pay no income taxes on payments received from principal. In addition, if the beneficiary is a widow, she receives under federal law a $1,000-a-year income tax exemption on payments of interest. This, however, has nothing to do with estate taxes.

The costs of estate planning. Having your will drawn and getting advice on your estate problems is probably the greatest bargain you can get from a lawyer. In fact, it's one of the greatest bargains you can get anywhere. If you were a millionaire, many law firms would be happy to draw your will and set up the trusts for a nominal fee, the reason being that they probably would be the attorneys for the executors and upon your death would have the legal work involved in a large estate that would then pay off handsomely in fees.

At the other extreme, a person with no particularly complicated problems probably could have a will drawn and obtain advice on such things as joint ownership for a fee of $25 up. A testamentary trust; that is one that would take effect upon your death, might cost $50 or even several hundred dollars depending on the work involved. If it was a living trust, the cost would be about the same.

These fees of $25, $50 or even several hundred dollars could actually provide savings of hundreds and even thousands of dollars. You work hard to earn that money, to save it and to invest it. In many ways, the problem of conserving it for your family is the easiest of all *if* you get at it in time and *if* you seek out the best professional advice and follow it.

advice
to a widow

A trust officer in a big city bank recently received an urgent telephone call from a young widow. Her husband had died only two weeks before, leaving her with $20,000 worth of life insurance. "What should I do?" she asked. "This salesman just called me again and says that I only have until three o'clock tomorrow to make the investment." The investment in question happened to be a mutual fund which, of course, could have been purchased at any time. It might just as well have been shares of stock, second-trust notes, a fancy new car or anything else that an energetic salesman figured he might foist off on an inexperienced person in an emotionally upset frame of mind.

In another case, a widow whose husband had died a year earlier happened to be talking to a tax lawyer and mentioned the very heavy burden of income taxes she was paying quarterly. He was somewhat surprised, as she was not employed and had very few investments. Upon inquiring, he learned that the company where her husband had worked had continued his salary for a year after his death. This was a gift to the widow, since she was doing nothing herself to earn the money. Yet a lawyer had advised her that she was required to pay income taxes on it. The tax lawyer got to work and managed to obtain a refund of over $3,000 for her. But this $3,000 was recovered only by the merest accident of a casual conversation.

These incidents point up one of the most difficult problems that come to investment counselors, bankers and others in the financial field. It is how to advise and, if possible, protect the widows who come for help in situations that often seem almost insoluble.

Here are some of the difficulties. In the first place, the widow is emotionally at sea. Her main support in life is gone. She desperately needs someone to whom she can turn for help and advice. In these circumstances, almost the first person who comes along and takes an interest in her is welcomed as a counselor. A widow will take advice on the most serious problems from friends, neighbors or relatives, not because of their business judgment and experience, but simply because she likes them.

One young widow was left with a bundle of securities that had been rather carefully selected by her husband. A neighbor was a lady who recently had become a "customer's man" in a local brokerage house. Her total experience in investments consisted of a quick course to enable her to pass the New York Stock Exchange requirements plus several months of sitting behind a desk in the brokerage office. She at once advised her widowed friend to sell certain securities and replace them with others. Very shortly, this widow had a trading account and was buying and selling with the abandon of a veteran, which was almost the worst possible thing she could do, considering that neither she nor her adviser had any basic investment know-how at all.

If the widow has at her disposal a fairly large sum, she becomes a magnet for people who have other intriguing ways for her to invest it. Very often a favorite relative is lurking about who has always wanted to start his own business. In one case a widow financed a nephew who wanted to open a hardware store. Once he got the store going, however, its day-to-day operation bored him. His failure to give the business his personal attention resulted in its eventual sale at a sizeable loss.

A widow has trouble realizing that she is a different person from what she was before her husband's death. She tends to want to go on with the same way of life, entertaining at dinner and perhaps maintaining a spare bedroom for weekend guests, even though this may be beyond her means. She may insist on an apartment in an expensive neighborhood to be close to old friends.

Or if she is living in the house that she and her husband had occupied over the years, sentiment often makes her loath to part with it, even though it may be too large and expensive for one person to maintain. There have been cases where a widow has borrowed money on a mortgage and undertaken large monthly payments in order to maintain a home that was larger than she needed and that had been clear of debt when she inherited it.

Perhaps an even more dangerous situation faces the widow whose husband owned his own business. Should she try to continue it or sell it? While she is making up her mind, the business easily can go downhill. Even if she offers it for sale at once, potential buyers, being more knowledgeable than she, probably will try to get it for less than it is worth. A strong sense of loyalty sometimes compels a widow to try to carry on a family business regardless of circumstances.

The most serious worry the widow has is how to obtain enough income to live on. Very often this causes her to seek an abnormally high yield on whatever money she inherits. A good conservative list of common stocks yields about 4%. Government bonds yield around 3¾%, while good preferred stocks might yield 4½%. If the widow's capital is limited, however, she can't get along on 4% or 4½% and desperately hopes to get at least 6% and preferably more. This is understandable, but the old investment maxim holds true: the higher the yield, the greater the risk.

In this dilemma, widows sometimes are tempted to put their money into such venturesome things as second-mortgage notes, which have notoriously high yields but are proportionately risky.

The proof of the risk is that such notes usually sell at a large discount in the open market. A $4,000, 6% second-trust note, for example, might sell for $3,000, an indication that the original holder isn't 100% sure he will receive the full amount due. If a person buys such a note at, say $3,000, he, or she, will receive not only 6% interest on $4,000 but also a capital gain of $1,000. The total of these amounts, spread over the life of the note, may bring a yield of 12%, 15% or even 20%, depending on the number of years the note has to run.

The big danger, of course, is that the home buyer who signed the note in the first place may default. If this happens, the holder of the first mortgage is paid off first, and the holder of the second-trust note gets what's left, if anything.

To show how vulnerable widows are, one lady whose husband had died and who wanted a high yield from her capital was persuaded to buy second-mortgage notes at face value, so that she received only 6% and failed entirely to get the 10%, 12% or 15% that she could have received if she had been given the benefit of the usual discount.

In many cities there are companies that make a practice of buying up second-mortgage notes at heavy discounts and reselling them at smaller discounts. This gives them a profit and passes the risk on to those who take over the notes. Companies of this sort often advertise that their customers have never suffered a loss. Just the same, several such companies have gone bankrupt.

Life insurance proceeds almost always make up a part of a widow's resources. Some insurance companies, anxious to get the settlement wound up, will pay a widow immediately in cash and fail to point out to her the various options that she could elect, such as leaving the money at interest or accepting it in the form of an annuity. One insurance man tells a story of how an insurance salesman years ago paid off a widow in cash, then turned right around and sold her an annuity on which he received a sales commission. She never knew that she could have elected the annuity in the first place and saved herself the commission.

All in all, women whose husbands die go through a miserable period. Not only do they suffer the loss of the person who gave them financial support and emotional security, but in addition there immediately flood in on them problems with which they could hardly cope even in the most favorable circumstances. These problems are not easy to solve even for trained financial men. There are no pat answers. However, the following suggestions should be useful to the widow and to those whose lot it is to try to help her.

The most pressing problem the new widow has is to get someone who can give her competent, unselfish and unbiased advice. This is not easy for two reasons. First, such people are not easy to find at any time. Second, a widow often is shy about "imposing on" another man although he would be happy to help.

Many a widow bravely tries to struggle along alone, causing her husband's old friends to think she is doing all right. One widow even tried to make out her own income tax return by simply using the same pattern that her husband had used the year before. The ensuing tangle with the Internal Revenue Service required unraveling by experts.

If the husband neither recommended any particular adviser to his wife nor designated one in his will, then the best bet usually is for the widow to go to her bank, or her husband's bank, and consult one of the officers. If the bank has a trust department, the trust officers probably are best equipped to make suggestions. And they will do so whether or not the widow intends to use their services. This is a sort of public service that good banks provide largely as a matter of public relations.

If the widow has no lawyer or investment adviser, the bank usually will make recommendations. A lawyer is necessary to handle the will, taxes and other problems. If there is money to invest, someone should be consulted who knows investments but who has no ax of his own to grind, that is, no interest in selling any particular security.

The course the widow should follow will depend on her age, whether she has dependent children, whether she has a job or can get one, how much property has been left her, whether it will provide an income and whether or not she can afford to continue to live in the same house or apartment that she and her husband occupied. In many cases, the widow can get a job. Her salary, plus some social security if she has minor children, will enable her to get along. But probably she will have to economize by moving to a house or apartment that is less expensive.

If the widow finds herself with any amount of capital above what is required to clean up immediate expenses, she has the problem of investing it. This is a tough one. Some widows, but all too few, have the business sense to handle their own investments. The widow of a Naval officer who inherited a modest sum of money when her husband died some years ago taught herself the principles of investing and studied the finances of companies listed on the New York Stock Exchange. By economizing and keeping her capital invested in growing companies, she did very well and now lives a pleasant life and is able to travel abroad every two years. But she is the exception. Most widows should put their money under professional management.

If a widow feels she has the patience to learn investing, and the will power to adopt a sound program and stick to it, she might consider these suggestions.

For amounts up to or in the neighborhood of $25,000: put the money into carefully selected investment trusts. It might be well to spread the money over two or three trusts. Those mentioned here have a fine record of capital growth, and this growth might be expected to continue if business conditions remain favorable. A few top-quality trusts are Lehman Corporation, State Street Investment Corporation, Tri-Continental Corporation, Consolidated Investment Trust and Chemical Fund. All of these can be purchased through brokerage houses.

Here are a few trusts that are more speculative than those listed above. And the yield is less, but the emphasis on growth is greater: National Investors Corporation, Putnam Growth Fund, Massachusetts Investors Growth Stock Fund, Fidelity Capital Fund, Inc. All may be purchased through brokers.

For amounts in the neighborhood of $50,000: put $30,000 into several of the investment trusts listed above, and put the other $20,000 into preferred stocks and/or bonds rated as "A" quality or better by Standard & Poor's. These preferreds and bonds will give a larger yield than common stocks or investment trusts, perhaps 4½% to 5%. Any respectable brokerage house can prepare a list and handle the investment.

For amounts in the neighborhood of or over $100,000: get professional advice either through a bank or by hiring an investment counselor.

Investment counseling firms. Such firms usually accept only amounts of $100,000 or over. Some even have minimums of $250,000 or $400,000. The usual annual management fee is ½ of 1% of the capital. A few smaller firms will accept amounts down to $25,000, but the fees may be proportionately high.

There are good firms and others that are mediocre. To check on a recommended firm, interview one or two of the firms' clients. Another way is to pick a firm that has proved its competence by the way in which it has managed an investment trust. Many firms manage either a mutual fund or a closed-end trust, and the growth and dividends are shown by published figures.

Or write to the Investment Counsel Association of America, 100 Park Avenue, New York 17, N.Y., and ask for the names of members in your area. This is a professional society with high ethical standards.

Trust departments of banks. A favorite trust arrangement is for the bank to pay the income to the widow in question and to permit her to draw upon principal in emergencies. In addition, if

she were to become ill, the bank would automatically be em-
powered to pay bills and generally handle her affairs. The trust
agreement, supplemented by a will, would also determine what
would happen to the principal upon the widow's death. It might
go to children, for example, in monthly payments or in specified
amounts upon their reaching certain ages.

Banks invest their trust funds conservatively, and the income
probably averages about 4%. The principal may be expected to
grow slowly during periods of rising stock prices.

Life insurance options. Modern life insurance policies generally permit the beneficiary to elect any one of several methods of
payment. The money may be taken in a lump sum, in a fixed
number of instalments, as a monthly income for life or as a
monthly income for life with a specified number of payments certain, even though the beneficiary were to die. Or the money may
be left with the insurance company at interest.

In many cases the purchaser of the policy already will have
designated the mode of payment, though even then the widow
may have the right to change it.

In others, the beneficiary must decide. Some insurance companies will automatically make a lump sum payment if the beneficiary fails to indicate another choice fairly promptly. The best
arrangement from the widow's point of view is that adopted by
several good companies. The money is put at interest automatically upon the death of the insured and continues to draw interest until the beneficiary makes a decision as to how the money
is to be paid.

Many widows whose husbands carried only small amounts of
insurance must perforce use it to pay doctor and hospital bills,
taxes, funeral expenses, and so on. But if the amount is fairly
substantial, some questions arise. Should the cash be drawn out
and invested in some other medium such as stocks? Or should it
be left with the company under one of the settlement options?
And, if so, which one?

In making a choice among options, it's important for the widow
to consult her husband's insurance adviser or some other insurance man she can trust. Selecting the option that will best fit in
with her family situation, other resources, tax problems, and so
on, can be a very complicated business. As an example, consider
how the age of the widow might affect a choice between leaving

money with the company to draw interest or taking it as an annuity for life.

The annuity tables now in use assume that today's young female will live for quite a long time. Therefore the monthly annuity payment for young widows is quite conservative. In some cases it is little more than the interest that would be received at today's rates if the money were left intact. Look at *Chart 43* and note that a young widow would do almost as well leaving her life insurance money at interest and converting it to an annuity, if that were her intention and if the company permits such conversions, at some later date when the payments would be larger. (The payments in the table are based on those currently made by a well-known mutual company; they include dividends and assume that 3.75% interest, the present rate, is earned.)

CHART 43
Monthly Payment

Age of beneficiary	$10,000 annuity 20 years certain	$10,000 left at interest
30	$33.19	$30.73
35	35.01	30.73
40	37.18	30.73
45	39.80	30.73
50	42.41	30.73
55	45.45	30.73
60	48.91	30.73
65	52.20	30.73

A widow aged 30 or 35 would be foolish, in the absence of a tax problem or other special situation, to elect the annuity option since she could receive almost as much without touching her principal. The relation between what she would get from the annuity and what she would get by leaving the money at interest will change somewhat with changes in interest rates and with the method by which the particular company computes dividends.

These figures on life insurance by themselves show how desperately the widow needs expert advice. And this need comes at a time when psychologically and emotionally she is least capable of seeking out those who could help her.

The hidden moral to this chapter is obviously that a husband should not only leave his affairs in order but also should leave his wife a list of advisers who will help her. If all men took this one step, it would go a long way toward solving one of the most difficult problems that widows have.

parting advice

As the investment counselor looks back over 30 years of managing other people's money, thoughts and memories crowd into his mind. Along with them come thoughts that he would like to pass on to his son, or some other person starting out on the long and difficult task of putting his savings to work and making them grow.

Cultivate skepticism. As an investor, you must decide whether you will manage your investment funds or hire someone else, either through buying shares in an investment trust, or retaining an investment adviser. In many cases, getting professional advice would seem best, providing care is used in selecting the trust or the adviser.

If you decide to manage your own funds, then you should read financial reports, economic projections by qualified men, writings on finance, and politics, social trends, taxes, labor, business, costs, profit margins, etc. Most everything that happens has its effect on securities. And each working day you should start with a new appraisal.

Nevertheless, in all your reading and studying, you should be skeptical. The financial statements are factual. Much of the rest is a matter of opinion and subject to the errors of human judgment.

Only after following an advisory service for some time should you be willing to trust its recommendations over your own judgment. Even then, the decisions should be your own so that your

judgments can be sharpened and you can accumulate investment
background and experience.

Cultivate perspective. Brokerage offices are full of confusion
and are not the best places to make sound financial judgments.
As the saying goes, "It is hard to get perspective if your nose is
glued to the ticker tape." Watching the tape tends to cause you
to join in mass judgments. And mass judgments feed on themselves. This has even resulted in a service based on "contrary
opinion," its projections being the opposite of what is generally
said or written.

Also, there is a theory that the smart investor should do the
opposite of what the small "odd lot" investors are doing. The
activity of odd lot investors actually is measured by a market
indicator computed for this purpose.

The benefits of good perspective have been seen by the authors in places as far apart as the north woods of Canada and the
isles of Greece. For example, a retired businessman made his
analysis of the business and market trend and then took off to
spend the winter in a cabin in the North, killing game and fish
for his food. In March he came in over the ice to prepare his income tax return. At this time he also reviewed his longer term
investment position. For years his record was amazingly good
until he succumbed to the advice of his banker, who, it so happened, was too close to the ticker tape.

Holdings of American securities by certain Greek investors
would be a credit to any investment adviser. The Greeks themselves, however, feel that we in America ought to do a better
job because we are nearer the scene of business activity. Yet
one reason they have done so well is that they are far enough
away not to be confused by the stock market chatter and supposedly surefire tips.

The investor sometimes can get a clearer view of what lies
ahead during a weekend in the country, or on a lake fishing. His
mind is then not battered by details nor his perspective clouded.

Be wary of predictions. The most experienced banker, broker,
economist or investment adviser can be 100% wrong when he
tries to peer into the future. In the spring of 1958 we wrote an
article stating that the time seemed propitious for accumulation
of common stocks. Even though this advice was somewhat gin-

gerly given, an officer of one of the largest banks in New York City called on the telephone and criticized the statement so violently that the editors hardly dared disagree with him aloud. Yet his own predictions of a deepening recession turned out to be completely wrong.

Give credit for good judgment where it belongs. When a man pulls off a coup by catching a short swing in a stock and doubling his money in a few months, he is credited with being brilliant. But when a man buys a stock like Gillette and holds it over the years until his investment has increased sixty-five-fold, the credit is more often given to "the long-term upward trend in stock prices."

Or, as one bank president said when being kidded for not having bought a group of stocks that were ten to one hundred times their cost twenty years ago, "Anyone could have bought them." But he hadn't bought them, nor had his trust department. Yet it all seemed so simple in retrospect. And if he had bought these stocks, would he have held them until they were ten to one hundred times the original cost?

How much is luck? Certainly it is a factor—yet luck is only part of the answer. The following can affect the investment result: the particular time when funds are inherited, the type of investment received, the position of stock prices in the cycle during the time in your life when you can really save. What you do, however, may add to or detract from your luck. Think of the investors who bought and held not growth stocks, but shares of street railways, or of some of the less successful railroads, or buggy businesses, or hat makers, or whatnot. Or Grandpa may have owned a farm in what is now Detroit, or outside of Chicago, or in the prairies of the Dakotas which are now part of the oil-heavy Williston Basin.

Back in the Thirties many of the younger men in the investment advisory field were suggesting stock purchases and making them for clients. They felt frustrated because they themselves did not have money with which to lay the base for their own fortunes. If they were lucky and saved, their chance came again in the late Forties. If the past is a guide, investors get several such chances in a lifetime. Unfortunately, the first chance may come before they have accumulated investment funds and the last at a time so late in life that they should not risk taking a heavy stock position.

Be patient, look far ahead. The greatest dangers to the individual are impatience and greed. When he buys a stock he usually wants to see it "move." A broker once said to an investment counselor, "Your problem and mine are quite different. Your purchases are made for the long pull. When I suggest a stock to a customer he expects to see action on the upside within a very short time."

At times the investor acquires stock in a good company within an industry that is currently facing difficult problems. It takes time for such problems to work out. Too often the individual does not have the patience to stay with his stock until it can fulfill its latent promise.

Greed often harms the investor by tempting him to grab a profit instead of letting it run. When gains are taken, taxes must be paid, leaving the investor less to reinvest. On top of this, he has to make the investment decision all over again.

Don't confuse the two ingredients that go into the investment decision. One is to determine in a broad sense where you should have your money invested; that is, what proportion should be in common stocks and what proportion in life insurance, bonds, preferreds and cash. The other is to choose the particular common stocks, preferreds and bonds to buy. Many a person has had success in making one of these decisions but not both.

In firms that manage large investment funds, one person may be known for his ability to sense the over-all business trend, while a completely different person may stand out as the best for selecting individual stocks. These men will likely be quite different in temperament. They will supply different major pieces to the investment jig-saw puzzle. Both are essential. Yet it is important that they keep from getting tensed up. Rather, they should keep so relaxed that their judgments may be reached by calm, unhurried, flexible, independent decision.

Feel. It is thought that to be successful in the investment field one should have what is called a "feel." An excellent example of a man who had this feel was the head of a large research office who spent two hours in July of 1937 trying to convince an associate that the firm should cut its holdings of stocks. He didn't quote facts and figures; he was at a loss for words, but he did have a conviction that things just were not right. Although he talked to only a few people, he had tried to pick those who he thought had a "feel." In this case he turned out to be 100% right.

Don't be ashamed to make small purchases. A widow who inherited a substantial amount of money used it to buy only three stocks. Her reason as confided to a friend was, "Certainly you wouldn't expect me to buy less than 100 shares." As a matter of fact, she would have been much better off spreading her money over more purchases. There is no stigma to buying odd lots and the odd lot charge is not great. If the selection is good and the stock appreciates, say 50%, the odd lot charge becomes insignificant. No one, regardless of experience, can pick exactly the right stock at the right time. Odd lot purchases can be the means of spreading the risk or conversely increasing the opportunity for gain.

The investor should never forget that substantial fortunes have been accumulated through small, careful purchases. Remember the story told earlier in this book of the man who started buying ten share lots of General Electric and Standard Oil of New Jersey. The result, years later, is a fortune that runs into the millions.

Don't invest with the idea of using profits or dividends for a specific purpose. The need to get a particular return from your investments on a particular date will warp your judgment and cramp your style. One reason the rich get richer is that they can let their investments ride; they can reinvest the dividends and add funds from time to time. The small investor craves financial security more than does the wealthy investor. This intense craving for security often causes the small investor to pay too much attention to dividend income. He should strive for the perspective of the wealthy investor who is perfectly willing to forego income providing his investment is showing a satisfactory compound rate of growth.

Never buy a stock expecting it to go up so you can meet a financial obligation of any kind.

"Don't tell me what you are recommending, tell me what you are buying." This old Wall Street adage makes sense. The investor who buys stock in a company should feel some assurance if he knows that the company's officers have bought the stock themselves, particularly if they have done it with their own savings as distinct from stock options.

Consolidated income can be valuable. Many a company owns all or part of other companies known variously as subsidiaries or affiliates. Very often the income from these subsidiaries or affiliates is not included in the income statements of the parent company. For example, many American companies have built plants abroad where labor costs are less. These plants not only sell their products abroad but ship them to this country. Particularly notable are American companies doing business in the Common Market in Europe. Unconsolidated income not only gives such companies a hidden value but often gives them more diversification than they would appear to have. Examples are Pfizer and Owens-Illinois Glass. Many may be found by looking through the pages of Standard & Poor's Listed Stock Reports.

Be wary of new issues. In recent years newly issued stocks have become popular with investors. Speculators use them as "trading stocks" because they move fast and erratically. But they are very difficult to appraise and are not recommended for the average investor. If bought at all, they probably should be bought via an investment trust.

Remember two of the ingredients that go into a rise in stock prices. The first may be a rise in earnings. The second may be a rise in investor confidence. If a company earned $1 a share ten years ago and earns $2 now, its price might be expected to have doubled. But in the meantime investor confidence in that common stock may have risen. A good many stocks that were selling at nine or ten times earnings in 1949 were selling for twenty to thirty times earnings twelve years later. Thus the company that earned $1 and once was selling for $10 a share, was later earning $2 and selling for $40 or even $60 a share. This increase in the price-to-earnings ratio was responsible for a good deal of the long bull market, particularly in top quality growth stocks.

In some cases this rise in investor confidence went to extremes. There have been companies selling for sixty times their original offering price without ever having shown any earnings at all. This book has not listed such stocks. They are hardly suitable for anyone but the seasoned speculator.

Don't underestimate the problems; be humble. Investing is a challenging occupation, or avocation, and it can be rewarding. But it is not a simple business. It can't be done successfully without real work and effort. Every political, social, economic and financial event has its effect on the price movements of stocks and bonds. The market renders its bloodless verdict on almost every event of importance that takes place in the world. The problem should be approached with a good deal of humility.

To voyage successfully in this sea of ever-changing prices and values, the investor must cultivate imagination, flexibility of mind and the ability to think clearly, independently and unemotionally. He who sets sail today has a favorable tide to help him along—the dynamic growth trend of America and the Free World. If he navigates skillfully and, like the companions of Ulysses, stops his ears against the sirens' song, the profits from his voyage should be many times the cost of setting the venture afloat.